Vision Critical Studies
General Editor: Michael Egan

D. H. Lawrence:
The World of the Major Novels

Vision Critical Studies published or in preparation:

E. E. Cummings
The Fiction of Sex: Themes and Functions
of Sex Difference in the C20th novel
George Gissing
Henry James: The Ibsen Years
The Silent Majority: A Study
of Working Class Fiction
Wyndham Lewis: Fictions and Satires

D.H. LAWRENCE:
THE WORLD
OF THE
MAJOR NOVELS

Scott Sanders

Assistant Professor of English,
Indiana University

VISION

Vision Press Limited
157 Knightsbridge
London SW1X 7PA

ISBN 01 85478 402 0

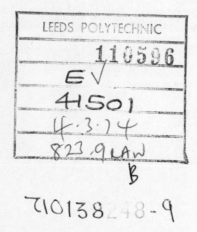

LEEDS POLYTECHNIC

110596

E √

41501

4·3·74

823.9 LAW

B

710138248-9

© 1973 by Scott Sanders

All rights reserved

Printed in Great Britain
by Clarke, Doble & Brendon Ltd
Plymouth
MCMLXXIII

To T.M.S., who stayed on the land and thought it good, and to his son who hungered for the city.

Contents

CONTENTS

Editorial Note

Vision Critical Studies will examine mainly nineteenth century and contemporary imaginative writing, delimiting an area of literary inquiry between, on the one hand, the loose generalities of the "readers' guide" approach and, on the other, the excessively particular specialist study. Crisply written and with an emphasis on fresh insights, the series will gather its coherence and direction from a broad congruity of approach on the part of its contributors. Each volume, based on sound scholarship and research, but relatively free from cumbersome scholarly apparatus, will be of interest and value to all students of the period.

M.E.E.

Author's Note

In the footnotes to the text I have used the following abbreviations for works by Lawrence:

CL   *The Collected Letters of D. H. Lawrence*, 2 vols., ed. H. T. Moore (London and New York, 1962).

CP   *The Complete Poems of D. H. Lawrence*, ed. Vivian de Sola Pinto and F. Warren Roberts (London and New York, 1964).

Fantasia   *Fantasia of the Unconscious* (New York, 1922; London, 1923).

PI   *Phoenix:* The Posthumous Papers of D. H. Lawrence, ed. Edward D. McDonald (London and New York, 1936).

PII   *Phoenix II:* Uncollected, Unpublished and Other Prose Works by D. H. Lawrence, ed. H. T. Moore (London and New York, 1968).

PSY U   *Psychoanalysis and the Unconscious* (New York, 1921; London, 1923).

SCAL   *Studies in Classic American Literature* (New York, 1923; London, 1924).

9

Acknowledgements

I recognize debts of scholarship and friendship in many quarters.
To Graham Hough, Mark Spilka, F. R. Leavis, Mary Freeman and H. T. Moore, who wrote the first comprehensive studies of Lawrence in the nineteen-fifties, I owe the settler's debt to the pioneer.

As a humanist I am grateful for the thought and example of George Morgan and Raymond Williams.

To Graham Hough and Mark Spilka I am grateful for advice, criticism and guidance through the early stages of my research; and to Mark Schorer and T. R. Henn for their continuing interest in my work.

I am indebted to the British people and the British Parliament for a Marshall Scholarship, which enabled me to live in their country and to begin work on this study. I am indebted to the Danforth Foundation for a Graduate Fellowship and to Indiana University for a Faculty Research Fellowship, which enabled me to complete this book.

Patrick Parrinder, Michael Egan, Eric Homberger, Martha Vicinus, Lee Sterrenburg, Murray Sperber and Patrick Brantlinger generously read my arguments and argued my ideas, and my wife offered judicious editorial suggestions at every stage. For the intellectual sharpening they forced upon me I am thankful.

I wish also to thank Laurence Pollinger Ltd. and the Estate of the late Mrs Frieda Lawrence for permission to quote from Lawrence's published works.

Introduction:
Literary Consciousness and Social Reality

We continue to inhabit the psychic landscape of Lawrence's fiction; the fissures between instinct and conscience, between worker and ruler, between primitive and modern, between desire and reason divide us still. This book maps that troubled landscape, and traces in its contours the shape of Lawrence's own experience of the world.

The nature of my argument is implicit in the double title above. I have tried to show the stages of development in Lawrence's consciousness and its links with real life. Focusing upon the five major novels, I have treated his fiction as a coherent, evolving response to concrete historical circumstances: the class division between his parents; his own alienation from all social groups; the increased mobility and consequent rootlessness of individuals; the decay of organized religion and the cultural death of God; the spread of education; the growth of cities; the advance of industry; the apparent triumph of science over nature; the invasion of private life by the mass media, by the market and by the state; the rise of the working class to at least a semblance of power; the socialist and fascist revolutions; the war. Lawrence's style, his themes and the basic categories of his thought were rooted in these economic and political developments, which were transforming European society during the early decades of this century.

The changes which Lawrence wrought in the novel form—in characterization and narrative structure—are part of that general reorientation of thought about the nature of man and society that we associate with the names of Marx, Weber and Durkheim in sociology, with the futurists and surrealists in art, with Darwin in biology, Frazer in anthropology, and in psychology with Pavlov and Freud. Lawrence responded in part to the works of these men themselves, but in larger part to the historical developments which their thought mirrored. History made it impossible for a sensitive young

11

writer any longer to believe in the omnipotence of reason, in the harmony between social classes, in man's remoteness from the animal kingdom or his proximity to the kingdom of heaven. Industrial blight, urban squalor and wars challenged Victorian faith in steady social progress, in the benevolence of technology and in the perfectability of man. Science no longer appeared so objective, the established order of society no longer appeared either natural or divine. Primitive modes of thought and feeling, supposedly long since banished, showed up like trace elements in the consciousness of modern man. The rational, free individual appeared to occupy a diminishing territory, threatened from the outside by relentless economic forces, and from the inside by the chaotic forces of the unconscious.

The frustrations and dislocations of Lawrence's own life coincided with these broadscale changes in thought and society, changes which in the last third of the century we are still trying to assimilate. From this coincidence between public and private traumas his works derive much of their continuing interest and power. The shape of Lawrence's life has been painstakingly documented by H. T. Moore, Edward Nehls and Emile Delavenay.[1] I have rehearsed these familiar materials only where they seemed absolutely necessary for a proper understanding of the evolution of Lawrence's ideas—for example in treating the social alienation which lies behind *Sons and Lovers,* or the wartime crisis recorded in *Women in Love.* Because the various elements of Lawrence's doctrine have been thoroughly scrutinized by Graham Hough, Mark Spilka, Mary Freeman, Eugene Goodheart and Mark Schorer, among others,[2] I have been able to concentrate upon viewing the

---

[1] Moore, *The Life and Works of D. H. Lawrence* (New York, 1951) and *The Intelligent Heart: The Story of D. H. Lawrence* (New York, 1954; London 1955); Nehls, *D. H. Lawrence: A Composite Biography* (Madison, Wisconsin, 1959); Delavenay, *D. H. Lawrence, the Man and His Work: the Formative Years, 1885–1919* (London and New York, 1971; original French edition, Paris, 1970). I have found Delavenay's fine study particularly useful, and only regret that it was not available at an earlier stage in my own work.

[2] Hough, *The Dark Sun* (London, 1955; New York, 1957); Spilka, *The Love Ethic of D. H. Lawrence* (Bloomington, Ind., and London, 1955); Freeman, *D. H. Lawrence: A Basic Study of His Ideas* (New York, 1955); Goodheart,

ideas as parts of a total system, one that evolved under the pressure of internal logic and external events.

When Lawrence's ideas are treated as a coherent system (anticipating for a moment the studies which are to follow), it becomes apparent that his world-view is constructed from a fundamental opposition between nature and culture. All of the more familiar dichotomies in his work—mind/body, social self/natural self, instinct/idea—are reducible to this radical conflict between the demands of culture and the demands of nature. This equivalence among the basic categories of his thought might be represented as follows:

NATURE	unconscious	body	natural self	instinct
CULTURE	conscious	mind	social self	idea

We shall see in the course of our study of *Sons and Lovers* that these psychological divisions mirrored the social divisions which Lawrence had observed as a child in the industrial Midlands:

NATURE	miners	working class
CULTURE	managers	ruling class

Then in *Women in Love*, as I shall argue in the third chapter, we can observe Lawrence translating his fundamental contrast into political terms:

NATURE	mechanism	aristocracy
CULTURE	organism	democracy

The Utopian Vision of D. H. Lawrence (Chicago, 1963); Schorer, "Fiction with a Great Burden," *Kenyon Review*, XIV (Winter, 1952), pp. 162–8, "Technique as Discovery," *Hudson Review*, I (Spring, 1948), pp. 67–87, "Lady Chatterley's Lover," *Evergreen Review*, I (1957), "Women in Love," *Hudson Review*, VI (Spring, 1953). All but the first of Schorer's essays were reprinted in his *The World We Imagine* (New York, 1968; London, 1969).

In *The Plumed Serpent* this contrast is translated once again, this time into religious and anthropological distinctions:

NATURE	dark races	pagan	primitive
CULTURE	white races	Christian	modern

In our study of *Lady Chatterley's Lover*, finally, we shall observe that the nature/culture opposition lies behind Lawrence's distinction between the truths of fiction and the truths of science, between spontaneous form and aesthetic form, between the eloquent animal world of silence and the all-too-human world of language:

NATURE	fiction	spontaneous form	silence
CULTURE	science	aesthetic form	language

The chapters that follow will put flesh on this skeletal summary, showing the radical interconnections between Lawrence's psychological, social, political, aesthetic and religious views. Although Lawrence habitually translated social facts—class conflict, the division of labor, alienation, the war—into metaphysical theories about the nature of man, his ideas were never static, never simply a reflection of social reality. On the contrary, his novels record the workings of a flexible penetrating mind coming to grips with an unstable world. The categories of his thought shifted continually, as he responded to events, and as he struggled to reconcile the opposite terms of his dialectic. In *Women in Love*, for example, under pressure of the war, he sought a midpoint between the African way (nature, body) and the Arctic way (culture, mind). In *The Rainbow* he searched for a compromise between the natural self and the social self, while in *The Plumed Serpent* he strove for a reunion between the primitive and the modern. His was a mind quick to perceive contradictions, and keen to erase them.

All the ills of modern man, according to Lawrence, showed up in sexual relations. The miseries of frustrated love had always been a dominant theme in the bourgeois novel; many of the greatest nineteenth century fictions were built upon it. But Lawrence surpassed even Flaubert and Tolstoy, Stendhal and Hardy in the degree of his concentration upon the state of love. For him sex was the frontier of the naked self; here the individual discovered his limits, as he was thrust by an impersonal force beyond the confines of the ego. Here was the boundary between nature and culture. Viewed from one perspective sex provided initiation into society, an acceptance of mate, family and community. Through courtship and the conventions of lovemaking one became part of society. Viewed from the opposite perspective, sex offered an escape from the world, an exit into the pre-social, even pre-human mysteries of the flesh. Through passion one became part of nature. Within the course of *The Rainbow*, as we shall see, Lawrence shifted from the first perspective to the second. Both views of sex are latent in all of the novels: on the one hand it miniatures community, on the other hand it denies community.

Lawrence was divided by the same contradictory impulses. In the end his yearning for community prevailed over his yearning for isolation, but not before he had given vent to some of the most bitterly misanthropic sentiments to be found in modern literature. During the most savage years of his pilgrimage, from about 1915 to 1925, he temporarily lapsed from outrage over man's present state into contempt for man himself. Because it was during these same years that he articulated his doctrine in its most explicit form, many of his ideas were tainted by this misanthropy and distorted by his own strained social position. Although these lapses were balanced by the sane and compassionate works which preceded and followed that turbulent period of his life, they cannot be treated merely as aberrations. His radical individualism easily veered over into solipsism. His moral urgency could degenerate into intolerance, his oracular pose into elitism. Behind the prophet lurked the hero. I have drawn these connections wherever I discovered them in Lawrence's work. Some will doubtless consider the result too harsh, others too gentle. A man preoccupied with contradictions, Lawrence invites such contradictory responses.

Like Shelley and Wordsworth, with whom he shares a deeper affinity than with such representative moderns as Joyce or Proust, Lawrence appealed to the freedom of nature against the restraints of culture. Like Godwin and Blake, he used the rhetoric of nature to attack the fetters imposed by society. But that very appeal involved him in a contradiction, for he could only depict the majesty of nature through the means of culture, even while he was attacking those means. Attempting to defend the unconscious against the conscious, the physical against the mental, he could employ no other weapons than those provided by the mind. He agreed with Bergson in seeing an essential incongruity between the fluid, continuous quality of inner experience, and the static, segmented quality of language. Any attempt to reconstruct this inner experience through the use of symbols would inevitably distort the reality. In the oldest religions, wrote Lawrence, "the whole life-effort of man was to get his life into direct contact with the elemental life of the cosmos . . . to come into immediate felt contact . . . sheer naked contact, *without an intermediary or mediator.*"[3] Such was Lawrence's own goal, often repeated; yet he was one of the most eloquent mediators, one of the finest poets of the inarticulate emotions, that our century has produced. His whole effort was directed toward translating the mutest of physical experiences into the alien realm of language. Like Carlyle who wrote volumes in praise of silence, Lawrence wrote volumes in defense of the inarticulate. We shall uncover various ramifications of this basic contradiction as we examine the separate novels.

Language is our chief means of establishing a sense of identity. It enables us to objectify our deepest meanings, to communicate our subjectivity to others, and, at the same time, to ourselves, so that we "experience" ourselves as something extended into the public realm in the form of text or speech. But Lawrence used language for a very different purpose. Over against the conscious, isolated self he set the unconscious, undifferentiated being, the natural process, the matrix of life out of which the individual emerges. To use Freud's terms, he set the ego against the id. But the id is not an identity at all, rather a name for the unknown, a territory of obscure forces, the dark and silent basement of the self. All of Lawrence's works exhibit a greater interest in the shadowed basement than in the sunlit house. His prime subject was the undifferentiated process rather than the isolated ego.

In other words, Lawrence was a true heir to Freud. Compared with the stark and savage evocations of the unconscious in *The Rainbow*, say, or *Women in Love*, the work of Proust, Mann,

[3] "New Mexico," PI 146–7.

16

Virginia Woolf and even Joyce appears tame and civilized. In Lawrence's fiction we observe a bolder researching and deformation of the self, equal in extent to the visual reinterpretations of personality undertaken by Picasso and Kandinsky, or the psychological reinterpretations suggested by Pavlov and Freud. While Joyce, Proust and the others explored the stream of *consciousness*, a comparatively placid medium littered with the debris of western civilization, Lawrence was exploring the unconscious, a turbulent medium harboring strange fishes.

Lawrence also ventured beyond his great contemporaries by explicitly connecting the revolt of the instincts with the revolt of the lower orders. During several periods of his life he ventured beyond Freud as well, to suggest that political and economic freedom must accompany any genuine psychological liberation. Honouring our repressed desires, translated into social terms, meant enfranchising the miner, textile worker and peasant. This side of Lawrence I admire. When free from anxiety and bitterness, he shared the essential humanist "demand for a free development of a many-sided, integrated man."[4] The deepest impulse behind his work, as in Blake, was a desire for the liberation of man from all chains, whether imposed by society or by the mind

The political implications of Lawrence's fiction, ranging from anarchism to totalitarianism, have seemed to me important, both in view of their historical context and in view of the stress which Lawrence himself placed upon them. Accordingly I have sought to articulate the views of society, the models for human community, implicit in his novels and essays. Originating in social experience, the basic categories of his thought were transformed in his imagination to re-emerge as patterns for some future society.

Few artists deserve the compliment paid to Byron by Bertrand Russell, who made him the subject of a chapter in his *History of Western Philosophy*. If a philosophy entails systematic and logically articulated ideas about the basic questions of human existence, then it is doubtful whether many artists have ever had one, and it is certain that Lawrence did not. Yet, as any reader soon discovers, he did hold certain firm beliefs about the character of man, nature and community, beliefs which he demonstrated in his fiction,

[4] Georg Lukács describes the humanist principle thus in *Writer and Critic and Other Essays* (London, 1970; New York, 1971), p. 70.

and which he set forth energetically if not systematically in the fictions that he wrote, interspersed among the essays and poems, from about 1908 until his death in 1930. Through even the flimsiest, most hurried of his prose, as through the finest, we detect the workings of a mind deeply concerned about the quality of life, and seeking to teach us how to perceive things more truly, how to live more fully. By focusing upon the social origins and political implications of the ideas which structure Lawrence's fiction, I honor his repeated claim that every artist must build upon a metaphysic, and upon that metaphysic must be judged.

A NOTE ON METHOD

It should be evident from what has already been said that I consider literature to be a social product, arising, like every cultural artifact, out of the dialectical interaction between a particular historical consciousness and a particular social reality. Study of this interaction has become the province of the sociology of knowledge, of which the sociology of literature is one branch. The present book has drawn many of its questions and concepts from these two disciplines. Implicit in my study of Lawrence is a sociological theory of the novel and a dialectical method of literary criticism which I plan to develop in a subsequent essay. In my thinking about the relation between literary consciousness and society, I have been helped and influenced by the work of Karl Mannheim, Georges Gurvitch, Peter Berger, Thomas Luckmann, Robert Escarpit and especially Raymond Williams, Lucien Goldmann and Georg Lukács.[5] The common intellectual ancestor of

[5] Mannheim, *Ideology and Utopia: An Introduction to the Sociology of Knowledge* (London and New York, 1936); Gurvitch, *The Social Frameworks of Knowledge* (New York and Oxford, 1971; original French edition 1966); Berger and Luckmann, *The Social Construction of Reality: A Treatise in the Sociology of Knowledge* (New York, 1966; London, 1967); Escarpit, *The Sociology of Literature* (London, 1971; original French edition 1958); Williams, *Culture and Society* (London and New York, 1958), *The Long Revolution* (London and New York, 1961) and *The English Novel from Dickens to Lawrence* (London and New York, 1970); Goldmann, *The Human Sciences and Philosophy* (London, 1969; original French edition 1952); "Introduction aux premiers écrits de Georges Lukács," in Georges Lukács, *La Théorie du roman* (Paris, 1963), and *Pour une sociologie du roman* (Paris, 1964); Lukács, *The Historical Novel* (London, 1962; New York, 1965;

all these men was of course Marx, whose theses about the relation between man's consciousness and his social being have inspired the modern cultural sciences. In my study of Marx I have benefited from Frederick Jameson's discussion of twentieth century theories of dialectical criticism, *Marxism and Form*.[6]

A comprehensive theory of the novel would analyze every component of the dialectic between the writer and his society. Beginning with the text, one would require an adequate stylistics to describe the verbal structure of the work; a sociology of book production to describe the life of literature as a commodity, as something that is manufactured, printed, marketed and consumed; a structural analysis of narrative; and a psychoanalytic theory of character. As for the audience, one would require thorough studies in reading publics, their tastes and motivations. One would need to know what psychological and social functions literature serves, how it selects its readership, and how it supplements or complements other cultural artifacts. With the help of semiology one could place the novel in relation to other symbol-using activities, and with the aid of anthropology and cognitive psychology one could judge the permanent role of artistic creation within the psychic economy of man. To describe the formation of the writer's consciousness we must turn to psychoanalysis and social psychology. And finally, in order to account for the social origins of the world-views which structure literary texts, we need a more powerful sociology of knowledge.

My object in this book is to attempt some of this analysis, to identify some of these connections, for one major novelist who has left us a graphic record of the interaction between individual psyche and history. In Lawrence's novels we encounter in heightened form the essential pressures, fears and hopes of our age.

original German edition 1955); *History and Class Consciousness: Studies in Marxist Dialectics* (London and Cambridge, Mass., 1971; original German edition, 1923).

[6] Jameson, *Marxism and Form* (Princeton, 1971).

1

Society and Ideology in *Sons and Lovers*

In 1913 Marcel Proust, the son of an heiress, was at work upon *A la recherche du temps perdu*; James Joyce, the son of a bankrupt small investor, tax collector, landlord, was at work on *A Portrait of the Artist as a Young Man*; Thomas Mann, descendant of prosperous merchants, the son of a Senator, was beginning *Der Zauberberg*; and D. H. Lawrence, the son of a miner, was revising *Sons and Lovers*. Each man was living in exile from his own past, struggling to make sense of his own life. Proust had secluded himself in a cork-lined room; Joyce had fled Ireland for Trieste where as teacher of the earth's languages in a stateless city he was to become the exemplary exile; Mann had deserted the north German burgher town of his childhood for a country retreat in Bavaria. But of the four writers Lawrence had travelled furthest from home; his exile was the most radical. For at the very time he was describing in his novel the life surrounding Eastwood's mines and Nottingham's mills, he was teaching grammar to middle-class boys in a south London suburb, hobnobbing with writers and editors, dining with members of the Royal Academy, lunching with Lady This and Lord That; and while revising his novel he was travelling on the Continent with another man's wife, mother of three, the daughter of a German baron.

The novel of education, or *Bildungsroman*, was a venerable and distinguished genre at the time these four men set out, on the chaotic eve of world war, to explain their own development. Proust could look back to the confessional writings of Montaigne, Rousseau and Stendhal. The precedent of Goethe cast its shadow over Thomas Mann. For Joyce, in addition to Goethe's *Wilhelm*

Meister, there was Samuel Butler's *The Way of All Flesh* and George Meredith's *Richard Feverel.* Lawrence's novel of education was clearly conceived within this tradition—through its earliest drafts it was entitled *Paul Morel*—but his development from infancy into manhood was significantly different from that of Joyce, Mann or Proust. The father of Proust was a renowned professor of medicine; the father of Mann was a public official; even Joyce's father had been three years at college and had acted upon the stage. But Lawrence's father, who had quit school as a child to work in the mines, was barely literate. True, the mother (who was a well-read woman, even a schoolteacher) stands at the center of *Sons and Lovers*; but it is the father who haunts Lawrence throughout the later novels. In *The White Peacock*, a first novel which significantly translates the Lawrences into the middle class, and in a previous draft of *Sons and Lovers*, the drunken father is dispatched early on. By the final draft he has become a troubling presence, and he was to become more so in succeeding novels. The novice writer began as the son of a miner rather than the son of a former schoolteacher, he was celebrated in London as a prodigy from the grimy coalfields of northern England, rather than as a product of the Education Acts of 1870 and 1902. That was the social identity with which Lawrence began, and which he never fully cast off. Neither Proust nor Joyce nor Mann had such a distance to travel from his social beginnings to the act of writing, nor for that matter had anyone else of equal stature among Lawrence's contemporaries.

Thus for Lawrence the very act of writing a *Bildungsroman*— with its emphasis upon the development of consciousness in an isolated, artistic hero—divorced him from his father and his father's people. But could a man so divorced treat his past without distortion? Could a young writer who had attained (by means of education, native genius, and the social aspirations inherited from his mother) to a place amidst the middle-class intelligentsia and aristocratic dilettanti of London; who had already written two novels featuring well-born and rather saccharine young heroes and heroines; who had spurned his farm girl sweetheart and had run off with a lady; who had journeyed so far intellectually from his father and even his mother, from Eastwood, from childhood—

22

could such a man write objectively about the experience of growing up in a working-class community?

In my judgement he could not, or at any rate did not. No one rivals Lawrence in the vividness with which he evokes the atmosphere of that industrial village, or the warring atmosphere of the home. But when it comes to passing judgment on that life, particularly upon Walter Morel, who is the only member of the family truly integrated into the mining community, Lawrence systematically distorts the picture. It is the nature of this distortion which interests me, because I believe that it provides a key to all of Lawrence's subsequent thought. Let me describe briefly what I mean, and then leave the remainder of the chapter for elaboration.

We view the world of *Sons and Lovers* with a double vision: through the eyes of the boy who has experienced this life on his own senses, and through those of the alienated artist who is striving to account for his social isolation, and to derive some message from his past.[1] The artist faithfully records the boy's memories of historic people, providing us with the raw data for interpreting their feelings and actions in terms of their social situation. But the narrator makes little use of this data. Although it is easy to describe the underlying social matrix which binds together the people and places of the novel's world, Lawrence generally ignored the social existence of his characters, as if some astigmatism had blinded him to the historical forces at work in their lives. The conflict between the father and mother, for example, which is clearly grounded in class differences, is translated into moral terms, as a struggle between bad and good, and

[1] Throughout I treat Paul's alienation as parallel to Lawrence's own. I believe this procedure needs no special justification. There is sufficient evidence for the parallel in the memoirs by Jessie Chambers, Ada Lawrence and Helen Corke, in the *Collected Letters* and essays, in the contemporary stories collected in *The Prussian Officer* volume, and in the biographies by H. T. Moore and Edward Nehls. One need not slight the novel's objectivity and coherence to recognize the personally cathartic role which it played in Lawrence's development. As he wrote to a correspondent in 1913: "I felt you had gone off me a bit, because of *Sons and Lovers*. But one sheds one's sicknesses in books—repeats and presents again one's emotions, to be master of them" (CL 234). My argument is that he presented them without fully mastering them.

then into psychological terms, as the conflict between unconscious and conscious, and finally into an opposition between body and mind. Similarly the discontent of womenfolk in *Sons and Lovers*, which is clearly part of the contemporary ferment for women's emancipation, is reduced to purely physical terms, so that social grievances are interpreted as sexual frustration. Strife between men and women is not linked to the difference in their status, but to a clash between their a-historical "natures," which becomes formalized in the course of Lawrence's thought as the opposition between the female principle and the male. In each case social categories are transformed into psychological categories, which harden into a metaphysic. In the chapter that follows I am concerned to trace the early stages of this transformation.

1 *The Formation of Paul Morel*

Except for William, the eldest son who has gone away to work in London, the Morel children remain at home, and with their mother they share the long evening wait for their father to come back from the mine:

> In the winter nights, when it was cold, and grew dark early, Mrs Morel would put a brass candlestick on the table, light a tallow candle to save the gas. The children finished their bread-and-butter, or dripping, and were ready to go out to play. But if Morel had not come they faltered. The sense of his sitting in his pit-dirt, drinking, after a long day's work, not coming home and eating and washing, but sitting, getting drunk, on an empty stomach, made Mrs Morel unable to bear herself. From her the feeling was transmitted to the other children. She never suffered alone any more: the children suffered with her.
>
> Paul went out to play with the rest. Down in the great trough of twilight, tiny clusters of lights burned where the pits were. A few last colliers struggled up the dim field-path. The lamplighter came along. No more colliers came. Darkness shut down over the valley; work was gone. It was night.
>
> Then Paul ran anxiously into the the kitchen. The one candle still burned on the table, the big fire glowed red. Mrs Morel sat alone. On the hob the saucepan steamed; the dinner-plate lay waiting on the table. All the room was full of the sense of waiting, waiting for the man who was sitting in his pit-dirt, dinner-less, some mile away from home, across the darkness, drinking himself drunk. Paul stood in the doorway.

'Has my dad come?' he asked.

'You can see he hasn't,' said Mrs Morel, cross with the futility of the question.

Then the boy dawdled about near his mother. They shared the same anxiety. Presently Mrs Morel went out and strained the potatoes.

'They're ruined and black,' she said; 'but what do I care?'

Not many words were spoken. Paul almost hated his mother for suffering because his father did not come home from work.

'What do you bother yourself for?' he said. 'If he wants to stop and get drunk, why don't you let him?'

'Let him!' flashed Mrs Morel. 'You may well say "let him."'

She knew that the man who stops on the way home from work is on a quick way to ruining himself and his home. The children were yet young, and depended on the bread-winner. William gave her the sense of relief, providing her at last with someone to turn to if Morel failed. But the tense atmosphere of the room on these waiting evenings was the same.

Paul is bewildered by his mother's suffering, which he shares with the other children, for he does not yet understand why, in terms of Mrs Morel's values, it is such a grave affair for a husband and father to linger at the pub. Although he sides with her against his father, Paul has not yet fully internalized the values on which her judgment is based. In this episode we see him learning, along with his brothers and sisters, to view the world as his mother views it—a learning process that covers the first half of the novel.

Mrs Morel's feelings dominate the scene. They cause a hitch in the children's play, they imbue the kitchen with a sense of tension, of waiting. Aside from her disgust with Morel on account of his drinking and his dirt, a feeling which we are told is transmitted directly to the children, she injects into the apparently trivial incident her perpetual anxiety over money matters. Years after describing this scene, Lawrence was to write a poem entitled "Poverty":

> Being born among the working people
> I know that poverty is a hard old hag,
> and a monster, when you're pinched for actual necessities.

Feeling pinched, the mother and children begrudge every penny squandered by the father, and for the same reason they celebrate even the smallest of treats for themselves—the cornflower-blue dish, a new black bonnet, oil paints, a restaurant meal, a fistful of flowers, an umbrella. That the candle in this scene is tallow rather than wax, that it is used to save the gas, and that there is only one—all this is meant and is felt to contrast with Morel's self-indulgence. Perhaps having to make do with what one had, perhaps the feeling that even the smallest purchases were triumphs over poverty, perhaps the dearth of gews and gaws in that miner's house helped make Lawrence preternaturally aware of the household objects—the pot steaming on the hearth, the plate forsaken on the table, the lonely candle—which furnish *Sons and Lovers*. This ability to depict with vivid concreteness the physical surroundings, whether natural or man-made, which shape life and thought, remained one of the most remarkable features of Lawrence's writing to the end. He admired the same ability in Cézanne, observing that in still-life the painter always respected and sought to evoke the appleness of apples, in landscape the hillness of hills; here was a kindred spirit who acknowledged the tough sinewy otherness of the physical world.

The home atmosphere of revulsion mixed with fear—revulsion towards Morel's character and fear that he might fail to support his family—obviously infects the children, as the bitterness and anxiety of elders work upon young people in Ibsen or Dickens. For Paul, dominated by his mother's feelings, the very night seems agitated. Consider the second paragraph: the paratactic syntax breaks the night up into a sequence of disconnected, fragmentary impressions; nothing hangs together; the world reflects Mrs Morel's disturbed feelings, the causes of which Paul does not yet comprehend. The encounter between mother and son emerges as a specific instance of what happens on those long winter nights when Morel is late in coming home, a specific instance that sums up a crucial phase in Paul's development, as he drifts away from his father and clings ever more closely to his mother. No time is indicated other than an evening in winter. Even the portion of Paul's childhood in which such a scene might have occurred can only be judged approximately. It epitomizes the "waiting evenings," a category of experience rather than a specific event. Hence the scene is less important as a biographical detail than as a concentrated image of a general condition. This is typical of Lawrence's practice throughout *Sons and Lovers*, which like all his other novels has little of what is conventionally called plot: Paul grows up, goes to work in Nottingham, has two love affairs, loses his mother and one brother to death. Rather than complexity of action, we are presented with an account of Paul's *formation*, of the living conditions, parental attitudes, work and friendships which shape his character. In scenes such as this one, general trends—in this case the progressive estrangement between husband and wife, together with the effects of that estrangement on their children—are distilled in the form of brief but intense human encounters.

Throughout the novel, as in the scene before us, dialogue is presented with an almost Biblical economy. Mrs Morel says really very little about what she feels or why ("Not many words were spoken."). Most of what she communicates to her son is nonverbal. Gesture, facial expression, posture, tone of voice, nervous activity, arrangement of objects, narrative commentary of all sorts—these are the principal means by which the most powerful feelings are communicated. Characters in the novel rarely speak more than three sentences at a time, generally only one, and that one usually quite simple. Yet Lawrence manages to create, by means of narrative devices, the impression of a powerful if inarticulate interplay of emotions between his figures, who seem to be groping for language. One need only recall the dialogue in Austen or late James, where characters externalize highly complex feelings in long, syntactically complex discourse; or the dialogue in George Eliot and Hardy—where even rustics, however rambling their speech, are in full verbal possession of their thought and emotion —to recognize, in terms of English literary conventions, how inarticulate the people of *Sons and Lovers* really are. If they seem more eloquent than the taciturn creatures of Hemingway, this is because Lawrence amply supplements speech with narrative. Dialogue in *Sons and Lovers* really exposes less about fixed personalities than about relationships, and about identity in the process of formation. But these are always intensely personal, one-to-one relationships, and because they are inarticulate they encompass little beyond the immediate issue of personal feelings. Hence the concentration of dialogue on feeling, spoken as it is by characters who are largely unconscious of their relation to the larger forces and conditions of their environment, tends to mask the broader social context within which individual relationships revolve. The

27

gulf between language and experience, particularly between the impersonal terms of social discourse and the extremes of personal experience, remains visible in all of the novels, but is especially prominent in *The Rainbow* and *Lady Chatterley's Lover*.

Few words need be exchanged between mother and son: because so much is understood, so much can be left unspoken. Already the two have drawn very close together in feeling and outlook: "When she fretted he understood, and could have no peace. His soul seemed always attentive to her." Paul's emotions come by reflection from his mother, from her suffering and anxiety, her brooding and impatience. By repeating for Paul the same images, almost the same language that has been used to describe Mrs Morel's feelings, Lawrence emphasizes this connection:

> The sense of his sitting in his pit-dirt, drinking, after a long day's work, not coming home and eating and washing but sitting, getting drunk, on an empty stomach, made Mrs Morel unable to bear herself.
>
> *   *   *
>
> All the room was full of the sense of waiting, waiting for the man who was sitting in his pit-dirt, dinner-less, some mile away from home, across the darkness, drinking himself drunk. Paul stood in the doorway.

Mrs Morel's response to people, her ideas, her categories of judgment, even her metaphors creep into Paul's speech, and they permeate the narrative description of his thought. Thus he argues her views on political questions, lacking opinions of his own; he echoes her verdict on Morel, the drunken wreck; and he parrots her assessment of Miriam. It is she who forces Paul to view his own father's work as bestial, and therefore to despise the man himself, treating the miner's fate within the industrial system as proof of his personal weakness.

Morel is necessarily excluded from the linguistic domain shared by mother and son. Unable to speak as they do, he cannot conceive reality as they do. Among the many scenes which could be chosen to demonstrate this contrast in outlook and the corresponding contrast in language, I take the one in which William's career is at issue:

28

Then, when the lad was thirteen, she got him a job in the 'Co-op.' office. He was a very clever boy, frank, with rather rough features and real viking blue eyes.

'What dost want ter ma'e a stool-harsed Jack on 'im for?' said Morel. 'All he'll do is to wear his britches behind out, an' earn nowt. What's 'e startin' wi'?'

"It doesn't matter what he's starting with,' said Mrs Morel.

'It wouldna! Put 'im 'i th' pit wi' me, an' e'll earn a easy ten shillin' a wik from th' start. But six shillin' wearin' his truck-end out on a stool's better than ten shillin' i' th' pit wi' me, I know.'

'He is *not* going in the pit,' said Mrs Morel, 'and there's an end of it.'

'It wor good enough for me, but it's non good enough for 'im.'

'If your mother put you in the pit at twelve, it's no reason why I should do the same with my lad.'

Mrs Morel clearly controls the scene, as indeed she controls the entire novel; her word is law, and she makes no pretense of hiding the fact from her husband or children. The difference in authority is reinforced by the difference in speech: Mrs Morel speaks the language of the narrator, Morel speaks the language of Bestwood streets. Her refined speech—for thus it sounds in the ears of Bestwood—fascinates the young Morel, who thinks it foreign and lady-like, and it distinguishes her from the working-class neighbors with whom she is never at ease. The husband's Derbyshire dialect has the contrary effect of identifying him with the community. Following the mother in all things, the children have learned her speech, which Paul in particular feels to be the medium of educated discourse. Bound within the regional dialect, Morel is equally bound by the local assumption that the son should accompany his father into the mine. A stranger to that dialect, Mrs Morel is free to envision another role for her sons: they are to be gentlemen. Lawrence always despised that upper-class accent which he referred to contemptuously in a poem as "The Oxford Voice," and it is true that his own writing derives much of its energy from the rhythms of working-class speech; yet by contrast to the language of his father, his own was educated, refined, middle-class— not Oxford English, certainly, but "Standard" English. Despite the obvious affection with which the miner's dialect is imitated, in this scene and elsewhere, it remains, like dialect in Dickens, a language of *imitation*, represented from the outside by a narrator whose scope of expression and whose range of concepts far surpass the limits of the miner's speech. (We find this opposition between "standard" English and Derbyshire dialect used to a much different effect in *Lady Chatterley's Lover*.)

Although Paul takes over much of his mother's language, he quickly outstrips her in learning, ideas and expressiveness. She does not care about Schopenhauer, she does not understand his art, she reads no Baudelaire. Eventually he surpasses her range of speech, as he has surpassed Morel's. For talk about ideas he must go to Miriam, who is also finally not articulate enough to satisfy him, driving him to complain of her wordless and cloying emotion. However much he extolls silence, however halting his speech, Paul is continually pressing toward an articulation of all those feelings—about love, God, nature, death, the blood, sex—which Lawrence argued could not be translated without distortion into language. And this paradox lies at the heart of all Lawrence's work: he could only use verbal means to explore those dimensions of experience which, he maintained, were incompatible with language. For Paul the achievement of integral personality, the process of individuation in Jung's sense, is intimately bound up with self-expression. According to the linguistic norms established for the voices of Mrs Morel, Paul and the narrator, Walter Morel appears to be a limited character, with only a vague sense of his condition or his identity, because his capacity for self-expression is so limited. In this case the linguistic limits to self-realization reflect social, economic, educational and occupational limits: the circumscription of language is only one symptom of a general circumscription of life.

As the scope of Paul's learning expands, as his ideas mature, as his ambitions stretch into further reaches of life, then like the Brangwens in *The Rainbow* he grows restless within the bounds imposed by his social origin. The growth of his expressiveness, together with the increasing complexity of thought and feeling attributed to him, which gradually converge toward (without actually matching) the linguistic standards set by the narrator, record the development of a totally alien sensibility within the Bestwood ethos. The mother's influence turns Paul against his father, then education and life in the city wean him away from his mother. So long as she lives, Mrs Morel remains the source of Paul's ambitions, she prompts him to that struggle into consciousness which eventually carries him not simply beyond his father's class, but beyond her own, indeed beyond all human groups whatsoever. His utter despair after her death is only partially explained, in Freudian terms, as the anguish of Oedipus over the dead Jocasta. It is also the despair of the isolated intellectual, the more isolated because he started out as the son of a miner rather than the son of a bourgeois:

> Beyond the town the country, little smouldering spots for more towns—the sea—the night—on and on! And he had no place in it! Whatever spot he stood in, there he stood alone. From his breast, from his mouth, sprang the endless space, and it was there behind him, everywhere. The people hurrying along the streets offered no obstruction to the void in which he found himself.

The declassed artist, he belongs nowhere. True, at the end Paul turns toward the town, a gesture which commentators have interpreted as negative or positive according to their temperaments. By either interpretation, the group with which Paul can identify remains to be discovered, beyond the confines of the novel. That is largely the subject of *The Rainbow*, where the quest for social involvement fails. By *Women in Love* that quest has been abandoned, the sensitive and isolated man having accepted his estrangement from society.

The hero of *Sons and Lovers*, like Stephen Dedalus in *A Portrait of the Artist as a Young Man* or like Julien Sorel in *Le Rouge et le Noir*,[2] extricates himself from a limiting social background. But not to move into any new community—and this is symptomatic of Lawrence's dilemma as an isolated intellectual. Although the hostility between individual and society is not as marked here as it becomes in later novels, Lawrence's fundamentally individualistic perspective, shying away from social commitment, focusing on personal growth in opposition to the growth of community, is

[2] "I often think Stendhal must have writhed in torture every time he remembered *Le rouge et le noir* was public property," Lawrence wrote in January of 1912 (CL 94), in the midst of recording his own history for public consumption. There are more similarities between Paul Morel and Julian Sorel than one of names to suggest that Lawrence may well have had Stendhal in mind when writing *Sons and Lovers*. Julien Sorel repudiates his peasant origins, aspiring to rise socially by means of his intelligence, but is unable, in the course of his rise,·to identify with any other social group.

already dominant. What is problematic in *Sons and Lovers* is individual character and personal relationships, rather than community, the larger society within which character and relationships develop. The highly personal nature of the material, so close to him in time and feeling, doubtless hindered him from recognizing the broader social and historical coordinates of individual lives in *Sons and Lovers*. At the same time, because this material is given, because it is for the most part autobiographical, features of contemporary society force themselves into the novel willy-nilly. Engels, and Lukács after him, called this phenomenon "the triumph of realism": the writer presents a fuller view of reality than his ideology would seem to allow for. Stated contrariwise, the novel provides evidence for judgments which are radically at odds with the author's own. I will examine some of this evidence in the following section.

The first half of *Sons and Lovers* is built of scenes such as the two just discussed, each one focusing on a moment of conflict within the family, each one adding an increment to the distance which separates Gertrude and Walter Morel. Several of the plays which Lawrence was writing at this time, in particular *A Collier's Friday Night* (echoes of Robert Burns: one of Lawrence's pet projects at this time was a biographical novel about that other plebian writer), were essentially dramatizations of such moments of strife and tension. Both in their structure and in the human conflicts which they represent, these two scenes reflect the narrative practices and ideological issues which shape the novel as a whole.

2 Class

We have seen that the difference in speech between Walter and Gertrude Morel, marking as it does their differences in class background and education, corresponds to an underlying conflict in outlook and aspiration. Mrs Morel comes from solid bourgeois stock, stout Congregationalists all. In the memory of her grandfather, a failed lace manufacturer, she possesses an image of lost social eminence that might be regained. From her father, an engineer whose chief concern seems to have been the size of his salary, and who was well-educated and stern-minded, she formed her ideal of manhood. As a young woman she had all but married one John Field, "the son of a well-to-do tradesman," also an educated man who aspired to the ministry and settled upon merchandising. She is well-educated herself, having taught school for some time. This side of her character emerges in chats with the vicar over starched table-cloths, in her activities with the Women's Guild, and in her promotion of the Morel children's education. Through her sons, for whom she wants middle-class jobs, comfortable homes and "ladies" to wive, she attempts to regain some of the status which she has lost through marriage to Morel.

Morel on the other hand, who left school at age ten to work in the mine, is barely literate, spelling painfully through the headlines and seeing no value whatsoever in the reading of books. He has no use for Mrs Morel's religion, preferring the pub to chapel, and fails to understand either her highfalutin ideas or Paul's art. Unlike his wife, he does not feel specially pinched by poverty, never dreams of clawing his way into the middle-class, nor does he envision a very different future for his children. Little beyond Bestwood attracts him, and little within Bestwood repels him.

Morel clearly does not live up to Mrs Morel's ideal of manhood, and she communicates her judgment to the children. In scenes other than those we have already considered the children learn from her to mock their father's manners, to belittle his work at the mine, to sneer at his lack of formal education and in general to degrade his manhood. Even though specific grievances often emerge during money squabbles, it is evident that something more basic than customary domestic wrangles over shillings and pence—vital as shillings and pence are—has motivated this total assault upon Morel as father and husband. Of course he scants her budget, but so do the other miners when times are bad. It is far more significant that he does not share her education, religion, social aspirations, aesthetic training, economic motivations, manners, language, moral views or political interests. Their marriage is wrecked by differences that are primarily social rather than personal.

In the scene discussed above, where William's career is at issue, Mrs Morel calls attention to these differences by contrasting herself with Morel's mother: she is not going to put *her* sons down the pit, whatever the old lady had decided to do with the likes of Walter. In the opening chapter these women meet, and from that encounter we learn that while living in a rented house, sitting on mortgaged chairs and eating off mortgaged tables might suit old Mrs Morel, it is far from suiting Gertrude Coppard Morel. Such a cramped financial state pinches her bourgeois soul. She had persuaded herself, we are told, that she was marrying a financially independent man, owner of two houses and a houseful of furniture, possessor of a bank account, a miner with the drive to "get on." As it happened she married a man indebted, Marx's classic laborer, owner of nothing but his body.

Her disenchantment with the marriage dates from this experience: "She said very little to her husband, but her manner had changed towards him. Something in her proud, honourable soul had crystallized out hard as rock." Because she remains aloof from the other miners' wives, who beard her for having put a stop to Morel's career as dancing master, and by implication for having fettered his free spirit with her puritan scruples, she feels increasingly isolated, "miles away from her own people." Her own people, of course, are the ministers, engineers, teachers and the like whom she knew as a girl. We are told that this marks the beginning of their marital battle, a beginning which Lawrence depicts with perfect clarity in social terms. But then what conclusion does he draw?

> She fought to make him undertake his own responsibilities, to make him fulfil his obligations. But he was too different from her. His nature was purely sensuous, and she strove to make him moral, religious. She tried to force him to face things. He could not endure it—it drove him out of his mind.

The narrator has translated social differences into moral and psychological terms: the wife is responsible, aware of obligations, bearing the reformer's burden; the husband is irresponsible, blind to obligations, the crude soil which she is to cultivate; he is sensuous, the body; she is religious, the spirit. Two pages later we read:

> Nevertheless, she still continued to strive with him. She still had her high moral sense, inherited from generations of Puritans. It was now a religious instinct, and she was almost a fanatic with him, because she loved him, or had loved him. If he sinned, she tortured him. If he drank, and lied, was often a poltroon, sometimes a knave, she wielded the lash unmercifully.

34

The pity was, she was too much his opposite. She could not be content with the little he might be; she would have him the much that he ought to be. So, in seeking to make him nobler than he could be, she destroyed him. She injured and hurt and scarred herself, but lost none of her worth. She also had the children.

Their differences in expectation are translated into valued "opposites": she has a high moral instinct, he by implication has a low; he sins and she redeems; he is content with mediocrity while she aspires to noble heights; she strives to shape him, he remains the passive clay; although he is destroyed, she, miraculously, loses "none of her worth." The passage, like the novel as a whole, assumes Mrs Morel's purpose and standards. Thus concrete differences between particular human beings, differences which are comprehensible in social terms, serve as the basis for constructing a metaphysic which opposes the body to the mind.

Time after time in those early pages Lawrence proffers moral or psychological explanations of incidents which he has already given us evidence for interpreting sociologically. Consider the hair-clipping scene in the opening chapter. Borrowing clothes from her sisters, Mrs Morel arrays baby William in white coat and hat, complete with ostrich feather, and she lets his hair burgeon in curls to complete this transformation of the miner's son into Little Lord Fauntleroy. One morning Morel takes the boy aside and clips his hair. No son of *his* should be considered a sissy in the village—but this is precisely what Mrs Morel wanted, because the child's appearance was a prop for her performance as lady in the mining community. In his description of the aftermath, however, Lawrence ignores this social dimension, referring to the incident as an "act of masculine clumsiness." Morel appears totally cowed, his wife appears the martyr.

Having taken the pledge at the time of his marriage, Morel resumes his drinking after these early battles, but not more heavily than many miners, so we are told, nor anything stronger than beer. In various scenes we learn that the pub offered him a form of community, free from authority, that could be found neither in mine nor home. His pub-sitting was a regular part of the miner's life, a compensation for numbing and back-breaking work, often the only social activity other than chapel (where Noncomformist ministers reconciled an embittered flock to their barren pasture) which was available to an uneducated and exhausted man in an industrial village. Despised by his wife, shut out from his family, Morel has added reason for drinking. But in scene after scene, when he appears drunk and brutal, we hear nothing of his reasons for drinking, but only of his ruin and of his wife's bitter suffering. After these early scenes, which pretend to justify the father's damnation by the mother, and, following her, by the children, Lawrence treats Morel from the outside as a broken man who is responsible for his own ruin, one who is redeemed only in fleeting moments by his singing or tinkering. The narrator's judgment is consistent with that of the mother: "his manhood broke," "he broke himself," he became "more or less a husk," he "fell into a slow ruin," he "lapsed slowly," he "denied the God in him."

There seems to be a division between the narrator who is compassionately recording the miner's life, and the narrator who is judging that life. After all, the triumph of realism is also Lawrence's triumph as a writer: he conveys a sense of the pressures, deformations and joys of life in that mining community with a loving attention and a vigor of language which is unrivalled in English literature. In a scene midway through the novel Morel observes his own body while bathing, a body prematurely aged, twisted and broken from years of hacking at the coal-face and from scores of accidents, a body scarred blue with coal-dust, and instead of damning the mines which have crippled him, "he felt the ruin he had made during these years. He wanted to bustle about, to run away from it." Lawrence simultaneously records a fact and implies a judgment. That Morel *felt* responsible for his own ruin seems convincing and disturbing. But the narrator by his silence at this point appears to accept this judgment, implying that Morel's social fate, a fate shared with millions of laborers, was a sign of personal guilt.

The narrator consistently views the father through the mother's eyes:

> As he bent over, lacing his boots, there was a certain vulgar gusto in his movement that divided him from the reserved, watchful rest of the family. He always ran away from the battle with himself.

Lawrence was later to use the contrast between reserve and gusto as a means of distinguishing the neurotically repressed middle-classes from the instinctive and sensuous common people. But here the miner appears "vulgar;" elsewhere we have found him described as a "knave", "poltroon," "nasty" and "brutal". When he returns home sweaty and exhausted from the mines, to find the Congregational minister sipping tea over a table-cloth in the kitchen, and when he is treated as a crude beast by his wife, Morel understandably grows furious. The minister is one of Mrs Morel's "own people," he is an educated man, a spiritual man, possessed of proper manners. He is a reincarnation of John Field, a middle-class substitute for her husband. Enough has passed before to persuade us that Morel appreciates the significance of the minister's presence and of his wife's behavior; certainly the reader does. Yet the narrator endorses Mrs Morel's opinion that, by fussing and complaining, the miner is just showing off; even young William is made to hate him, "with a boy's hatred for false sentiment, for the stupid treatment of his mother." We are told that as Morel ages he acts in increasingly "dirty and disgusting ways," but all we learn of this behavior is that "His manners in the house were the same as he used among the colliers down pit." Yet what was the determining reality for this miner, cut off from the rest of his family, if it was not that gathering of colliers down pit? His ways were disgusting from Mrs Morel's point of view, according to her middle-class upbringing, and it is this point of view which Lawrence employs throughout the novel, in matters great and small.

Even Morel's lack of education is turned against him. In one important scene Paul reluctantly tells his father of winning a prize in a writing competition for a child's paper:

> Morel turned round to him.
> 'Have you, my boy? What sort of a competition?'
> 'Oh, nothing—about famous women.'
> 'And how much is the prize, then, as you've got?'
> 'It's a book.'
> 'Oh, indeed!'
> 'About birds.'
> 'Hm—hm!'

And that was all. Conversation was impossible between the father and any other member of the family. He was an outsider. He had denied the God in him.

The breach between father and son appears as an educationally conditioned difference in language. What after all is Morel to say about famous women, resurrected from histories and dressed up in an essay? What conversation is he to make about the prize book which he cannot read? Still a child, Paul has already outstripped his father in formal if not in practical knowledge. Nor is that surprising in view of the miner's upbringing. Yet this demonstration of Morel's educational backwardness (previous scenes have demonstrated his drunkenness, his brutality, his ignorance of bourgeois manners and his indifference to bourgeois culture, his refusal to stand up for his own rights and his inability to "get on" at work) is made occasion for the judgment that he is *personally* guilty of failing to become a whole human being: "He had denied the God in him." Although it is difficult to see how any but an exceptional man could have overcome his disadvantages—poverty, inadequate education and limited class expectations, work that is physically exhausting while mentally undemanding, cramped housing and political impotence—nevertheless Mrs Morel condemns him for failing to achieve precisely this miraculous escape. Paul accepts her class-bound judgment. Lawrence, having himself freshly escaped at the time he wrote the novel, accepted it as well.

In making that judgment Mrs Morel applied what can best be called a 'bourgeois' perspective, wholly consistent with her Protestant ethics, a perspective which treats the individual as the unit of success or failure, without regard to the conditions which shape him, without regard to the collective social reality within which he dwells. Like St Paul, whom her father admired more than any other man, and like the great Reformation theologians who looked to St Paul for their authority, Mrs Morel held the individual responsible for his salvation or damnation. Her individualist perspective dominates the book, as her feelings dominate Paul, as her values dominate the Morel household. Suffering from the capitalist ethic on the job and from the Protestant ethic in his own home, Morel neatly illustrates Max Weber's proposition of a link between the two spheres of ideology. Both the religious and the economic ideology treat mankind as a collection of atomic individuals, each person seeking his own salvation or profit, motivated solely by rational self-interest—according to Adam Smith's formulation—

each isolated Robinson Crusoe remaining solely responsible for his worldly condition. Thus both William and Paul make their escape, such as it is, alone, leaving their community unchanged; their alienation would seem to be the natural state of man according to Mrs Morel's individualist perspective.

For Lawrence, writing *Sons and Lovers* between 1910 and 1913, before experiencing the mass insanity of the War, before really understanding his characters' problems as problems of contemporary society, this individualist perspective was convincing. After all, had he not scrambled out of the working class, had he not escaped the industrial system, had he not wooed a lady? Individual autonomy, at least for those who were willing to give a tug at their own bootstraps, seemed to him a proven fact. Enjoying an exile's comparative social independence, he exaggerated man's freedom, since anyone estranged from the conditions and institutions of his society, whether physically exiled like Rousseau, or emotionally like Blake, is prone to stress man's freedom rather than his bondage. Of course the exile is at once the most and the least free of men; his very isolation from all social groups prevents him from effectively acting upon his ideas.[3] Such isolation commonly leads—as has been shown by Émile Durkheim, who named this condition *anomie*—to frustration and disgust, equally with oneself and one's society. Like Swift and Orwell, two other emotional exiles, Lawrence was by spells the aloof yet penetrating observer, and the misanthrope, manifesting by turns the profoundest concern for his countrymen and the most consummate disgust, each alike the fruit of social isolation.

Lawrence's exaggerated sense of individual autonomy led him to distort his representation of reality—especially in *Sons and Lovers*, but to a varying degree in all his novels—by isolating personal existence partly or wholly from social existence. Although *Sons and Lovers* abounds in references to social conditions and historical movements, these are not used to account for the quality, the changes and crises, of individual lives. That is to say, Lawrence explains the problems of his characters psychologically rather than historically, in terms of a personal rather than a collective past. When in a later essay he wrote that "I feel

[3] I am indebted to Raymond Williams' discussion of the psychology of exile in *Culture and Society, 1780–1850* (London and New York, 1958).

it is the change inside the individual which is my real concern. The great social change interests me and troubles me, but it is not my field,"[4] he posited a dichotomy between individual psychology and social existence which would have seemed alien to George Eliot, Dickens or Austen, and to all of the great Continental realists such as Stendhal, Balzac or Tolstoy. Of course he was entitled to occupy himself primarily with subjectivity, and did so, but when he set himself the task of *explaining* subjectivity, or of passing judgment on individuals, he often failed, as in the case of Morel, to take the social dimension into account.

Morel's failure should be grounds for criticizing the industrial and economic system which has maimed him, rather than for criticizing the man. Mrs Morel's bitter repudiation of her married state expresses more than class prejudice. Her outrage and Morel's ruin were to be translated by Lawrence into a basic critique of the social order which had produced this humanly degraded way of life. This woman is determined not only to help her children escape the financial straits in which she finds herself, but also to liberate them from the brutal working conditions and from the domestic squalor which the industrial order has imposed upon generations of Morels. To her son she transmits both outrage and frustration, and she teaches him to defend precisely those values which the industrial system—with its associated politics, economics, housing and schools—denies. The son of Mrs Lawrence was to protest—in plays and essays and novels—the evil which had been committed against the human spirit in Eastwood's mines and streets. When Lawrence returned to the same emotional terrain at the end of his life, in *Lady Chatterley's Lover* and "Nottingham and the Mining Country," he judged his father differently. He had become aware by that time of the larger social forces which had intersected in the lives of the Morels, Leivers and Dawes, and in particular those forces which had mutilated his father.

I have dwelt upon the conflict between Mr and Mrs Morel because it is the clearest example in the novel of a socially and historically comprehensible problem which is nevertheless interpreted by Lawrence in personal, psychological terms, and because it demonstrates the triumph of Mrs Morel's individualist per-

[4] "The State of Funk," PII 567.

spective, which rules the novel as a whole. The class differences between Mr and Mrs Morel are evident. The novel "follows this idea," Lawrence wrote to his agent in 1912, "a woman of character and refinement goes into the lower class, and has no satisfaction in her own life."[5] Lawrence was very much aware of the corresponding class differences between his own parents, and he frequently referred to this social conflict, built into his family, as a means of explaining certain aspects of his own character and thought.

> My mother was a clever, ironical delicately moulded woman of good, old burgher descent. She married below her. My father was dark, ruddy, with a fine laugh. He is a coal miner. He was one of the sanguine temperament, warm and hearty, but unstable: he lacked principle, as my mother would have said. He deceived her and lied to her. She despised him—he drank.[6]

He wrote those words late in 1910, while his mother was dying. In a later poem, much of the sympathy which he had once felt toward his mother's class having vanished, he wrote more bitterly of the social fissure which had divided his childhood:

> My father was a working man
> and a collier was he,
> at six in the morning they turned him down
> and they turned him up for tea.
>
> My mother was a superior soul
> a superior soul was she,
> cut out to play a superior role
> in the god-damn bourgeoisie.
>
> We children were the in-betweens
> little non-descripts were we,
> indoors we called each other *you*,
> outside, it was *tha* and *thee*.[7]

Aware though he was of this parental class conflict, I do not believe Lawrence fully realized how very near the heart of his work

[5] Letter to Edward Garnett, CL 160. 14.xi.12.
[6] Letter to Rachel Annand Taylor, CL 68. 15.xi.10.
[7] These are the first three stanzas of "Red-Herring," *Collected Poems*, p. 490. Compare the late "Autobiographical Sketch" (PII 300–1). On the question generally, see Ada Lawrence, *Young Lorenzo* (Florence, 1932).

that conflict lay, how fundamentally the contrast between his father's life and his mother's ideas had influenced his own representation of reality.

3 Four Frustrated Women

As in the case of Morel, so with the principal women of the novel, the account which Lawrence gives of individuals and of personal relationships often ignores or even contradicts the interpretation which is suggested by the objective social existence of the characters involved. There are no satisfied women in *Sons and Lovers*, and the most important four—Mrs Morel, Mrs Leivers, Miriam and Clara—are downright frustrated. All of them squirm in the cramped circumstances which they have been allotted by marriage or birth. All of them seek to escape the narrow bounds of their existence, either through education, religion, political activity or through men. Lawrence never acknowledges these connections among his womenfolk, because he treats their problems as personal and therefore explicable in terms of their separate pasts or their unique personalities, which appear isolated from each other and from their social context.

But the frustration of these four women certainly has a common source: during the latter decades of the nineteenth century and the first decades of the twentieth, women's education expanded faster than the social opportunities which were available to them; their political awareness increased while they remained politically impotent; their rising self-estimate conflicted with their low status in society. These contradictions in the social condition of women issued, during the decade before the war, in a militant and violent feminist movement. The period 1903–1914 was the heyday of Mrs Pankhurst's Women's Social and Political Union. Like their counterparts at that time in the trades unions and the Irish Home Rule Movement, the suffragettes resorted to violence out of frustration with a dawdling Parliament and a lethargic populace. There were suffrage riots throughout Europe during the years 1906–1914, involving unenfranchised men as well as women in Prussia, Italy and Austria. Demonstrations by suffragettes in London had become so common during the years which Lawrence spent as a teacher in Croydon, where he drafted *Sons and Lovers*, that he treated them in his letters as a normal part of the political landscape. It is against this historical background of feminist unrest and dissent that his four frustrated women must be viewed.

Mrs Morel's case has already been discussed. Her husband having failed to live up to her bourgeois ideal, she seeks to realize her social aspirations through her sons. William is broken by the strain, and Paul very nearly so. The elder son's exhausting study, his passion to advance in his work, his hectic rise through the social circles of Bestwood, Nottingham and London, even his destructive hunger to marry that tawdry "lady," derive from Mrs Morel's ambitions. The same ambitions motivate Paul, if not with William's intensity. The two sons are forced by their mother and by their own education to repudiate their father's values and way of life. "I've never had a husband," Mrs Morel complains to Paul, but what she means is: Morel is not what I wanted him to be, nor has he enabled me to become what I wanted myself to be. The claim she makes on her sons—first William and then Paul—is not just emotional, but also ethical, social, vocational. The result is a crippling interdependence between sons and mother, which has usually been explained in Freudian terms. But such a psychological account ignores the social causes of Mrs Morel's frustration and of Morel's inadequacy as a father figure.[8] This frustration is never more evident than in her descent towards death. What is tragic in Mrs Morel's dying is not the torture, nor death itself, but rather the fact that she has failed while living to realize the freer existence which she has imagined for Paul, and that she dies just at the moment when her son shows promise of fulfilling at least some of her expectations.

About Mrs Leivers we are told little, except that she finds housewifing on the farm a bitter chore, and that she charges every aspect of life with religious significance:

> The mother exalted everything—even a bit of housework—to the plane of a religious trust. . . . Paul was just opening out from

[8] Lawrence acknowledges the crippling nature of this attachment in essays and letters, as well as in the novel. This theme is taken up in the play, *The Daughter-in-Law* and in several stories in *The Prussian Officer* volume. Little of substance has been added to the Freudian interpretation of the novel presented by Alfred B. Kuttner in *Psychoanalytic Review*, III, No. 3 (July, 1916); but compare the elaboration by D. A. Weiss, *Oedipus in Nottingham* (Seattle, 1962).

childhood into manhood. This atmosphere, where everything took a religious value, came with a subtle fascination to him.

It is precisely this religiosity which makes her farm life bearable, by giving meaning to menial work, and dignity to an existence which she considers brutal, for she is exhausted by the labor and repelled by the crudeness of her menfolk. Mrs Leivers transmits to Miriam her distaste for this life, together with her compensating religion. Marx and Nietzsche were agreed in criticizing this tendency of Christianity to rationalize a painful social existence or to compensate for poverty of life. The Congregationalism of Lawrence's mother, like most Nonconformist sects of the industrial north of England, had the effect, because it was so puritanical, of transforming straitened circumstances into the conditions of virtue. Paul never recognizes this compensatory function which religion serves for the Leivers women, nor is it fully acknowledged by Lawrence, who treats this intense religiosity as an accidental trait of the mother, which is bequeathed with damaging consequences to the daughter.

Such is the background for Miriam's frustration, which is whetted by her education and by her contact with the larger world of Nottingham through Paul. Jessie Chambers, who served as model for Miriam, records in her memoir that she felt rebellious when her own education was cut short, because she feared that her ignorance would doom her to remain on the farm. "Right from infancy I had been aware of a world that glimmered beyond the surrounding world of fact, and I dreaded lest the circumstances of my life should shut me out, compel me to live, as it were, in the dark. . . ."[9] Paul, who has no intention of sinking into the colliery life of his father, resents the fact that Miriam cannot let herself merge happily and unconsciously into life on the farm. Lawrence translates her distaste for the farm into psychological terms as an aversion to the physical. She cannot bear to hear that the mare is in foal, we are told, because she is unable to accept her own sexuality; whereas she is clearly rejecting a whole way of life, in which mares are forever in foal, brothers are cruel and brutal, muddied floors wait to be scrubbed, meals to be cooked, errands to

[9] *D. H. Lawrence: A Personal Record* (London, 1935; New York, 1936), p. 46. We recognize in her words the yearning of the Brangwen women of *The Rainbow*.

be run. She is an educated Cinderella who resents serving as drudge to her farming menfolk; like Paul she yearns to escape by the one means available to her—her mind. Thus when Lawrence criticizes her for being too spiritual, too hungry for knowledge, too earnest, too restless, he is condemning in her precisely those impulses which alienated him from his own social origins. The opposition between body and mind which he invokes as explanation is a metaphysical cloak dragged in after the fact. Neither Paul within the novel nor Lawrence without respects Miriam's social aspirations, but must reduce them to sexual frustrations. A man can give himself entirely to his work, says Paul, and therefore what a man does with his life is important, but a woman can only give to work "the unimportant part of herself." She must seek fulfillment through a man, as the fictional Mrs Morel and the historical Mrs Lawrence had done.

Miriam's isolation and the influence of her mother adequately explain that sexual timidity which angers Paul—who also holds the girl responsible for his own timidity, which in fact derives from his attachment to *his* mother. The sexual attitudes of both the boy and girl, their fears and expectations, are largely shaped by their mothers, for both of whom marriage has been a painful ordeal. But Lawrence ignores the effects of the frustration which was common to the two wives. He also underrates the importance of Mrs Morel's ambition that Paul marry a "lady"—a category which Miriam does not fit. The mother "frankly *wanted* him to climb into the middle class, a thing not very difficult, she knew. And she wanted him in the end to marry a lady." She has implanted the same desire in William, who ruins himself for the stupid, careless and vain Miss Western, because she is genteel, she is a lady. By claiming that Paul acquires his sexual inhibitions from Miriam, Lawrence underestimates the impact upon the son of Morel's failure to satisfy Gertrude, for Paul fears the same kind of inadequacy.

A good many of the nicest men he knew were like himself, bound in by their own virginity, which they could not break out of. They were so sensitive to their women that they would go without them for ever rather than do them a hurt, an injustice. Being the sons of mothers whose husbands had blundered rather brutally through their feminine sanctities, they were themselves diffident and shy.

45

Once again their marital conflict is described as an opposition between masculine brutality and feminine delicacy, as if these were inherent qualities of man and woman, rather than socially conditioned differences. Mrs Morel suffers less from a physical brutality than from a social one: her notions of home, marriage, work, financial independence, fatherhood and success are outraged by the miner's life. Miriam's brothers appear crude to her, not because they are men, but because they are farmers, and seem content to remain so. Preferring a metaphysical or psychological explanation to a sociological one, Lawrence is reluctant to explore the basis in social existence for the factors which he does stress: Paul's love for his mother, Miriam's religiosity, and the sexual immaturity which they share. Each of these traits stems in part from class conflicts, as we have seen, or from the contemporary predicament of women. Even Miriam's possessiveness could be explained in terms of the girl's desire to escape into a freer life through Paul, seeing him, as his mother sees him, to be a way out. In terms of psychological differences alone, therefore, the conflict between Paul and Miriam is not comprehensible.

The fourth frustrated woman is Clara Dawes. Like Mrs Morel, she is unhappily married to a man whom industrial work and scanty education have brutalized. Like Miriam, she has sought to escape her position through education, with the result that she finds factory labor more confining and demeaning than before. Unlike the other two women, however, she is a militant feminist, seeking to achieve the collective advancement of women and to regain a sense of her own dignity through the feminist movement. Which is not to say that Mrs Morel is wholly a stranger to the movement: she writes papers for the Women's Guild, to the amazement of her children, and she joins with the other members of the Guild in criticizing the quality of Bestwood life, to the annoyance of the menfolk. Yet Lawrence treats Clara's association with the feminist movement as a casual or amusing fact about her, even though that feminism is a direct expression of the historical situation which binds together all of the frustrated women in the novel. Once again his individualist perspective suppresses the actual social connections between characters and events.

Perceiving Clara, in the light of his own needs, as a sensual object, Paul is unable to allow due weight to her social aspirations. Instead he interprets her social frustrations as sexual frustations, her desire for education, meaningful work and a dignified place in the community as a mask for sexual yearning. Accordingly he returns her at the end to Baxter Dawes, his own amorous attentions having "healed" her, although her social situation is more cramped then ever. Lawrence clearly reveals the narrowness of Paul's perspective, without however suggesting any alternative view, when the young man brushes off his mother's concern for Clara's reputation by arguing that people "know she's a suffragette, and so on"—"and so on" meaning that because Clara "lives separate from her husband, and talks on platforms" she "hasn't much to lose," "her life's nothing to her." Paul has in fact *used* Clara, without regard to her needs or desires as a person, and without respecting the broader movement for women's emancipation in which she is involved; for one of the goals of that movement, as Clara herself proclaims, is to abolish those attitudes which justify the exploitation of women. Although she satisfies Paul's animal needs, Clara is no more a lady than Miriam is, and so she cannot satisfy his social ambition. Lawrence's own position at the time he was writing *Sons and Lovers* made it difficult for him to present without distortion the humbler, less articulate social aspirations of a Miriam or a Clara. His success as scholar, teacher, writer and, most recently, lover, doubtless made the persistent frustration of such women more puzzling. The woman he loved of course, was Frieda Weekley, with whom he was living abroad while completing the novel, a woman who by virtue of family estates and pedigree was aristocrat enough to satisfy the notion of "lady" entertained by the son of a Nottingham miner.

Women in search of liberation, defying social restrictions, were to remain central figures in Lawrence's fiction to the end: Ursula and Gudrun Brangwen in *The Rainbow* and *Women in Love*, March in *The Fox*, Alvina Houghton in *The Lost Girl*, Lou Witt in *St Mawr*, Kate Leslie in *The Plumed Serpent*, and Connie Chatterley in *Lady Chatterley's Lover*, to name only the major figures. Already in January of 1913, before finishing *Sons and Lovers*, Lawrence was hard at work upon *The Insurrection of Miss Houghton*, later to become *The Lost Girl*, in which he depicted a heroine struggling to free herself from her lower-middle-class origins. It is significant that in his next completed novel, *The Rainbow*, it is the women rather than the men who are anxious to lead a fuller life, who escape in hope and imagination from the limiting conditions in which their husbands are mired. "My mother's generation was the first generation of working-class mothers to become really self-conscious," Lawrence wrote in an "Autobiographical Fragment":

the woman freed herself at least mentally and spiritually from the husband's domination, and then she became that great institution, that character-forming power, the mother of my generation. I am sure the character of nine-tenths of the men of my generation was formed by the mother: the character of the daughters too.[10]

His childhood experience of frustrated women, of the yearning and discontent which impelled the feminist movement, left an impression so deep upon his imagination that it could still be traced in his last novel.

I point to the general condition underlying these four cases of frustration, not to suggest that Lawrence should have written a sociological study of feminism, nor to deny the individuality of his women characters, but rather to indicate that he suppressed the connections which were *there*, implicit in his material, in the structure of the society on which *Sons and Lovers* is based. I am of course bringing Lawrence to bear witness against himself. His brilliant portraits of the simmering Mrs Morel, the resigned Mrs Leivers, the yearning Miriam, the sullenly frustrated Clara, provide us with rich social evidence that contradicts his explicit judgements. Once again, as in the portrayal of the conflict between Mr and Mrs Morel, narrative description which is grounded in concrete social experience undercuts the individualist perspective which governs the novel as a whole.

4 Origins of the Dichotomy: Body vs. Mind

We have observed that the conflict between Walter and Gertrude Morel is often described in the novel as an opposition between flesh and spirit, an opposition which is reflected by differences in speech: Morel's language is highly sensory and formulaic, presenting a direct account of his emotional responses to immediate experience; Mrs Morel on the other hand demonstrates that, while sharing her husband's capacity for concreteness, she possesses the additional capacity for abstraction, for transcending the

[10] "Autobiographical Fragment," PI 818.

present situation towards past and future, for articulating something more than immediate sensations. By the time of writing *Studies in Classic American Literature*, Lawrence had come to view the analogous contrast between his own parents as the paradigm of conflict between body and mind:

> My father hated books, hated the sight of anyone reading or writing. My mother hated the thought that any of her sons should be condemned to manual labour. Her sons must have something higher than that. She won. But she died first. He laughs longest who laughs last. There is a basic hostility in all of us between the physical and the mental, the blood and the spirit. The mind is 'ashamed' of the blood. And the blood is destroyed by the mind, actually.[11]

Here manual labor is explicitly opposed to labor of the mind. Morel's work is almost purely physical; the role of planning, purpose, control—of *consciousness*—is minimal. Only at night or on holiday, when he is mending boots or blacksmithing, does Morel become the conscious, self-directing craftsman idealized by Ruskin and Morris; but these are only sparetime activities, fitfully pursued. He is not a craftsman but an industrial worker. Mental functions in the mines have been transferred to the owners and managers. Like Mrs Morel, they are the educated ones, and they are the ones whose projects and orders are carried out by men such as Morel. There is in the mines a *functional* division between body and mind, which corresponds—as Marx and other nineteenth-century critics of industrial civilization observed—to the division of labor between workers and managers.

This division was for Lawrence the dominant feature of industrial society; it crops up again and again in his writing. Aside from the account of opposition between workers and owners in *The White Peacock* and *Sons and Lovers*, the manager reappears as a creature of dominating will and mind in such characters as Tom Brangwen, Jr., Gerald Crich, Clifford Chatterley, Fraser (in *The Daughter-in-Law*), and the mine owners of *Aaron's Rod*.[12]

[11] *Op. cit.*, p. 81.

[12] In his *English Social History 1914–1939* (New York and Oxford, 1965), A. J. P. Taylor observes that the mine-owners in the 1920s, who made a practice of wringing every ounce of coal and every minute of labor from exhausted miners, and who starved out the strikers, "were about the least worthy element in the British community" (p. 248).

The manager achieves his apotheosis in the superman, a figure, owing as much to Nietzsche as to Carlyle, which Lawrence was to sketch in essays from wartime onwards, and was to outline skeptically in such characters as Don Ramon (*The Plumed Serpent*) and Kangaroo. Contrasted with the managers is a mass of brutish, sensual workers, sluggishly physical creatures. There are the colliers of *The Rainbow*, "hanging about in gangs and groups, or passing along the asphalt pavements heavily to work," who "seemed not like living people, but like spectres;" and in *Women in Love* the "half-automatized colliers," who have "a look of abstraction and half-resignation in their pale, often gaunt faces;" and in *Lady Chatterley's Lover*:

> the colliers trailing from the pits, grey-black, distorted, one shoulder higher than the other, slurring their heavy ironshod boots. Underground grey faces, whites of eyes rolling, necks cringing from the pit roof, shoulders out of shape. Men! Men! Alas, in some ways patient and good men. In other ways, non-existent. Something that men *should* have was bred and killed out of them.

The managing elite execute the mental functions of planning, designing, controlling, coordinating, while the laboring masses perform the corresponding physical functions in accord with the will of others. This functional difference is reinforced by differences in education, in class culture and in living conditions.

Lawrence was recording a social fact, the product of a particular organization of labor, which he knew at first hand from the mining villages and industrial cities of the Midlands in which he spent the first half of his life. In his dualism of body and mind, a dichotomy which is fundamental to all his thought, he reproduced this social fact; the structure of concepts corresponds to the structure of functions in the industrial system. What he took to be a natural and inevitable conflict, I am suggesting, was neither natural nor inevitable, but socially produced; and I am suggesting further that this mistaking of the social for the natural is another sign of his neglect of the historical dimension. Of course the mind-body division is as old as philosophy, and it figures in many of those thinkers—notably Schopenhauer, Nietzsche, Bergson and Freud—whose ideas were familiar to Lawrence. But the interesting question is not to determine which tradition of thought influenced him, but *why he reacted to reality in this way*, why this particular mode of thought seemed to account for life as he experienced it. The notion that mind and body are deadly antagonists accords with Lawrence's experiences of social reality, as it figured in the conflict between his parents, which was primarily a function of class differences, and in the effects of mine work on hundreds of men like his father. His belief that the domineering mind is destructive of the flesh corresponds to the actual effects of Mrs Lawrence on her husband, and of the managers on the workers.

When Paul insists that ideas are the province of the middle classes, and physical warmth the preserve of the common people, he merely reflects his experience of the Morel family, of Bestwood and of Nottingham. For the middle classes include the managers, teachers, doctors, lawyers, clergymen and others who specialize in mental activity; and the common people are those whose task is physical. The class distinction runs along the divisions of labor. (The same dichotomy reappears in the opening pages of *The Rainbow*.) Lawrence's lifelong attempt to reintegrate the physical and mental in his characters was thwarted by the surviving—in fact widening—divisions in society itself, which were only aggravated by the 1914–1918 War, as we shall observe in the chapter on *Women in Love*. As the years and books rolled on, the categories of body and mind tended to crystallize in his thought. Just as Nietzsche rewrote the past in order to emphasize the struggle between Dionysus and Apollo within us and as Freud ransacked literature and myth to exhibit the conflict between id and ego, so Lawrence reinterpreted history and theology to explain the division of man into flesh and spirit. Whatever metaphysical status he attributed to that dichotomy, however, whatever mythical genealogy he concocted, the dualism itself is grounded in his social existence, and acquires its power as a critical tool from that grounding.

Such dualism is politically hazardous, because in its extreme form it lends itself to the view that society is *naturally*, rather than historically, divided into two classes—the conscious elite and the laboring masses. In his wartime essays, and in such middle-period novels as *Aaron's Rod*, *Kangaroo* and *The Plumed Serpent*, Lawrence himself was to express sympathy with such a view. Anyone who cares about the quality of life among laboring people, as Lawrence did, and yet who persists in thinking of them as mindless, passive, incapable of changing their own condition, might

51

naturally gravitate towards totalitarian ideas—the conscious elite, the benevolent despot, the superman dictator must save the masses. (I will return to this aspect of Lawrence's own thought in my discussion of *Women in Love*, where the issue is more sharply focused.) His attitude toward the common people was not that of educated disdain—as it was for Flaubert and Baudelaire, whom he was reading during his apprenticeship as a writer—but of concern mixed with fear. Although he could safely identify with the isolated lower-class hero—the gamekeeper, Leatherstocking, peasant, miner—Lawrence was unable to identify *with the lower class*. Whenever miners or peasants, soldiers or trade-unionists congregate in his fiction, they become threatening. No longer vital, emotional individuals, they merge into a new dehumanized creature which Lawrence calls the "masses." As Raymond Williams has taken pains to argue in his *Culture and Society 1780–1950*, no such creature exists; use of the word "masses" simply denotes a refusal to deal with the diversity of social groups and individuals, either out of fear or contempt. For Lawrence, I am suggesting, the dominant emotion was one of fear—fear of being reabsorbed into the working class in which his father toiled, and from which he himself had emerged; fear of being identified with that class of people whom his mother had taught him to despise.

When called up for one of several army medical examinations to which he submitted during the war years, Lawrence felt a momentary attraction to the working lads who shared his barracks, but then he shunned this temptation as "a decadence, a degradation, a losing of individual form and distinction, a merging in a sticky male mass. It attracts me for a moment, but immediately, what a degradation and a prison, oh intolerable."[13] Lawrence's characters are haunted by the terror of merging, of losing their identities, of being "degraded" by membership in some large human group, as they are haunted by the equally strong desire to merge, to escape the ego. These are the two poles of Lawrence's own response, not just to the "masses," but to all social groups:

> I don't want to act in concert with any body of people. I want to go by myself . . . and be houseless and placeless and homeless and landless, just move apart.[14]

[13] Letter to Dollie Radford, CL 456. 29.vi.16.
[14] Letter to Mark Gertler, CL 548. 16.iii.18.

I should love to be connected with something, with some few people, in something. As far as anything *matters*, I have always been very much alone, and regretted it.[15]

He established his own individuality by becoming a declassed intellectual; he escaped into isolation, and was never able to commit himself again to any social group. Late in life he was to acknowledge that

what ails me is the absolute frustration of my primeval societal instinct. I think societal instinct much deeper than sex instinct—and societal repression much more devastating. There is no repression of the sexual individual comparable to the repression of the societal man in me, by the individual ego, my own and everybody else's.[16]

Coming from a man who wrote obsessively of sexual ailments, that is a significant confession. Unlike the other literary intellectuals who were busy, during the first few decades of this century, propounding an ideological distinction between mass civilization and minority culture—I have in mind T. E. Hulme, Wyndham Lewis, Ezra Pound, T. S. Eliot, F. R. Leavis—Lawrence derived no comfort from the notion of belonging to an educated elite, for he felt at least as much contempt for the conscious minority as fear of the masses. No social fact about Lawrence is more important than his complete isolation, a result of the *déclassement* which is recorded in *Sons and Lovers*.

5 Reified Society, Reified Nature

Although Lawrence's critique of industrial society has not yet become explicit in *Sons and Lovers*, the raw materials, the conditions which he would later condemn, are all there. During the nineteenth century, as the scale of economic organization increased, as automation fragmented the work process, as control over the process itself receded ever further from the worker and as the relations between workers became increasingly mechanized, the individual human being was reduced to the role of an instrument of production. We can observe the effects of these economic changes upon the life of Bestwood. The men become interchange-

[15] Letter to Rolf Gardiner, CL 928. 22.vii.26.
[16] Letter to Trigant Burrow, CL 989–90. 13.vii.27.

able tools in the production process. There is no opportunity for creativity in their work, nor does their labor seem to produce any durable results, since the indistinguishable tons of coal are quickly consumed. Slack times in the pit mean hard times in the home, and there is no redress. The penniless and the powerless in the novel are intimidated by train stations and restaurants, by waitresses and paymasters; they queue for Saturday morning charity treatment at the doctor's surgery; like Mrs Morel they develop "that peculiar shut-off look of the poor who have to depend on the favour of others." Paul's feeling of terror and humiliation when fetching his father's pay expresses a child's dread of the "system;" when first seeking work as a lad fresh out of school, he balks at entry into the "business world, with its regulated system of values, and its impersonality," because this means becoming a "prisoner of industrialism." In order to work, a man must submit to an alien system, which operates according to its own impersonal laws.

The working people of Bestwood have little sway over those forces which fundamentally shape their lives—supply and demand on the market, weather, pay offers, strikes, government decisions, educational policy, development of industrial uses for coal, accidents in the mine, or the distribution of resources in the earth's bowels. They are not masters of their condition, either individually or collectively. As a group they function within an encompassing political and economic system over which they have practically no control. For them the larger society has become, to use Marx's term, reified: it seems to be a substantially independent world, inhabited by irrational, unpredictable and uncontrollable forces which determine people's lives while remaining oblivious to their desires.

There are striking similarities between this experience of society and Lawrence's representation of nature as an autonomous process over which the individual has no control, but in which he is deeply enmeshed by virtue of his animality, his existence as a physical creature. This is the view of nature which is implicit, for example, in the scene in which Paul and Miriam confront a rose tree at evening:

> It was very still. The tree was tall and straggling. It had thrown its briers over a hawthorn-bush, and its long streamers trailed thick

right down to the grass, splashing the darkness everywhere with great spilt stars, pure white. In bosses of ivory and in large splashed stars the roses gleamed on the darkness of foliage and stems and grass. Paul and Miriam stood close together, silent, and watched. Point after point the steady roses shone out of them, seeming to kindle something in their souls. The dusk came like smoke around, and still did not put out the roses.

The rose tree is an active subject, the master of transitive verbs, and is not simply alive but *independently* alive, acting on the young lovers who are bound together, as they themselves acknowledge, by something common in nature, something which they recognize to be continuous with their own passions, instincts and desires, something that calls forth a response from their "souls." As we shall see in our study of *The Rainbow* in the following chapter, where the stylistic expressions of this view of nature are discussed in detail, Lawrence's human agents for the most part respond passively to impersonal forces which transcend them and which, in sexual relations particularly, are overwhelming.

This subjection of the human to impersonal nature recurs in passages throughout *Sons and Lovers*: the account of Paul and Miriam's first sexual encounter, in which a cherry tree, a sunset and a fir register the harmony between the course of external nature and the course of their young blood; the scene by the flooded Trent, where the surging river functions as objective correlative for the emotions that master Clara and Paul; the scene in which Paul emerges from lovemaking to hear peewits scream:

It was all so much bigger than themselves that he was hushed. They had met, and included in their meeting the thrust of the manifold grass-stems, the cry of the peewit, the wheel of the stars;

and finally another lovemaking scene in which he merges in consciousness with the encircling natural world:

Just as he was, so it seemed the vigorous, wintry stars were strong also with life. He and they struck with the same pulse of fire, and the same joy of strength which held the bracken-frond stiff near his eyes held his own body firm. It was as if he, and the stars, and the dark herbage, and Clara were licked up in an immense tongue of flame, which tore upwards and upwards.

55

After one such encounter Paul reflects that "It was as if they had been blind agents of a great force": the natural process, like the social, becomes reified, appearing as an autonomous realm of irrational and impersonal forces. Just as unpredictable and uncontrollable social forces rule the lives of common people, so natural forces govern the course of personal relationships. The one realm of impersonal forces is no more hospitable than the other. And just as economic forces reduce human beings to instruments of production, so instinctual forces reduce human beings to instruments of gratification.

Thus Paul justifies his calculated use of Clara by arguing that their intercourse is mutually rewarding—yet she is nonetheless his instrument, serving his needs. To his mother he confesses that, "Sometimes, when I see her just as *the woman*, I love her, mother; but then, when she talks and criticizes, I often don't listen to her." When Clara charges him with treating her as an object, rather than as a person with her own needs and desires, he excuses himself by appealing to the relentless urge of passion. His relationship with Miriam, though fuller, is corrupted by the same instrumental attitude:

> He had always, almost wilfully, to put her out of count, and act from the brute strength of his own feelings. And he could not do it often, and there remained afterwards always the same sense of failure and of death.

When in a fit of pique he accuses her of trying to "absorb" him, he is merely echoing his mother's jealous sentiments. Although Lawrence was later to swear by the "truth" of judgments uttered spontaneously and passionately (basing his faith on the instincts), the judgments which actually appear in his novels, as in the present instance, often merely express unexamined prejudices. When Paul declares an end to his love affair with Miriam—which for his part has been based on intellectual and sexual domination—he is shocked by the girl's bitterness, since he has justified his actions all along by reference to the holy and undeniable passions. In its crudest forms this appeal to the sanctity of instinct becomes in the later Lawrence a variety of sexual determinism, differing little in its ethical implications from the biological determinism of the Social Darwinists. The instrumentalization of human beings and the mechanization of personal relationships is equally vicious, whether enforced by an industrial-economic order, or by a natural order.

At the time Lawrence was writing, the term "nature" had two principal meanings, which might be called the scientific and the romantic. According to the first interpretation, which derived from Kepler, Galileo, Newton and Kant, and which sustained biological and physical research throughout the nineteenth century, "nature" was an orderly system of laws which governed the universe, a system which was unalterable but which, since it was accessible to reason, could be harnessed by man for his own purposes. According to the second interpretation, which derived in its modern form primarily from Rousseau, and which appealed especially to the Romantics, "nature" was the opposite of system; it represented all of those forces which escaped man's reason, which defied his effort of reducing the world to order. The difference between these two interpretations has often been described, rather vaguely, as that between mechanical and organic views of nature. Given these terms, we can say that Lawrence appealed to the organic against the mechanical, but that very appeal, in the extreme form it reached in *Women in Love*, say, or *The Plumed Serpent*, could become mechanistic. His realm of uncontrollable forces, his "nature," is none the less reified for being irrational. In the very process of opposing the mechanistic world-view which he took to be characteristic of science, Lawrence was tempted to substitute a reified vision of his own.

Because he was increasingly to use nature as an antidote to society, it is important to recognize at the outset these disturbing symmetries between the social and natural orders, symmetries which suggest that the image of nature in the novel is in its main outlines a projection of the experience of society. The reified natural process corresponds to the reified social process. Already in *The Rainbow* characters were to be divided into natural and social dimensions, parallel to the division between body and mind, and nature was to become, and remain, a sacred preserve, sacred precisely because of its independence from society. The less control men had over their life in society—particularly those men who, like Lawrence, were unable to commit themselves to any collective action, and thereby to merge their individuality into the group—the greater their need to believe in some autonomous realm, perhaps of nature, which would remain immune to the pressures of history. Lawrence's conception of nature therefore tended to develop in dialectical opposition to his experience of contemporary society, with the result that distortions of the social order tended to become mirrored in the natural order.

The sentimental education of a working-class boy, the lives of a mining family, a farming family and a suffragette: these appear to be the chief subjects of *Sons and Lovers*. We are presented with the drama of "an organic disturbance in the relationships of men and women," to use Dorothy Van Ghent's phrase,[17] and with the Oedipal dilemma of a miner's son. But these materials have an historical content which Lawrence, on account of his psychological focus, did not fully acknowledge. That is to say, the true underlying subject of the novel is a larger historical reality, the movements and qualities of which are concretely focused in the lives of individual characters, who are "typical" in the sense defined by Lukács.[18] The psychology of these characters can be interpreted as a response to social conditions; their motives and behavior are comprehensible in terms of their social existence. Whether we examine Mrs Morel's frustrated bourgeois aspirations, Morel's brutalization, Mrs Leivers' bitterness, Miriam's compensating religiosity, Clara's feminism, Dawes's demoralization, or the middle class values and emotional lameness of Paul, we find evidence of crucial trends in contemporary society: the deprivations of working class life; the increasing mechanization of society which was to result in the horrors of the 1914–1918 War; the conflict between bourgeois and proletarian ideologies which would lead to revolutions after the war; the proliferating sense of *anomie*; and the movement of women for emancipation. To claim this is not to deny the richness of the novel's world, but on the contrary to indicate the ground of its coherence, to reveal the matrix of social trends which gives it unity. Indeed the novel derives its significance as much from this larger historical reality as from the individual lives through which history is concretely grasped. Although Lawrence focuses on personal relations and

[17] *The English Novel* (New York, 1953), p. 247.
[18] See in particular his Preface to *Studies in European Realism* (Preface: Budapest, 1948).

subjectivity, it is a subjectivity permeated by social forces, which registers the stress of growing up within a working community that was being transformed by industry, the schools, and the awakening of social consciousness.

Furthermore, Lawrence's own psychology, like that of his characters, is rooted in the social and moral conditions which govern the world of *Sons and Lovers*. Like them, his values and thought developed within the bounds of a specific social existence. His ideas and his art, whatever enduring interest they may possess, represent first and foremost a coherent response to a concrete historical situation. In this chapter I have suggested certain correspondences between the plane of consciousness and the plane of social existence: the origins of Lawrence's individualistic perspective in bourgeois ideology, with his consequent substitution of psychological for historical explanation; the relation of his mind/body dualism to the dualism of mental and physical functions enforced by the division of labor; the additional parallel between the mind/body dualism and the conflict (practical and ideological) between middle and working classes; the similarity between the representation of nature and of society, each realm being impersonal, autonomous and irrational, and each one reducing the individual to the status of an object in a process which he cannot control. There is at least this much similarity between the structure of his social experience and the structure of ideas which he uses to account for that experience.

I have suggested that Lawrence was relatively unaware, at this point in his development, of the larger social implications of his characters' problems, that he was for the most part unconscious of the image and critique of society which is implicit in *Sons and Lovers*—a limitation of vision due to the immediacy, intimacy and subjectivity of the material from which the novel is built, and due also to his acceptance of his mother's Puritan and bourgeois perspective. In *The Rainbow* he sought to overcome this isolation of personal experience, not however by integrating the individual into society, but by immersing him in nature. Whereas in *Sons and Lovers* he was largely unconscious of the impact of society on the individual, in *The Rainbow* he was to become acutely conscious, and was to regard the social world as the enemy of private life.

2

Nature vs. society in *The Rainbow*

Lawrence always stressed the nature in human nature. Like birds and wildflowers, his characters are prey to the forces and subject to the laws of the natural order. Whereas realism in the English novel before him had generally emphasized men's social experience and historical context, he stressed men's physical experience and natural context. There were precedents, to be sure, in Emily Brontë and Hardy, both of whom served him as models, and in such Naturalists as George Moore (and of course Zola in France and Dreiser, Crane, London and Norris in the United States); but none of his predecessors had ventured so deep into the unconscious in search of the natural man. Already in his first three novels nature frames and measures personal relationships. In *Sons and Lovers*, as we have seen, Paul justifies his actions by appeal to instinct; with his women he speaks in a language of natural things, of flowers and moons and trees. Only in the love-making scene by the flooded river Trent, however, where the lovers descend from the "ordinary level" of the "public path" to mingle their passion with that of the river, does Lawrence explicitly oppose the realm of flesh and flowers to the realm of social existence; and even this degree of opposition is largely due, as I have suggested, to his individualistic focus: it expresses indifference towards society rather than hostility.

At the end of that novel Paul felt isolated, adrift; although immersed in the world he "had no place in it." Lawrence himself sensed the need, in the absence of God and community, for membership in some order which transcends the individual. In a letter of December, 1914, while he was in the midst of revising

The Rainbow for the last time, he announced that he no longer accepted the belief that " '*I* am all. All other things are but radiation out from me,' " preferring now "to try to conceive the whole, to build up a whole by means of symbolism, because symbolism avoids the I and puts aside the egotist; and, in the whole, to take our decent place."[1] The whole in which man is to take his decent place is not society but nature, which Lawrence conceived in religious terms; individuals in *The Rainbow* are integrated into an encompassing natural process which in turn is opposed to society. Paul's need for transcendence is thus answered, but not his need for community.

1 Nature in Man

The rendering of human passion within the sympathetic embrace of a natural landscape is one of the most striking features of *The Rainbow*. Reading about Tom's courtship of Lydia, about the sheaf-gathering ballet of Will and Anna, or about the wind-swept climax of the love-affair between Ursula and Skrebensky, one feels that here Lawrence's genius is distinctly at work. By giving this last passage a closer look, we can identify certain of the linguistic means which Lawrence used to shift the focus of living and loving from society to nature:

> He came to her finally in a superb consummation. It was very dark, and again a windy, heavy night. They had come down the lane towards Beldover, down to the valley. They were at the end of their kisses, and there was the silence between them. They stood as at the edge of a cliff, with a great darkness beneath.
>
> Coming out of the lane along the darkness, with the dark space spreading down to the wind, and the twinkling lights of the station below, the far off windy chuff of a shunting train, the tiny clink-clink-clink of the wagons blown between the wind, the light of Beldover-edge twinkling upon the blackness of the hill opposite, the glow of the furnaces along the railway to the right, their steps began to falter. They would soon come out of the darkness into the lights. It was like turning back. It was unfulfilment. Two quivering, unwill-

---

[1] Letter to Gordon Campbell, CL 302. 19.xii.14. On the symbolism which Lawrence built up in *The Rainbow*, see Mark Spilka, *The Love Ethic of D. H. Lawrence* (Bloomington, Ind., and London, 1955), Chapter 5, and the excellent article by S. L. Goldberg, "*The Rainbow*: Fiddle-Bow and Sand," *Essays in Criticism*, XI (1961), pp. 418–34.

ing creatures, they lingered on the edge of the darkness, peering out at the lights and the machine-glimmer beyond. They could not turn back to the world—they could not.

So lingering along, they came to a great oak-tree by the path. In all its budding mass it roared to the wind, and its trunk vibrated in every fibre, powerful, indomitable.

"We will sit down," he said.

And in the roaring circle under the tree, that was almost invisible yet whose powerful presence received them, they lay a moment looking at the twinkling lights on the darkness opposite, saw the sweeping brand of a train past the edge of their darkened field.

Then he turned and kissed her, and she waited for him. The pain to her was the pain she wanted, the agony was the agony she wanted. She was caught up, entangled in the powerful vibration of the night. The man, what was he?—a dark, powerful vibration that encompassed her. She passed away as on a dark wind, far, far away, into the pristine darkness of paradise, into the original immortality. She entered the dark fields of immortality.

When she rose, she felt strangely free, strong. She was not ashamed—why should she be? He was walking beside her, the man who had been with her. She had taken him, they had been together. Whither they had gone, she did not know. But it was as if she had received another nature. She belonged to the eternal, changeless place into which they had leapt together.

Her soul was sure and indifferent of the opinion of the world of artificial light. As they went up the steps of the foot-bridge over the railway, and met the train-passengers, she felt herself belonging to another world, she walked past them immune, a whole darkness dividing her from them. When she went into the lighted dining-room at home, she was impervious to the lights and the eyes of her parents. Her everyday self was just the same. She merely had another, stronger self that knew the darkness.

This curious separate strength, that existed in darkness and pride of night, never forsook her. She had never been more herself. It could not occur to her that anybody, not even the young man of the world, Skrebensky, should have anything at all to do with her permanent self. As for her temporal, social self, she let it look after itself.

Through passion Ursula gains access into the immense powers of nature. Like the adept of Zen Buddhism, her isolate, conscious self is extinguished in nature, to be replaced by a new self which

participates in this larger ordering. Thus she escapes the creep-
ing *anomie* which had overcome Paul Morel. No longer merely
daughter or student or teacher, she is something at once more
rudimentary and more grand, a physical creature, a nexus of vast
and incomprehensible forces. Every major character in *The Rainbow* comes eventually to this realization, by way of sexuality or
otherwise, for in the world of Lawrence's fiction this is the customary rite of initiation.

The love-encounter takes place in literal and semantic obscurity.
The dark has edges; the night is heavy, palpable. Within the
enveloping darkness the feeble lights and sounds of society merely
emphasize the surrounding gloom. Beldover itself, with its spawn
of industrial squalor, is swallowed in the blackness. Ursula and
Skrebensky are absorbed along with the oak into the "powerful
vibration of the night." Feeling themselves, like Paul and Clara,
"blind agents of a great force" they cease for the moment to exist
as isolate, self-directing individuals and become phases or nodes
of a larger vibration.

The process of reification which we detected in *Sons and Lovers*
has thus reached a more advanced state in *The Rainbow*. Loss of
self-control recurs in the experience of every figure in the novel.
People are possessed by demons, they lapse into spells, drown in
floods; they are overcome by speechlessness, absorbed into fields
of force, bewitched by the moods and motions of the natural
world. All through history, Lawrence informs us in his Preface to
Movements in European History (1921), men have been the
puppets of their instincts; our comings and goings merely express
the powerful forces at work in the unconscious, and therefore the
nineteenth-century positivists were deluded in seeking a rational
history. History is a joke which nature plays on society.

In *The Rainbow* nature invariably dwarfs society, which appears
remote, frail and hostile. Ursula and Skrebensky dread returning
to the "machine glimmer"—that industrial, urban, political and
public world which Mellors in *Lady Chatterley's Lover* would
think of bitterly as "that sparkling electric Thing outside there."
Society becomes the enemy. No more will Ursula respect "the
opinion of the world of artificial light," precisely because it is
artificial, a small clearing feebly lit by the arc lamp of human
consciousness, regulated by science, but surrounded by wild beasts

wheeling in darkness. (One detects in Ursula's defiance a revolt against the Nonconformist puritanism of Mrs Lawrence. Appropriately enough, the National Purity League, which took censorship action against *The Rainbow* in 1915, was headed by a man who was, like Mrs Lawrence, a Congregationalist.) Not only are most of Lawrence's love-encounters transferred physically to another environment—to woods, moors, rivers, clearings and beaches—they are also transferred ethically into another framework of values. The old framework lingers, however, as an implicit code against which his characters revolt. It abides here in the notion of shame, in the world's opinion, in the established order of the home, in the eyes of train passengers and parents.

When Ursula returns to the world of artificial light it is the discovery of the range of her own physicality, her immersion in "the whole darkness," which distinguishes her from the uninitiated train passengers. Darkness, at first an aspect of the physical atmosphere, no more than a black space, an absence, through which a train's headlight can sweep, comes to stand for the wondrous domain of sexual experience. Thus Lawrence transforms landscape into emotional terrain (the gloomy meadows surrounding Beldover became "the dark fields of immortality"), a transformation he effects so often that we begin to doubt whether the division between inner, psychic world, and outer, natural world is really valid. By such means he assimilates Ursula's emotional state to the natural environment, and divorces both from society. Paul and Clara also defy social mores in their lovemaking beside the flooded Trent, but in their case the opposition to society remains conventional—the breaking of sexual taboos. Whereas here in the relationship between Ursula and Skrebensky the opposition has become radical. Nature and society represent wholly different systems of value, and offer wholly different grounds for identity.

Like the feeble lights engulfed by darkness, Skrebensky's four irrelevant words only intensify the silence. Human speech seems inadequate or unnecessary. Here as in the entire novel there is little correspondence between what the characters feel and what they can say about those feelings. Like his master Tolstoy, whose *Anna Karenina* lay behind both *The Rainbow* and *Women in Love*, Lawrence had an uncanny ability for depicting the nonverbal communication between people, as we have already observed in the silent speech between Mrs Morel and her son. Riffling through the pages, one is struck—in contrast to a novel by Austen or George Eliot or James—by the scarcity of dialogue, by the disparity between speech and inner life (a disparity which Henri Bergson during the same years was incorporating into a fashionable metaphysic). Lawrence's characters are often inarticulate by nature, yet many of the intense emotional states and complex psychological processes which lie outside their range of speech lie outside the range of all common speech. Venturing into a linguistic no man's land, he had to blaze his own trails. T. S. Eliot's complaint in the *Four Quartets* (account taken for differences of temperament) might apply to Lawrence as well:

> And so each venture
> Is a new beginning, a raid on the inarticulate
> With shabby equipment always deteriorating
> In the general mess of imprecision of feeling,
> Undisciplined squads of emotion.

"Darkness"—the appropriate leitmotif for a book which challenged the Enlightenment confidence in reason and language—refers not only to that in human experience which is irrational but to that which is *unsayable*. Yet a scene such as the present one is an invasion of the darkness: Lawrence has brought to the experience all the tools of the novelist. What his characters could not have said, he has written. Thus while he attacked Freud's mythology of psychic processes, because it pretended to articulate the "darkness" of the unconscious, and thereby advanced the imperialistic claims of reason, Lawrence himself was busily subduing the disorderly instincts to speech.

Description of human physicality had at the time when Lawrence was writing small space in the established uses of language. Of course the animality of *homo sapiens* had been for some time at the center of scientific speculation about man, whether one considers the biology of Darwin, Huxley and Haeckel, the sociology of Wilfred Pareto (with his notion of animal "residues"), the anthropology of Frazer, or the psycho-mythology of Freud himself. In *The Ego and the Id* Freud tells us he borrowed the German form of the id (*das Es*) from Nietzsche, who used it in a similar sense to designate "whatever in our nature is impersonal

C
65

and, so to speak, subject to natural law."[2] Nietzsche, the advocate of Dionysos, glimmers through Lawrence's prophetic writings, as he glimmers through the products of his generation. Thus Lawrence's claim for recognition of man's animality was by no means a lonely cry.

The passage which we have been considering, which is typical of his writing in this respect, gives us the impression that he was struggling to extend the boundaries of language, to encompass more of man's purely physical experience. The repetitions and restatements suggest a halting, circling attempt to grasp an experience which for Ursula is unprecedented. The progression from "dark . . . vibration" to "dark wind," to "pristine darkness of paradise," to "original immortality" and finally to "dark fields of immortality" suggests a mind driven in a frantic search for an adequate expression of an intense but verbally elusive experience, even as that experience unfolds. With Bergsonian fidelity to the contour of emotion, the text records the effort towards articulation—like the chisel-marks left in stone by Michelangelo, the texture of brush-strokes on a canvas by Van Gogh. The writing proceeds, both in individual scenes and in the whole novel, with its layered structure of generations, by what might be called bracketing, as that word is used in artillery: he fires short, long, to one side, then to the other, constantly in search of the proper range, each shot, each formulation refining slightly our perception of the target.

But the ultimate experience eludes the verbal chase. For Lawrence it was a matter of principle—and of vivid personal experience—to maintain that human physicality finally evades the reach of language, like a fox, footloose in wilderness. To have presented this love-encounter with the syntactic cat's-cradles of late James, with Flaubert's razored diction, or with the Byzantine mythologism of Joyce would have been to assert the dominion of the verbal and the conscious over the wordless and unconscious life of the body. A passage of the sort we have been considering marks the boundary of articulation, where Lawrence's most distinctive powers as a novelist were concentrated.

Nature is speechless, society verbal. The life of the "social self" is communicable in ordinary language, that of the "perman-

[2] Freud, *The Ego and the Id*, trans. Joan Riviere (New York, 1962), p. 13.

ent self" is not. The contrast between nature and society coincides with the division between silence and language:

NATURE	natural self	body	SILENCE
CULTURE	social self	mind	LANGUAGE

In *The Rainbow* every comparison between the two dimensions awards precedence to nature. Man is first of all a physical creature —only derivatively is he a creature of society or history. Ursula and Skrebensky's past, their communal relations, all that pertains to their "social" selves is irrelevant to their experience: they have been led to this conclusion by the logic of their emotions. They are subjected for the moment wholly to the experience, and to the natural forces which through their sexuality they apprehend.

The opposition between society and nature is one of the dominant structuring principles of the novel. For the Brangwens society is an alien order which drives its railroads and digs its canals into the Marsh Farm; an alien world which Tom visits on market days; to which Will is only tenuously connected (even then after long indifference) by his craft instruction; and which Ursula first enters, then spurns, as a teacher. One is born into nature—one must join society. The social self is defined by the ethical and linguistic conventions of society, but the natural self is grounded in experiences which trespass those conventions. The attitude of indifference towards society in *Sons and Lovers* becomes one of defiance in *The Rainbow*, and in *Women in Love* one of horror. From *The Rainbow* onward the antagonism between social and natural man was to remain one of the dominant features of Lawrence's thought.

He was especially preoccupied with this psychological split in his wartime essays, notably the *Study of Thomas Hardy*, *The Crown*, "Education of the People" and "Democracy." In the latter, refering at one point to a female character in an American novel, he formulates the split in borrowed Freudian terms:

> The *ego* is obviously a sort of second self, which she carries about with her. It is her body of accepted consciousness, which she has inherited more or less ready made from her father and grandfathers. This secondary self is very pernicious, dictating to her issues which

are quite false to her true, deeper, spontaneous self, her creative identity.

Nothing in the world is more pernicious than the *ego* or spurious self, the conscious entity with which every individual is saddled. He receives it almost *en bloc* from the preceding generation, and spends the rest of his life trying to drag his spontaneous self from beneath the horrible incubus. And the most fatal part of the incubus, by far, is the dead, leaden weight of handed-on ideals.[3]

Although he conflates superego and ego here, his meaning is clear: the social self, bearer of community consciousness, player of social roles, is false, pernicious, spurious; the natural self, spontaneous and creative, precedes and transcends the community, it blossoms from a wholly different stratum of being. Skrebensky, Harby, Tom,Jr. and Maggie Schofield represent a type of person whom Lawrence sees as given over partly or wholly to the mechanical second self. Psychoanalysts have consistently distinguished this social self, the being-in-the-world, from some primary natural self. For Freud of course the socially-imposed self was the superego; for Jung it was the *persona*; for Wilhelm Reich the "character defense structure;" and for R. D. Laing the "false-self system."[4] Lawrence's own view was closest to that of Reich, who considered the social self a crippling and vicious imposition upon the spontaneous, animal self.

In terms of Marx's anthropology, Lawrence was much more interested in natural man than in species man, in the biological substratum than the specifically human. Marx's own emphasis was precisely the opposite—which accounts in part for Lawrence's impatience with the political and economic preoccupations of the socialists. Yet the root of his concern was not so different from that of Marx; both were spurred to criticize society by outrage over the condition of industrial workers. The criticism which was

[3] "Democracy," PI 710–1. A discussion of the social self/natural self contrast, as it appears in the essays, will be found in Baruch Hochman, *Another Ego: The Changing View of Self and Society in the Work of D. H. Lawrence* (Columbia, S.C., 1970).

[4] The sources for Freud and Jung are familiar. See especially Freud's *The Ego and the Id* and Jung's *Two Essays on Analytical Psychology* (1955; written 1917–28). For Reich and Laing I am referring to *Character Analysis* and *The Divided Self*, respectively.

implicit in *Sons and Lovers* becomes explicit in *The Rainbow* in Lawrence's remarks on the miners of Wiggiston:

> Like creatures with no more hope, but which still live and have passionate being, within some utterly unliving shell, they passed meaninglessly along, with strange, isolated dignity. It was as if a hard, horny shell enclosed them all.

The shell, the false self, has been imposed by the industrial system; the passionate being, the natural self, remains hidden within. At the end of the novel Ursula envisions a time when in each person the true natural self will burst through its shell and industrial civilization be swept away. Whereas for Marx the cause of suffering and dehumanization among workers was a particular form of society, a particular organization of industry, for Lawrence in his more extreme moments industry itself, society in whatever form, appears as the devil to be damned.

In its radical form the psychological split becomes schizoid. We can recognize many of Ursula's traits in Laing's description, in *The Divided Self*, of schizoid vacillation between intensive self-consciousness and the desire to become invisible, dissolved, "a passive thing penetrated and controlled by the other."[5] Her craving to annihilate Skrebensky may be viewed in Laing's terms as the defense mechanism of an "ontologically insecure" person, so uncertain of her own identity that she must destroy the other or reduce him to the status of an object, for fear of disintegrating under the impact of his personality. Lawrence's tendency to see only two possibilities for the self—either complete isolation or complete merging—is one of the key features of the schizoid personality. However, as both the title and argument of Wylie Sypher's book, *Loss of the Self in Modern Literature and Art*, suggest, Ursula's radical uncertainty about her identity may be schizoid but it is also one of the characteristic ailments of our century. Proliferating bureaucracy, increasing urbanization, industrialization, mobility and division of labor have widened the gap between public and private selves. Robert Musil's man without qualities, Franz Kafka's anonymous Joseph K., Beckett's bodi-

---

[5] Op. cit., p. 113. Laing's theories, of course, must be applied with caution, since they show the influence of literary study—including Sartre and Lawrence himself—as well as clinical study.

less voices, exhibit the plight of the individual who is alienated from all forms of community, and who is also unable to identify himself in relation to any transcendent order, whether biological or theological. We have identified the beginnings of Lawrence's own social alienation in *Sons and Lovers*, his *déclassement* and his experience of industry as the hostile imposition of some external authority. Dissatisfied with society, therefore, in *The Rainbow* he recommends nature for his transcendent order.

2 *Effects of the Unconscious in Everyday Life*

Like the writings of Freud, *The Rainbow* had an unsettling effect on Lawrence's contemporaries, for it described, even celebrated, the violent eruption of the unconscious into the tranquil pastures of ordinary life. Consider for example this hectic interlude in the marriage of Tom and Lydia:

> And he remained wrathful and distinct from her, unchanged outwardly to her, but underneath a solid power of antagonism to her. Of which she became gradually aware. And it irritated her to be made aware of him, as a separate power. She lapsed into a sort of sombre exclusion, a curious communion with mysterious powers, a sort of mystic, dark state which drove him and the child nearly mad. He walked about for days stiffened with resistance to her, stiff with a will to destroy her as she was. Then suddenly, out of nowhere, there was connection between them again. It came on him as he was working in the fields. The tension, the bond, burst, and the passionate flood broke forward into a tremendous, magnificent rush, so that he felt he could snap off the trees as he passed, and create the world afresh . . . he felt a stupendous power in himself, of life, and of urgent, strong blood.

By exaggerating emotions Lawrence renders inexplicable what we normally accept as vicissitudes of love. Such terms as "wrathful," "solid power of antagonism," "mad," "stiffened with resistance," "will to destroy," "passionate flood" and "stupendous power" magnify and thereby mystify the fluctuations which attend all human relationships. People once again appear as the passive objects of their emotions: "Then suddenly, out of nowhere, there was connection between them again. It came on him. . . ." Imagined during a period of stormy relations with Frieda, as we can judge from contemporary letters and from the volume of poetry

Look! We Have Come Through!, all the man-woman relationships in *The Rainbow* oscillate according to their own eccentric, unpredictable periods, between the poles of union and division, love and hate, tenderness and anger, in a manner reminiscent of *Anna Karenina*. By this oscillation Lawrence suggests, in a way rarely achieved, the inevitable and mysterious day-to-day mutations in love.

To register the impact of turbulent emotions he frequently disrupts syntax, as the Expressionist painters distorted the image and exaggerated line. Thus of Will Brangwen:

> If he relaxed his will he would fall, fall through endless space, into the bottomless pit, always falling, will-less, helpless, non-existent, just dropping to extinction, falling till the fire of friction had burned out, like a falling star, then nothing, nothing, complete nothing.

In refusing to yield to the unconscious he resembles Skrebensky, who is willing to surrender himself to his nation but not to his passion. For their fear of the darkness, for their refusal to yield, both men are condemned: Skrebensky as a complete failure, Will, after his bout of sensual initiation with Anna, as but a partial success. For Will religious ecstasy takes the place of sexual ecstasy. In the account of his response to Lincoln Cathedral we again encounter distortion of syntax and parody of coital rhythms:

> Here the stone leapt up from the plain of earth, leapt up in a manifold, clustered desire each time, up, away from the horizontal earth, through twilight and dusk and the whole range of desire, through the swerving, the declination, ah, to the ecstasy, the touch, to the meeting and the consummation, the meeting, the clasp, the close embrace, the neutrality, the perfect, swooning consummation, the timeless ecstasy. There his soul remained, at the apex of the arch, clinched in the timeless ecstasy, consummated.

Words and phrases succeed each other according to the logic of metaphoric association and synonymy, rather than the logic of syntax. The hypnotic repetition so characteristic of Lawrence has the effect not only of impressing upon the reader certain key terms, but also, like slow-motion in the film, of retarding the action and focusing our attention on certain intense emotional states. Thus he distinguishes stylistically between inner or psycho-

logical time—what Bergson called *la durée*—and the outer chrono-
metric time of science. As in the sheaf-gathering scene between
Will and Anna, or the scene in which stampeding horses frighten
Ursula, rhythmic repetition appears to break down the linear-
temporal sequence, and to expand the moment in an hallucinatory
way, evoking what Lawrence liked to call the "fourth dimension" (a term perhaps culled from newspaper accounts of Einstein's
theory of general relativity, which was published in 1915, the
same year as *The Rainbow*).

Psychic eruptions are commonly represented in the novel by the
sort of linguistic features we have been observing: syntax is dis-
rupted; characters are transformed into objects; qualities of feeling are hypostatized as autonomous processes ("surge," "flow,"
"wind"); words lose their cognitive meanings in combination ("one
fecund nucleus of the fluid darkness"); repetition and metaphoric
association displace syntactic relations; certain words recur like a
tic or an obsession; and the rhythms of phrases suggest coitus
rather than speech. Such words as "swoon," "hypnotized,"
"lapsed," "spell" and "possessed" crop up continually, announc-
ing loss of self-control to overwhelming forces which are "dark"
and "unknown" in that their sources are buried in the unconscious. Throughout *The Rainbow* the ordinary experiential world,
which the mind seems to control and language to describe, is
threatened by another order of experience, before which the mind
yields and language fails.

The intensity which Lawrence infuses into these extraordinary
experiences would be dissipated by ordinary speech, and so his
characters hold their peace; but theirs is not an impoverished
silence, like that of Beckett's figures, the silence of the overly-
conscious. Their reticence masks an excess of experience rather
than a dearth. Most of what the narrator tells about their inner
life could not be told by the characters themselves. I have suggested that this is mainly a consequence of Lawrence's attitude towards his material: he refused to subordinate the ungovernable
and fathomless order of nature to the control of language. But it is
also partly a consequence of the native inarticulacy of the characters themselves. Choosing to create people who by his measure
were closer to the physical springs of life, Lawrence at the same
time chose men and women who were incapable of saying much

about those springs. For them the realms of darkness and silence correspond.

From the "passionate flood" which bears him along, Tom receives a sense of power, a sense of connection with some violent force—the power which Ursula discovers in the "vibration of the night," in the cell nucleus, in the stampeding horses, in moonlight; which Anna during her pregnancy identifies as the procreative Lord; which Will experiences as the thrusting hand of God. Indeed the world of *The Rainbow*, like the paintings and compositions of the Futurists, whose manifestoes Lawrence read while revising his novel, is saturated with power. People seem to dwell in a field of force, interacting with each other and with their environment through "will," "influence," "presences," "spells," "impulses," "trances," "power," "electricity" or "magnetism"—the metaphors mixing the occult with physics. We are presented with a dynamic model of man and nature (in the best tradition of nineteenth-century science) in which the conscious, self-directing individual is connected, through myriad modes of force, with his fellows and his surroundings. The dynamic model becomes even more prominent in *Women in Love*, and it is worked out with intricate physiological detail in *Psychoanalysis and the Unconscious* (1919–20) and *Fantasia of the Unconscious* (1921). Although social forces exist in the world of *The Rainbow*—as manifested with appalling cruelty in industrial Wiggiston and in Ursula's school—the more powerful forces are natural. In *Women in Love*—mainly, I believe, on account of the World War—the balance shifts in the opposite direction. History, the public world, becomes a nightmare from which the characters, like Stephen Dedalus in *Ulysses*, are trying to wake.

Lawrence's creatures inhabit an unstable world. Violent forces lurk just below the surface of consciousness. "Psychology has split and shattered the idea of a 'Person'," E. M. Forster wrote in 1939, "and has shown that there is something incalculable in each one of us, which may at any moment rise to the surface and destroy our normal balance."[6] The creator of the Marabar Caves, brooding on the eve of another world war, recognized that depth-psychology had undermined faith in the isolate, conscious individual, whose impulses were wholly accessible to introspection—

[6] *What I Believe* (London, 1939), pp. 6–7.

in short, had discredited the central tenet of bourgeois ideology, around which, as Ian Watt has shown in *The Rise of the Novel*, the novel form crystallized. Simultaneously with Proust and Joyce and Gide and Hesse, but after his own fashion, Lawrence was reconceiving the person in fiction. In a well-known letter of 1914 to Edward Garnett he wrote that

> you mustn't look in my novel for the old stable *ego*—of the character. There is another *ego*, according to whose action the individual is unrecognisable, and passes through, as it were, allotropic states which it needs a deeper sense than any we've been used to exercise, to discover are states of the same single radically unchanged element.[7]

Identity, which had appeared so stable a commodity in George Eliot, Jane Austen, Dickens and even Hardy, had become unstable —subjected from the outside to violent social forces, from the inside to the powerful beasts of the unconscious. Lawrence had come to feel that the image of the coherent, conscious self depicted by almost all previous English novelists (Laurence Sterne and Emily Brontë are major exceptions, and they stand therefore outside all formulations of the "Great Tradition"), was, as Bergson pointed out, merely a fiction which served to make sense of the flux of experience. He was less interested in the social self, the "stable ego," than in the animal self immersed in nature. Depth-psychology, with its questioning of reason and its emphasis upon the impersonal forces at work on the individual, an emphasis shared by the new science of sociology, was among the most powerful influences at that time behind the artistic experiments of Picasso and Kandinsky, the attempts at expressionism in music by Schoenberg, and the crisis in epistemology which preoccupied Weber in sociology, Einstein in physics and Russell and Wittgenstein in philosophy.

Lawrence's work stands in the midst of this reorientation of thought about the role of consciousness and the nature of identity. Among his novels *The Rainbow* marks the decisive shift in his

[7] CL 282. 5.iv.14. Many critics have offered an interpretation of the novel which begins from this quote: see in particular Julian Moynahan, *The Deed of Life: The Novels and Tales of D. H. Lawrence* (Princeton, 1963), Chapter 2; and Keith Sagar, *The Art of D. H. Lawrence* (Cambridge, 1966), Chapter 3.

thinking from the individualistic focus of *Sons and Lovers* to the animistic and finally religious perspective of his mature writings.

What I have called Lawrence's bracketing procedure—his movement by metaphor, synonymy, repetition, approximation—is exhibited on a broader scale in the narrative structure of *The Rainbow* itself.[8] In the movement from generation to generation (perhaps owing something to *Buddenbrooks*, which Lawrence had read by 1913) there is a progressive widening of the terms of reference and a broadening of consciousness on the part of the characters, as there is a physical movement away from the isolated Marsh Farm into the industrial city. But despite this genuine expansion of the novel's world, despite its passage from the agrarian nineteenth century to the urban twentieth, each of the three successive generations restates essentially the same set of problems: the attempt to define a man-woman relationship that will be mutually fulfilling; the struggle for a sense of self that does not depend upon the domination of other people; the search for a compromise between the claims of nature and the claims of society. Not every generation achieves the same degree of success in solving these problems, but every generation undergoes very much the same trials. The rhythms of courtship, sexual initiation, struggle between man and woman, violent oscillations in love, and experimental encounters with the social world, recur in the life of every major figure in the novel. Even the language in which these crucial experiences are presented varies no more from generation to generation than it does within the career of any one character. Many of the passages so far examined could conceivably have been drawn from the account of any of the three generations —which is only to support Lawrence's claim that in the novel he was less concerned with representing the isolated individual than with discovering the generic: each generation is unique in its experience, but on a deeper level it represents in another form "the same single radically unchanged element."

No single metaphor, no single generation, defines the man-woman relation—but collectively they suggest its contours. In each successive cycle Lawrence returns to the same issues, even as he expands his vision to take more and more of contemporary society

---

[8] Compare the useful article by Roger Sale, "The Narrative Technique of *The Rainbow*," *Modern Fiction Studies*, V (1959).

within his scope. And so in the novel's structure we detect the
pattern of repetition coupled with variation, of recurrence coupled
with growth, that we have also found in the language of a brief
passage or an entire scene. Lawrence himself, in remarking on the
style of Giovanni Verga, described this pattern exactly:

> Now the emotional mind, if we may be allowed to say so, is not
> logical. It is a psychological fact, that when we are thinking
> emotionally or passionately, thinking and feeling at the same time,
> we do not think rationally: and therefore, and therefore, and there-
> fore. Instead, the mind makes curious swoops and circles. It touches
> the point of pain or interest, then sweeps away again in a cycle,
> coils round and approaches again the point of pain or interest.
> There is a curious spiral rhythm, and the mind approaches again
> and again the point of concern, repeats itself, goes back, destroys
> the time-sequence entirely, so that time ceases to exist, as the mind
> stoops to the quarry, then leaves it without striking, soars, hovers,
> turns, swoops, stoops again, still does not strike, yet is nearer,
> nearer, reels away again, wheels off into the air, even forgets, quite
> forgets, yet again turns, bends, circles slowly, swoops and stoops
> again until at last there is the closing-in, and the clutch of a decision
> or a resolve.[9]

This "curious spiral rhythm" is so characteristic of the way
Lawrence's mind operates (the style of the passage illustrates the
argument) that it can be shown to permeate every layer of his
work, from the most local to the most general. Here Lawrence
provides a rationale for his repetitions—whether of word, phrase,
scene, character or the general movement of a book: he is not
engaged in a logical argument, nor is he concerned with exhaus-
tively specifying a milieu or a life; rather he is engaged in refining his own vision of the human condition, in defining what is
essential, in identifying the generic.

In the cycles of our moods, in the periods of the physical world,
and in our own bodily life, we discover the recursive rhythms of
Lawrence's prose. In his Foreword to *Women in Love* he himself
acknowledged this connection between language and experience:

> In point of style, fault is often found with the continual slightly
> modified repetition. The only answer is that it is natural to the
> author: and that every natural crisis in emotion or passion or un-

[9] "Preface" to Giovanni Verga's *Cavalleria Rusticana*, PI 249–50.

derstanding comes from this pulsing, frictional to-and-fro, which works up to culmination.

This defense of his recursive style clearly applies to the many passages in which the imitated rhythm is coital; but it applies equally well to the delicate accounts of day-to-day mutations in love between Tom and Lydia or Will and Anna. The spiral rhythms pursued by the "emotional mind," which Lawrence noted in the style of Verga, inform all levels of his own writing—the syntax of sentences, the pattern of scenes, and the narrative structure of the whole.

"This activity of the mind," he goes on to say in the passage on Verga, "is strictly timeless." Although the generations of Brangwens are temporally related to each other, they are also, like a sequence of metaphors, related atemporally by their common pattern. *The Rainbow*, like *Sons and Lovers* and *Women in Love*, derives much of its persuasiveness from this doubling and trebling of man-woman relationships, each one raising, while revealing different aspects of, very much the same questions. Indeed all the novels recast essentially the same characters, who fight through the same fundamental issues. Lawrence lacked—or at any rate refused to use—the exhaustive moral and social categories employed by Austen or George Eliot. Nor did he often proceed, as Flaubert or James did, by precise linguistic specification of motive and mood. Approximating rather than specifying, as if the experience he represented were not finally compatible with language, he wrote back and forth, character after character, book after book, across very much the same (admittedly ample) terrain, so that the novels collectively read more like a palimpsest than a series of discrete statements.

3 Man in Nature

The characters of *The Rainbow*, like those of Hardy's novels (which Lawrence studied with the painstaking care of an apprentice), are firmly planted in the loam of the earth. Their innermost experiences, their psychic development, their instincts and desires are represented as radically continuous with the forces of generation and the processes of change in the natural world.

The whole of the sheaf-gathering scene in the chapter "Girlhood of Anna Brangwen" could be cited as an incomparable demonstration of this link between psychological and natural rhythms. I quote only a few lines, beginning from the point at which, bearing his load of corn stalks, Will approaches Anna:

> Into the rhythm of his work there came a pulse and a steadied purpose. He stooped, he lifted the weight, he heaved it towards her, setting it as in her, under the moonlit space. And he went back for more. Ever with increasing closeness he lifted the sheaves and swung striding to the centre with them, ever he drove her more nearly to the meeting, ever he did his share, and drew towards her, overtaking her. There was only the moving to and fro in the moonlight, engrossed, the swinging in the silence, that was marked only by the splash of sheaves, and silence, and a splash of sheaves. And ever the splash of his sheaves broke swifter, beating up to hers, and ever the splash of her sheaves recurred monotonously, unchanging, and ever the splash of his sheaves beat nearer.

Here the reiteration of verbal units, the repetition of physical actions and the underlying coital pattern combine to express the mounting emotional tension between the lovers, which culminates a few lines later in a proposal of marriage. In small space, this prefigures the larger rhythms of their married life, the continual recurrence of love and strife between them. Unlike Walter and Gertrude Morel, for whom differences of class and education are basic, Will and Anna seem to fight over issues of sexual and spiritual domination. Although certain social causes for their struggle could be found—Will, like Walter Morel, is frustrated by his work; Anna, like Gertrude Morel, is anxious to make her husband over in her own image—they are not prominent in the novel. In comparison with *Sons and Lovers*, *The Rainbow* provides little of the data necessary for interpreting the feelings and actions of characters in terms of their social situation. The "natural" conflict, the organic disturbance between men and women in the novel, appears to be rooted so deep in individual character, to be so much a matter of the impersonal unconscious, as to escape social determination.

Consider as a second example the account of Lydia's reawakening, presented retrospectively in the second chapter of the novel. After Lensky's death, and after a period of depression and withdrawal from the world, she is restored to a zest for living and delicately prepared for Tom's courtship by the influence of nature:

. . . there was a strange insistence of light from the sea, to which she must attend. Primroses glimmered around, many of them, and she stooped to the disturbing influence . . . the light came off the sea, constantly, constantly, without refusal, till it seemed to bear her away, and the noise of the sea created a drowsiness in her, a drowsiness like sleep. Her automatic consciousness gave way a little . . . she found the bluebells around her glowing like a presence. . . . She went past the gorse bushes shrinking from their presence, she stepped into the heather as into a quickening bath . . . one morning there was a light from the yellow jasmine caught her, and after that, morning and evening, the persistent ringing of thrushes from the shrubbery, till her heart, beaten upon, was forced to lift up its voice . . . she would wake in the morning one day and feel her blood running, feel herself lying open like a flower unsheathed in the sun, insistent and potent. . . .

Once again we see a character reacting at first passively, and then willingly, to urging from the natural world. Again the "automatic consciousness"—the false self, social mask, persona, shell—which in Lydia's case has been toughened through suffering, must yield to the unconscious, to the forces of life within her and around her. The phrase "quickening bath" distills the essence of the passage, for Lydia is literally immersed in the "influences" and "presences" of nature. By such terms Lawrence intimates relations that develop unconsciously and involuntarily, between man and woman, or between man and nature.

Lydia's rebirth, a complex and verbally intangible process, is likened to the growth and blossoming of a flower. She emerges from this process sensitive to the urging of a new natural influence, that of Tom Brangwen, "the man who had come nearest to her for her awakening," "the image of power and strong life." The beau, the flowers and the sea manifest the same energy, the same urge, the same quickening. By thus presenting psychological processes in terms of natural ones throughout the novel, Lawrence suggests not just a metaphorical resemblance between the two, but an actual, fundamental connection. According to Lévi-Strauss mythic thought proceeds in exactly the same way, by accommodating human affairs to the patterns of nature—which might account for Lawrence's fascination with anthropological and occult treatments of myth. Through the early three novels culminating in *Sons and Lovers*, he generally followed the dominant nineteenth-century literary tradition of viewing nature from the perspective of man; but in *The Rainbow*, in part due to an increasing disgust with man's works, he came increasingly to view man from the perspective of nature, as one manifestation of the life-process.

This altered perspective is magnificently presented in those justly admired opening pages of the novel. For generations of Brangwen farmers, in daily contact with animals and land and weather, nature has set the terms of existence. Their experience only differs from Lydia's in being continuous:

> They felt the rush of the sap in spring, they knew the wave which cannot halt, but every year throws forward the seed to begetting, and, falling back, leaves the young-born on the earth. They knew the intercourse between heaven and earth, sunshine drawn into the breast and bowels, the rain sucked up in the daytime, nakedness that comes under the wind in autumn, showing the birds' nests no longer worth hiding. Their life and interrelations were such; feeling the pulse and body of the soil, that opened to their furrow for the grain, and became smooth and supple after their ploughing, and clung to their feet with a weight that pulled like desire, lying hard and unresponsive when the crops were to be shorn away.

They furrow the earth like lovers. The intercourse between sun and seed, between men and the fleshly soil, is analogous to the intercourse between man and woman—including the seasons of moods, the cycles of fertility, the periods of gestation and the terms of birth. Thus in Lawrence as in Donne human sexuality miniatures the cosmos.

Like Anthony Schofield, whose offer later in the novel of a purely physical marriage momentarily tempts Ursula, the Brangwen men, immersed in nature, are merely "one with it," whereas Ursula both "saw it, and was one with it. Her seeing separated them infinitely." It is this ability to see beyond the physical, to transcend the fever of procreation, which distinguishes the Brangwen women from the men. The loss of self-control, the yielding to the natural, which Lawrence represents as a brief and necessary interlude in sexual passion, has become a permanent condition of existence for the farmers of the Marsh. Throughout the novel nature remains the matrix of human life, but it is also the source of energies which enables men to transcend nature by constructing and inhabiting a social world. At the opening, the ideal relation between nature and society seems clear: to combine the natural vitality, sensual refinement and warm trust embodied in the life of Tom and Lydia on the Marsh Farm, with the intellectual adventure and communal involvement offered by the greater social world. But by the close of *The Rainbow*, as we shall see shortly, that relation has become extremely problematic. The tribulations of England during 1912–1915—a country rent by strikes, fearing revolution, mobilizing for war—lay behind this disillusionment.

Although Lawrence's perception of man as a part of nature is latent in the earlier novels, it only becomes fully manifest in *The Rainbow*. "This is a constant revelation in Hardy's novels," he wrote in that study of the elder novelist, begun in 1914, which revealed more about himself than about Hardy,

> that there exists a great background, vital and vivid, which matters more than the people who move upon it. . . . And this is the quality Hardy shares with the great writers, Shakespeare or Sophocles or Tolstoi, this setting behind the small action of his protagonists the terrific action of unfathomed nature; setting a smaller system of morality, the one grasped and formulated by the human consciousness within the vast, uncomprehended and incomprehensible morality of nature or of life itself, surpassing human consciousness.[10]

This is precisely Ursula's discovery, which encapsulates the view of nature and society in *The Rainbow*:

> This world in which she lived was like a circle lighted by a lamp. This lighted area, lit up by man's completest consciousness, she thought was all the world: that here all was disclosed for ever. Yet all the time, within the darkness she had been aware of points of light, like the eyes of wild beasts, gleaming, penetrating, vanishing. And her soul had acknowledged in a great heave of terror only the outer darkness. This inner circle of light in which she lived and moved, wherein the trains rushed and the factories ground out their machine-produce and the plants and the animals worked by the light of science and knowledge, suddenly it seemed like the area

[10] *Study of Thomas Hardy*, PI 419.

under an arc-lamp, wherein the moths and children played in the security of blinding light, not even knowing there was any darkness, because they stayed in the light.

From his knowledge of Freud and Herbert Spencer, and from his reading of Darwin's *Origin of Species*, T. H. Huxley's *Man's Place in Nature* and Ernst Haeckel's *The Riddle of the Universe*, Lawrence was familiar with the view of man which derived from evolutionary theory—man the biological species, distinguished from other animals only by certain frail and imperfect contrivances such as language, vulnerable to the instincts of lust or aggression which stirred inside him, a scarcely civilized creature capable of surviving only if he acknowledged and reconciled the beast within. Although Zola was certainly influenced by this biological view of man, as Balzac had been by an earlier version, Lawrence may be said to be the first major writer to attempt a thoroughgoing translation of this view into fictional terms. His vision of nature as a living "background" resembles Whitehead's conception of the universe as organism, or Bergson's notion of life as a stream impelled by the *élan vital*, or Teilhard de Chardin's account of the total life-process, all three formulations roughly contemporary with Lawrence's own.

In his novels every passionate encounter between man and woman, every stage in the struggle towards selfhood, every intimate contact with nature leads ultimately into "darkness" or the "unknown." It is as if he forced his characters through the medium of words to the boundaries of language, beyond which they could sense powers and orders of being which neither he nor they could name. This is precisely the dilemma implicit in all writing about God. The theologian can gesture towards the absolute, but cannot reduce it to words. Lawrence's characters— in harmony with Kierkegaard, Tillich and Buber—discover the Godhead within the depths of themselves. It is when he attempts to plumb those depths, when he tries to penetrate the "unfathomed distances" within the self, that his language shows the strain of translating the untranslatable. Dante's God is obscured by an excess of light, Lawrence's by an excess of darkness.

He attributes to his natural order many of the qualities, and much of the language, traditionally ascribed in Judeo-Christian cultures to God. This divinization of the life-process resembles the natural theology which developed in response to Darwin, and which found in the operation of immutable natural laws evidence of a God who comprises the whole of nature. "The universe is a great complex activity of things existing and moving," Lawrence wrote in *Apocalypse*, "and all this is God." His uncannily vital descriptions of nature bear out his pantheistic claim in *The Crown* that "We can only know the *revelation* of God in the physical world."

Nowhere is the essentially religious character of his natural vision more clearly manifest than in *The Rainbow*. Thus Lydia as a mature woman worships the sensual "Mystery"; Anna in her pregnancy dances tribute to her unknown procreative Lord; Will, whose sexual experiences are described in ritualistic terms, preserves his religious passion throughout the trials of his marriage; Ursula translates Christianity into physical terms, desiring Jesus for her lover; and Tom intuits an eternal infinite "greater ordering" in the birth of a child and in the wheel of stars. Many scenes in the novel, including most of those mentioned here, are ritual in the sense defined by Tillich: "symbolic forms in which the religious substance that supports our entire existence is represented in a unique way."[11] Nature for Lawrence is that "religious substance," which is shadowed forth in ritual scenes throughout his works, ranging from the exchange of flowers in *Sons and Lovers* to the brutal human sacrifices of *The Plumed Serpent*. In Christian theology the sacred penetrates the profane; here nature penetrates the human. Biology supplants theology. Fate gives way to natural law.

Thus in Lawrence, as in Rousseau and Wordsworth, nature

---

[11] *On the Boundary* (New York, 1966), p. 73. Lawrence wrote in a letter of 1913 that he was fascinated "to see art coming out of religious yearning," a fascination whetted by Jane Harrison's *Art and Ritual*, which he read in the autumn of that year. On Lawrence's use of ritual, see the works by Spilka and Moynahan already cited. On the religious dimension of Lawrence's fiction, see George Panichas, *Adventures in Consciousness: The Meaning of D. H. Lawrence's Religious Quest* (The Hague, 1964); Nathan A. Scott, *Rehearsals of Discomposure* (London and New York, 1952); and Phillip Rieff, *The Triumph of the Therapeutic: Uses of Faith after Freud* (London and New York, 1966), Chapter 7. Leavis discusses this aspect of *The Rainbow* in his chapter on that novel in *D. H. Lawrence: Novelist* (London, 1955; New York, 1956).

becomes the divine milieu. J. S. Mill was already complaining in his essay on *Nature* in the 1850s that appeals to a divinized "nature" were being substituted for discredited appeals to God by the followers of that woolly-minded Frenchman Rousseau. Like Freud and Lawrence's influential contemporary T. E. Hulme, Mill mistrusted nature, particularly human nature. Lawrence, on the other hand, like the Romantics before him and like Wilhelm Reich and Herbert Marcuse since, held that man is not inherently corrupt, but is corrupted by his institutions, particularly by those which repress his sexual impulses. For Lawrence this did not mean wholly ignoring Darwin's nature "red in tooth and claw"—after all in *The Rainbow* there are the stampeding horses and the wild beasts wheeling in darkness—but it did mean claiming that men were capable of living much more freely and finely and peacefully than their present society permitted.

His representation of the divine principle as a universal life impulse is consistent with a dominant mode of nineteenth-century thought: Hegel postulated a World Spirit, Carlyle a World Urge, Schopenhauer the will, Bergson the *élan vital* (which Shaw translated into the life-force), Freud and Jung the libido. Meanwhile the physicists were systematically interpreting all natural phenomena as various manifestations of some basic energy. Indeed physics had contributed during that century to the desacralization of nature, what Schiller called the "disenchantment of the world." Along with Ursula's professor at college scientists were asking, "May it not be that life consists in a complexity of physical and chemical activities, of the same order as we already know in science?" For the scientist, if not yet for the general public, nature had lost its mystery. It symbolized nothing, spoke no language.

It is apparent, then, that in *The Rainbow* Lawrence was responding both to the cultural death of God and to the desacralization of nature. When Tom Brangwen gazes at the stars, he sees not only hot gases in motion, but symbols of a "greater ordering." Natural theology served Lawrence as a means of restoring coherence and pattern to human existence—a pattern which he felt Christianity had once provided, but could provide no longer.

> So the children lived the year of Christianity, the epic of the soul of mankind. Year by year the inner, unknown drama went on in them, their hearts were born and came to fullness, suffered on the

cross, gave up the ghost, and rose again to unnumbered days, un-
tired, having at least this rhythm of eternity in a ragged, inconse-
quential life. But it was becoming a mechanical action now, this
drama.

The felt need for *some* "rhythm of eternity," for some sense of an
underlying pattern, an encompassing process, was a crucial impulse
behind Lawrence's work, an impulse which over the last century
has become increasingly urgent as our conventional versions of
God and our inherited social ideals have lost credibility. I am not
suggesting that Lawrence would have agreed with Arnold in viewing poetry or any other literature as surrogate religion; nor that
with I. A. Richards he would have hoped for literature to "save
us." I am only suggesting that through the novels, above all in
The Rainbow, he movingly communicated his intuition of a God
revealed in the natural order, and in the depths of the self. If one
accepts Marx's argument that men in the capitalistic industrial process who are alienated from the products of their labor, are to the
same degree alienated from "the sensuous external world," then
Lawrence's attempt to reconcile men with nature appears as a
necessary step in the reconciliation of men with their own
creations.[12] His representation of man as a part of nature should
be seen, therefore, not only as one aspect of a larger reorientation
of thought about man, which was spurred on by scientific speculation concerning the irreducibly animal component of human nature
(a reorientation associated with such pivotal figures as Darwin,
Frazer and Freud), but also as a response to the contemporary
crisis in religious and social ideology. The language of *Women in
Love* registers the effects of this crisis even more clearly, as I shall
try to show in the next chapter.

4 *The Conflict between Nature and Society*

By stressing man's physicality, Lawrence's thought appears at
times deterministic, at times anti-social. If human activity is
rooted in nature, as *The Rainbow* argues, then freedom becomes
problematic; as in any religious system, the notion of freedom
sorts ill with the notion of an omnipotent, omnipresent divine
order. If man, even though a creature of nature, still maintains

[12] *Economic and Philosophical Manuscripts of 1844*, in *Karl Marx: Early
Writings*, trans. and ed. T. B. Bottomore (New York, 1963), pp. 125–6.

a margin of freedom, then he can be held responsible for the exercise of that freedom. If he does not, then he cannot. Lawrence vacillates between one view of man's condition and the other.

Consider for example the case of Will Brangwen (which parallels that of Walter Morel in *Sons and Lovers*). He is criticized for worshipping the church, for refusing to take control of his own life, for being domineering and anti-social. But these faults and his obscure failure as man and husband are only symptoms, according to Lawrence, of a deeper organic disease:

> He must submit to his own inadequacy, the limitation of his being. . . . He was aware of some limit to himself, of something unformed in his very being, of some buds which were not ripe in him, some folded centres of darkness which would never develop and unfold whilst he was alive in the body. He was unready for fulfilment. Something undeveloped in him limited him, there was a darkness in him which he *could* not unfold, which would never unfold in him.

But if Will's failure is due to some inherent fault in his make-up then it is beyond his control or responsibility. If "there was a darkness in him which he *could* not unfold," can we distinguish his predicament from the helplessness of Ursula and Skrebensky, who, subjected to passion, "*could* not turn back to the world"? If not, we can no more blame Will for his failure as a man than Ursula and Skrebensky for their passion, or Tom for courting Lydia, or a flower for the shape of its blossom. Here Lawrence's two frames of reference conflict: conscious man, man the creature of culture, free within limits to choose the form of his life, must be judged by the values which that life embodies or fails to embody; but unconscious man, man the creature of nature, wholly subject to the forces stirring in the depths of "his very being," cannot meaningfully be judged at all.

For most of the novel, even when masterfully evoking the natural frame, Lawrence judges men as social beings, responsible to spouse and family and community for their actions. Yet there are lapses, as in Will's case, which are symptomatic of a growing tendency on Lawrence's part to reject society altogether in favor of nature. We sense this alienation from society in Ursula's fascination with "the strange laws of the vegetable world" in which she glimpsed "something working entirely apart from the purpose of the human world." She thus declares her allegiance to that great natural "background" which Lawrence admired in the works of Hardy, Sophocles, Shakespeare and Tolstoy. If natural impulses operate unconsciously, if they are experienced in their pristine form through sexuality, if their movements escape the bounds of language and the determinations of reason, then human consciousness and will are at best irrelevant to nature—and at worst inimical. All the social criticism in the novel hinges on this opposition between human will and natural processes. Whereas in *Sons and Lovers* the social critique remains largely implicit, in *The Rainbow* it becomes explicit, because Lawrence, following Rousseau and the Romantics, has discovered in nature a standard for judging society. Collective, purposive human effort, wherever it appears in the novel, is destructive. Human will in Wiggiston resides in the industrial machine, which reduces colliers and master alike to the status of instruments. In the earlier novel this instrumentalization was presented merely as a fact about Walter Morel's life; here it has become the basis for an indictment of the factory system. In Ursula's school the pupils are subjected to the will of the teachers, the teachers to the headmaster, the headmaster to the state; and that state seems to have very little notion about what it wants other than more production and more producers. Even the university seems to Ursula no more than "a little apprentice-shop where one was further equipped for making money . . . a little, slovenly laboratory for the factory."

Lawrence's manifest distaste for the fabric of man's social existence is condensed in Will's reaction to the steel and concrete sprawl of London:

> How had helpless savages, running with their spears on the riverside, after fish, how had they come to rear up this great London, the ponderous, massive, ugly superstructure of a world of man upon a world of nature! It frightened and awed him. Man was terrible, awful in his works. The works of man were more terrible than man himself, almost monstrous.

For Marx men's social relations combined with nature to provide the material conditions of life; ideology was the superstructure erected upon these foundations. But for Lawrence the cities and factories were themselves part of that usurping superstructure. In the contemporary essays collected in *Twilight in Italy*, he worries that industry, which had blighted the Midlands of his childhood, might spread like a cancer over all the earth: "It is the hideous rawness of the world of men, the horrible, desolating harshness of the advance of the industrial world upon the world of nature, that is so painful."[13] Whenever nature and society are compared in the novel, the natural invariably appears more powerful and more appealing than the social; and if we compare the complex and finely-rendered accounts of life at the Marsh presented in the early chapters, with the schematic and often perfunctory rendering of the "man's world" in the latter chapters, Lawrence's preference seems unmistakable.

The Marsh Farm, rich in life though it is, appears in the opening pages of the novel as a cage to the spirit. Its values guide all three generations in their quest for fuller life, but its own life is too circumscribed to satisfy the Brangwen women's longing for active participation in the thoughts and business of the social world. But no arena larger than the Marsh Farm yet consistent with its values ever emerges in the novel.

Judged by the standards of the Marsh, all other forms of life are found wanting: the industrial world of Tom, Jr., the world of humanistic learning feebly represented by Winifred Inger, the province of teaching scouted by Ursula at Brinsfield School, the University community of Nottingham, the serfdom inhabited by soldiers and civil servants such as Skrebensky.[14] The list is a long one, considering that all these aspects of contemporary society are introduced, assessed and rejected within the last hundred and

[13] *Op. cit.* (Penguin edition), p. 160. Originally published London, 1916.

[14] The novel's assault upon Skrebensky the soldier, and upon the sheepish citizenly virtues necessary in wartime, doubtless contributed as much as "obscenity" to the banning of *The Rainbow*. For example James Douglas, who was quoted in the censorship proceedings, wrote the following in the *Star* of 22 October 1915: "The wind of war is sweeping over our life, and it is demolishing many of the noisome pestilences of peace. A thing like *The Rainbow* has no right to exist in the wind of war. . . . The young men who are dying for liberty are moral beings. They are the living repudiation of such impious denials of life as *The Rainbow*." This, and other contemporary responses to the novel, will be found in R. P. Draper, *D. H. Lawrence: The Critical Heritage* (London and New York, 1970); documents relating to the censorship case will be found in the article by John Carter, "The Rainbow Prosecution," *Times Literary Supplement*, 27 February 1969, p. 216.

fifty pages of the novel. The haste is symptomatic. In the sketchy figures of Tom, Jr., Miss Inger, Skrebensky, Mr Harby, Maggie Schofield (this novel's feminist), Ursula's former headmistress and the mechanistic scientist, Lawrence pillories those aspects of contemporary society which he feared or despised. But these straw men are too frail to bear the burden of social criticism placed on them. Of course Lawrence's indignation is genuine: one need only read the description of industrial Wiggiston, or the account of the human waste caused by the school-system, to recognize the depth of his feeling. But it is indignation expressed more by the means of the essayist than by those of the novelist. Because these latter chapters are more schematic, because the representatives of the outer world are treated perfunctorily, the novel's social criticism, whether or not one sympathizes with it, carries less weight than the critique presented in *Women in Love*. One cannot fill out such a cardboard figure as Skrebensky by arguing that he is a prototype for Gerald Crich: within the economy of *The Rainbow* itself he is too slight a character to support the case which Lawrence appears to be making. The same applies *a fortiori* to the other representatives of the man's world, for they are even less substantial, mere paper to his cardboard.

One cannot validly conclude from the last third of the novel that contemporary society offered no form of living which would have been compatible with the values of the Marsh Farm. Perhaps in the England into which Ursula was born there were no humane forms of social involvement, perhaps there were no opportunities for engaging in the thought and activity of the man's world without abnegating the integrity of the self, without violating the norms of nature. Perhaps—but its seems doubtful. Movements for social change were rife in 1910–14 England: the Fabianism of Shaw and the Webbs, Mrs Pankhurst's feminism, the liberal reformism associated with Lloyd George, the scientific utopianism championed by H. G. Wells, the labour movement headed by Arthur Henderson, Sorelian syndicalism, revolutionary socialism. Lawrence was either uninterested in discovering acceptable forms of social involvement or incapable of imagining them. Of course he imagined much besides, and magnificently. But his failure to explore the possibilities of living within an urban and industrial world with anything like the richness or complexity which he demonstrated in exploring the agrarian and natural world is nevertheless a real limitation, and should be recognized as marking one boundary to his vision.

Although in the opening pages of the novel the permanent subjection of the Brangwen men to the forces of nature is rejected by the Brangwen women, who yearn to participate in the world beyond the ken of the Marsh Farm, the world of knowledge, "the far-off world of cities and governments and the active scope of man"—the world, that is, of man's collective life in society—and although this yearning endures through each generation, Ursula is left at the end with the Brangwen longing still unfulfilled. By the end, in fact, she seems wholly disillusioned with the man's world. Her early "fear and dislike of authority," her terror of the "power of the mob," her "fear that her undiscovered self should be seen, pounced upon, attacked by brutish resentment of the commonplace, the average Self," never disappears. This fear of society resembles Lawrence's own wartime terror of "merging in a sticky male mass." The two poles of Ursula's schizoid response to society are those of Lawrence himself: the yearning to play a part in the community, and the fear of being destroyed by the mob. Her passionate experiments with Skrebensky teach her to resent "the social imposition," to think of people as beasts "falsified to a social mechanism," to distinguish radically between her "social" and her "permanent" or natural selves. In her often violent rejection of society as an *imposition* on her natural self, in her failure, like Mellors in *Lady Chatterley's Lover*, to distinguish between the good and bad elements of that "thing outside," there is more than a hint of Lawrence's own latent tendency, already apparent in *Sons and Lovers*, to group "others" into a hostile mass, to identify society with cruel and anti-natural authority, and then to shun both with a fear that by the writing of *Kangaroo* would become paranoid.

In Ursula's dilemma—a young woman who is at once socially frustrated and fearful of losing her individuality—we perceive the condition of Lawrence himself, a condition defined precisely by Raymond Williams, in his account of George Orwell, as that of the exile, who is unable to commit himself to any society,

> because he can see no way of confirming, socially, his own individuality; this, after all, is the psychological condition of the

self-exile. Thus in attacking the denial of liberty he is on sure ground; he is whole-hearted in rejecting the attempts of society to involve him. When, however, in any positive way, he has to affirm liberty, he is forced to deny its inevitable social basis: all he can fall back on is the notion of an atomistic society, which will leave individuals alone. . . . To belong to a community is to be part of a whole, and, necessarily, to accept, while helping to define, its disciplines. To the exile, however, society as such is totalitarian; he cannot commit himself, he is bound to stay out.[15]

An internal exile during the war, afterwards a global wanderer, Lawrence continued to advocate liberation of the self, but could never commit himself to any form of community, in which alone freedom could be secured. The social models which he toyed with, and eventually discarded, were totalitarian orders headed by prophetic figures suspiciously resembling himself: the fascist movement of *Kangaroo*, the theocratic state of *The Plumed Serpent*, the aristocratic order proposed in the wartime essays, and even his ideal colony of Rananim, which was to have been peopled exclusively by disciples obedient to his will and ideas. In those wartime essays, notably *Study of Thomas Hardy, The Crown,* "Education of the People" and "Democracy," he formulated and reformulated his view, resembling that of Herbert Spencer, that all of nature is moving to separate the individual from the mass. Thus he arranges for nature to recapitulate his own social trajectory.

To be sure, Lawrence recognizes the dangers in Ursula's attitude, and he upholds the world of man even when his heroine is buried deepest in the world of nature. For example, the visible record of man's collective effort in Rouen, where she is holidaying with Skrebensky, wakes her from the sensual trance into which she has drifted:

> She followed after something that was not him. . . . The old streets, the cathedral, the age and the monumental peace of the town took her away from him. She turned to it as if to something she had forgotten, and wanted. This was now the reality; this great stone cathedral slumbering there in its mass. . . .

[15] *Culture and Society, 1780–1950* (Harmondsworth, 1961), pp. 281–2. Williams' ideas about the psychology of exile have been applied to Lawrence by Terry Eagleton, in his *Exiles and Emigrés* (London and New York, 1970), pp. 191–218.

She shares the Brangwen yearning for that "something" beyond: yet this is all we hear at this point of the man's world which she has temporarily forgotten; and this brief passage seems feeble in comparison to the several pages in which her sensual trance is described. Similarly, in her encounter with the stampeding horses —a scene which on one of its several levels of significance represents an experience of the fiercest impulses within the self, and therefore reveals to her the logical consequence of pursuing some purely physical fulfillment—she is saved by her vision of "the smaller, cultivated field . . . the highroad and the ordered world of man." Yet at the very end of the novel she can imagine no new order, only a sweeping away of the old. This closing glimmer, reflecting a hopefulness which Lawrence was expressing in letters to his new friend Bertrand Russell in the early months of 1915, letters in which he spoke passionately of revolution, seems little more than a gesture on Lawrence's part, for almost every image of the "ordered world of man" which he has presented in the novel has been negative; so he registers the danger of Ursula's temporary rejection of the social, but offers nothing which could give substance to her vision of the "cultivated field."

There remains the Marsh Farm, the literal cultivated field, which is presented with greater power and persuasiveness than any urban-industrial environment that Lawrence ever attempted. It is his Egdon Heath, the true protagonist of the novel. But like the pastoral world depicted in *The White Peacock*, and like the tattered farm country of *Sons and Lovers*, this natural retreat is under attack from industry—gutted by canals, sliced by railroads, slurred by smokestacks. Wild unspoilt rural England for Hardy was already a fiction, which Lawrence could no longer sustain. To have created that natural world in *The Rainbow* was a great achievement; but that alone does not fulfill the goal which Lawrence set himself in the opening pages—to imagine a form of social life that would transcend the natural world without violating its norms.

Ursula's temptation to desert society for nature (with its vegetable laws "working entirely apart from the purpose of the human world") haunts all of Lawrence's major characters. In *Women in Love*, for example, at one point Birkin escapes to the fir-trees, and thinks:

Why should he pretend to have anything to do with human beings at all? Here was his world, he wanted nobody and nothing but the lovely, subtle, responsive vegetation, and himself, his own living self.

But in the next line he resists the temptation, as Ursula has resisted: "It was necessary to go back into the world." In the late fable about "The Man Who Loved Islands," as in *The Rainbow* and *Women in Love*, Lawrence insists on the destructive consequences of isolating oneself from the world of man. Yet from the latter chapters of *The Rainbow* onwards, his characters are in constant flight from society, they observe the "ordered world of man," if they observe it at all, from ever greater distances.

So long as nature is not divorced from society, so long as it serves to point the direction in which society should change, it remains a convincing standard for Lawrence's social criticism. So long as he opposes nature to specific forms of society, to particular historical configurations, rather than to society as such, his vision seems penetrating and persuasive. But once man is divided up into radically opposed natural and social dimensions, as if the first were an alternative to the second, as if the second were somehow an unnecessary encumbrance on the first, as if man could return to a pre-social state of existence, then the concept of "nature" loses all value as a critical standard—for in this case nature is not proposed as a measure but as a substitute for society. Already in *The Rainbow* this division is marked. In *The Plumed Serpent* and *Lady Chatterley's Lover* it becomes almost absolute. But in *Women in Love*, even though its picture of man's world is shades darker than the image presented by *The Rainbow*, that division is broken down under the pressure of contemporary events.

3

Women in Love:
Study in a Dying Culture

"I think there is no future for England," Lawrence wrote in a letter of 17 November 1915, "only a decline and fall. That is the dreadful and unbearable part of it: to have been born into a decadent era, a decline of life, a collapsing civilization."[1] His stormy wartime writings are darkened by this cultural pessimism, and lightened only flickeringly by visions of a new heaven and a new earth. It was a pessimism shared by many of his contemporaries. Hofmannsthal, Yeats, Mann, Proust and Eliot were all disturbed by the passing of an old order to which they felt they belonged. A cynicism about the outer world coupled with an obsessive interest in psychic states characterized the work during these years of Gide, Hesse and Pirandello. Spengler's *The Decline of the West* appeared in 1918 and immediately became a best-seller. Freud's lifelong pessimism, aggravated by the war, issued after 1918 in a social theory that emphasized the necessity of repression and the savage power of Thanatos. In her diary for 1918, Beatrice Webb remarked that every citizen—exhausted by the war, terrified by the plague of Bolshevism, confused amidst the collapse of social ideals and alarmed by the rapidity of change—knew that "the old order is seriously threatened with dissolution without any new order being in sight."

Within this apocalyptic era *Women in Love* took its final shape, the gloomiest of Lawrence's works. We breathe here the atmosphere of Daniel, Mark and the Revelation to John, texts whose language had been drummed into Lawrence's consciousness from

---

[1] Letter to Constance Garnett, CL 383. 17.xi.15.

an early age, language to which he returned throughout his life in times of crisis.[2] In *Women in Love* we read of the Deluge, Sodom, the Dead Sea Fruit. We hear of the old idols being smashed, the avenging angels coming to sweep the sinful away, the fruit of man rotting upon the boughs of life. We come across flowers of dissolution and flowers of mud. Within these pages all is borne away on a river of corruption; mankind is a withered tree, a doomed species; he is the prey of the devil and of other assorted demons. The novel fairly teems with apocalyptic imagery. Gudrun and Loerke envision the world ending by a cataclysmic explosion, or by war, or by glaciation. Without specifying the means, Birkin also imagines universal annihilation. "The book frightens me," Lawrence wrote in a letter of 1916, "it is so end-of-the-world."[3] Casting around for a more fitting title, he thought of calling it *Days of Wrath, The Latter Days* and, in Latin, *Day of Judgment.*

Bunyan and Milton had responded in apocalyptic language to the Puritan Revolution and counter-revolution; Blake and Carlyle responded in similar terms to the French Revolution and to the first stirrings of labor revolt in England. They drew upon the non-conformist Biblical tradition which Lawrence knew so well through sermons and hymns and readings. He inherited both their imagery and their style of response to cultural crises (the affinity with *Sartor Resartus* seems especially close). But why did he take up their particular legacy? What lay behind his choice of the apocalyptic stance?

In his brilliant study of revolutionary messianism in medieval Europe, Norman Cohn has shown that mass apocalyptic delusions flourish in times of great social stress, marked by traumatic public events, among people who are economically insecure and have lost all social moorings.[4] I believe this observation applies equally well to Lawrence during the war years. His eschatalogical concerns, his

---

[2] Frank Kermode suggests detailed comparisons with the book of Revelation in his essay, "Lawrence and the Apocalyptic Types," *Critical Quarterly*, X, Nos. 1 and 2 (Spring-Summer, 1968), pp. 14–38. For a study of the theme of decay and corruption in Lawrence's works, with special attention to *Women in Love*, see Colin Clarke, *River of Dissolution: D. H. Lawrence and English Romanticism* (London and New York, 1969).

[3] Letter to Catherine Carswell, CL 482. 7.xi.16.

[4] *The Pursuit of the Millenium*, Second Edition (New York, 1961; London, 1970), pp. 73–4.

misanthropy, his abhorrence of the "masses," the radical instability of his characters, the verbal and intellectual violence which he manifests in *Women in Love*, can only be accounted for with reference to social and psychological factors of the sort Cohn suggests. The most pressing factor was the war. For Lawrence this European bloodbath came as no overnight wonder, no freakish disturbance of a placid world, but rather as the conclusion of a long process of cultural decay, the death rattle of a moribund civilization.

He grafted onto this public crisis a crisis in his own life. During 1915 and 1916, the first two full years of the war and the years in which *Women in Love* was finished, Lawrence's own fortunes were at their nadir. His health was bad. He was poor, and after the suppression of *The Rainbow* had every prospect of growing poorer. The ban made him as uncertain of his audience as of his finances. For a new audience he began looking toward America, and for money he looked toward friends. When begging and borrowing failed to produce enough income to support his meager household, he briefly toyed with the idea of returning to teaching, or even taking up some form of war work. During the same period he maintained a precarious social position on the fringes of the liberal aristocracy and the decadent London bohemia, two groups already moribund before the war. All his attempts at social involvement failed miserably. Unwilling to ally himself with any of the groups which actually gained in power during the war— the working class, the bureaucracy, the managerial elite—he magnified his own experience of declining social groups into tokens of the decline of the west.

Compounding this social and economic strain was the uncertainty of his sexual identity. During those wartime years he was torn, more savagely than at any other point in his career, by competing homosexual and heterosexual impulses. Homosexual themes stir just beneath the surface in *The Rainbow* and *Women in Love*; they figure openly in the next new work, *Aaron's Rod*, as they also figured, according to contemporary report, in the suppressed (and finally destroyed) wartime philosophical work called *Goats and Compasses*. A close reading of *Women in Love* suggests that Lawrence found this challenge to his sexual identity deeply unsettling.

This personal crisis fused with England's cultural crisis to produce the most deeply troubled and troubling of Lawrence's works. In the chapter that follows I am concerned to trace the violent, disturbing imprint left upon *Women in Love* by the war, by Lawrence's social frustration, and by his struggle against homosexual impulses.

1 *The Language of Violence*

A violent spirit broods over *Women in Love*. This is volcanic land, shaken by tremors, ridden by disease, inhabited by people who are unstable and destructive. Every character in the novel is subject to fits of ungovernable rage. Thus in the opening pages when Gudrun's emerald-green stockings provoke taunts from a member of the wedding crowd, she reacts with insane fury: "A sudden fierce anger swept over the girl, violent and murderous. She would have liked them all annihilated, cleared away, so that the world was left clear for her." The "rottenness in the will," the lust for "inexpressible destructiveness" that Gudrun detects in the miners of Beldover afflicts everyone in the book, particularly Birkin, who frequently echoes her dream of an earth cleansed of people: "I abhor humanity. I wish it was swept away. It could go, and there would be no *absolute* loss, if every human being perished tomorrow." When Birkin contradicts Hermione, he feels "waves of hatred and loathing of all he said coming out of her . . . dynamic hatred and loathing, coming strong and black out of the unconscious." Gerald, who bears the murderous mark of Cain, demonstrates his own passion for cruelty in his dealings with Minette, the mare, the miners, the rabbit and with Gudrun. Even Ursula, the most peaceable of the lot, occasionally succumbs to wild and irrational fury. Birkin's indifference to the drowning of a Crich child, for example, makes her feel "such a poignant hatred of him, that all her brain seemed turned into a sharp crystal of fine hatred. Her whole nature seemed sharpened and intensified into a pure dart of hate." Hermione's attack with the paperweight upon Birkin and Gerald's attempt to kill Gudrun are only the two most turbulent eddies in the current of violence which flows through the novel. Gudrun feels "an unconquerable desire for deep violence" against Gerald, which Gerald in turn feels against Gudrun and Loerke, Hermione feels against Birkin, and Birkin feels against mankind. Clearly these people are very much out of balance.

Throughout the novel sexuality is linked with violence. The drowning of the entwined lovers in "Water Party" is merely the most dramatic instance. Loerke, we are told, beats his mistress. In "Mino" Birkin applauds the tomcat which bullies its mate. Becoming himself the tomcat in "Continental," Birkin certifies his own manhood by subjecting Ursula to his will ("Her impulse was to repel him violently, break from this spell of mocking brutishness. But she was too fascinated, she wanted to submit . . . she gave way, he might do as he would.") In a spirit of viciousness and cruelty Gudrun taunts the bulls, Gerald tortures the mare, and both of them madden the rabbit. In each case the lovers make animals the victims of their battle for dominance.

When Gerald meets the kittenish Minette, one of the free-wheeling women who frequent London's bohemia, he immediately regards her as prey for his violent desires:

'How long are you staying?' she asked him.

'A day or two,' he replied. 'But there is no particular hurry.'

Still she stared into his face with that slow, full gaze which was so curious and so exciting to him. He was acutely and delightfully conscious of himself, of his own attractiveness. He felt full of strength, able to give off a sort of electric power. . . .

She appealed to Gerald strongly. He felt an awful, enjoyable power over her, an instinctive cherishing very near to cruelty. For she was a victim. He felt that she was in his power, and he was generous. The electricity was turgid and voluptuously rich, in his limbs. He would be able to destroy her utterly in the strength of his discharge. . . .

They talked banalities for some time.

This extreme contrast between the "banalities" exchanged on the surface and the play of violent forces beneath recurs throughout the novel. The sexual attraction, characteristically described in terms of elementary physics (magnetism and electricity appear over three dozen times in the novel) is colored by a sadism which transforms the woman into a victim, and the act of love into one of destruction. Allowance must be made, as always, for Lawrence's exaggeration, but, account taken, in this passage as in so many others throughout the book, the riotous emotions stirring beneath the placid surface seem wildly disproportionate to the occasion.

Everyone in the world of *Women in Love* suffers from this radical instability, major and minor characters alike, as if the violence unleashed in the outside world had been internalized, creating an impression of emotional volatility more characteristic of the great Russians (especially Dostoevsky, whom Lawrence was reading in 1915–16) than of the generally more restrained English. Surface action masks an undercurrent of violence; moods change rapidly; persons dissolve into impersonal forces; language runs quickly to extremes.

Aside from the literal mayhem of the trenches in France, there was in England, during those first years of the war when Lawrence was putting *Women in Love* into its finished form, a good deal of rhetorical violence. The labor movement was vociferous and threatening, particularly the syndicalist wing, which borrowed some of its language from George Sorel's *Reflections on Violence* (1908). Sylvia Pankhurst outflanked her mother to the left in her militant crusade for the emancipation of women. Speeches, newspapers and weeklies were choked with diatribes against the beastly Germans. Echoes of Futurism filtered in from Italy and Paris, of Dadaism from Switzerland—the former movement, in the vitriolic words of Marinetti, embracing violence and destruction, the latter denouncing the whole of contemporary culture. For a time in 1914 Wyndham Lewis's Vorticist movement swirled around a periodical appropriately entitled *Blast. Women in Love* partakes of this verbal strife. which preceded and accompanied the armed strife of the battlefields.

But the strain of disorder runs deeper in the novel. Personality has been reduced in quite a remarkable degree to a sequence of physical states. The interactions of the four main characters take on an almost mathematical formalism, corresponding on the verbal plane to the visual formalism of many post-Impressionist paintings. The book is even more stark and schematic than *Jude the Obscure*, its nearest spiritual predecessor among English novels—more stark because the crucial personal relationships have not only been isolated from society, but have become a substitute for any form of social involvement. Thus Lawrence continued the narrowing and intensifying process which he felt Hardy had begun, the process of reducing character to its physiological minimum. Indeed, the notation which he developed for representing sensory states was probably his greatest addition to the expressive resources of English.

In *Women in Love* this physiological notation achieves its purest form, a brand of psychic physics, in which states of being are presented as states of matter. Characters appear as solids, liquids and gases; they are likened to mud, clay, steel, radium and bronze. Gerald in particular passes through all the states of water, from ice to steam, achieving his apotheosis in the end as "cold, mute Matter." Under the stress of violent emotions, persons tend to dissolve into lumps of matter or lines of force, interacting by means of electricity, magnetism, friction, radio-activity or gravitation. The ideal love relationship, which was figured in *The Rainbow* by the balanced arch, appears in Birkin's love-ethic in terms of equilibrium, nodality, polarization, attraction and repulsion: "he wanted a further conjunction, where man had being and woman had being, two pure beings, each constituting the freedom of the other, balancing each other like the two poles of one force." He desires the "polarization of sex," which would allow man and woman to remain independent within the "polarized sex circuit." The marriage of Mr Crich is a perversion of Birkin's ideal, for instead of enjoying that state of balance and mutual freedom which he prescribes, the wife "was consumed in a fierce tension of opposition, like the negative pole of a magnet." The relation between Gerald and Gudrun reduces to the same algebra of force: "He and she were separate, like opposite poles of one fierce energy." Thus the actions and relations in the novel appear as physical phenomena, the work of forces over which individuals exercise neither responsibility nor control.

This reduction of states of being to states of matter harmonizes with Lawrence's futurist program, conceived in defense of *The Rainbow*, but more fully applicable to *Women in Love*:

the laugh of the woman is the same as the binding of the molecules of steel or their action in heat; it is the inhuman will, call it it physiology, or like Marinetti—physiology of matter, that fascinates me . . . I only care about what the woman *is*—what she IS—inhumanly, physiologically, materially. . . . You mustn't look in my novel for the old stable *ego*—of the character. There is another *ego*, according to whose action the individual is unrecognisable, and passes through, as it were, allotropic states which it needs a deeper sense than any we've been used to exercise, to discover are states of the same radically unchanged element.[5]

Loerke, with his love of machinery and his deification of industry, could be taken as a satirical portrait of the Futurist. Yet Lawrence himself at this time was fascinated by violence and destruction, obsessed with dynamism, with the play of forces and the permutations of matter, a fascination shared by the Futurists, whose work and theories he had been reading, and about whom he intended to write an essay. In early versions of his essays on Dana and Melville, he also praised the two American writers for displaying futurist qualities, claiming that they presented "events in the light of their extreme reality: mechanical, material, a semi-incoherent dream-rendering. . . . These two are masters of the sheer movement, of substance in its own paths, free from all human postulation or control."[6] The "savage desire to go to extremes" which he admired in Melville, and which attracted him at this time to classic American literature, describes equally well his own violent manner in *Women in Love.*

Precisely here, in his emphasis upon the physical basis of human existence and in his depiction of turbulent unconscious impulses, Lawrence's work differs most radically from contemporary experiments in fiction. True, Joyce and Proust and Virginia Woolf were also dissolving the "old stable ego" of the character, dismantling the "certain moral scheme" that he objected to; yet they remained for the most part at the level of *consciousness,* they explored memory, associations, perceptions, thoughts. But Lawrence dealt with more rudimentary layers of existence. He undertook more tenaciously than any other English writer of this century the function which Herbert Read, speaking for a generation raised on Freud, declared to be the unique responsibility of the artist: "to materialize the instinctual life of the deepest layers of the mind."[7] Association, memory, allusion, conscious connections of all sorts play comparatively little part in his fiction. Where the

[5] Letter to Edward Garnett, CL 282. 5.vi.14. For a fuller discussion of Lawrence's relation to Futurism, see Mary Freeman, *D. H. Lawrence: A Basic Study of His Ideas* (New York, 1955). For an examination of the symbolism and strategy of Lawrence's love ethic, see Mark Spilka, *The Love Ethic of D. H. Lawrence* (Bloomington, Ind., and London, 1955).

[6] *The Symbolic Meaning,* p. 237. Cf. SCAL 109, 127, 138.

[7] *Art and Society* (New York, 1966; London, 1967), p. 95.

characters of Joyce or Woolf or Proust are subject to the past, those of Lawrence live almost exclusively in the present, because instincts are not subject to history.

We have already observed in *Sons and Lovers* and *The Rainbow* the hazard of reducing states of being to states of matter. The deterministic overtones of this practice appear even more starkly in *Women in Love*. If the influences at work in the characters are impersonal, then Birkin and Ursula are no more responsible for their relative success in love than are Gerald, Gudrun and Hermione for their failure. Although the same physical metaphors are used to represent all love-relationships in the novel, only that of Birkin and Ursula—we are told—is a success. But on this linguistic level there is little to choose between them, for the rhetoric of matter and force is ethically neutral. By claiming a larger and larger role for the nonhuman, for the purely physiological influences in life, Lawrence granted man less and less conscious control over his existence. Of course it was precisely because he believed misuse of consciousness had bred the diseases of war and industrialism that he championed nature against society, instinct against reason. This opposition, which was still only tentative in *Sons and Lovers*, then more pronounced in *The Rainbow*, has become absolute in *Women in Love*.

Like a biologist Lawrence sought to provide knowledge of the nonhuman roots of human life; yet knowledge of that which is neither specific to man's nature nor subject to his control remains of doubtful use for moral argument. Encountering a similar impulse in Poe, who "never sees anything in terms of life, almost always in terms of matter . . . or in terms of force, scientific," Lawrence objects that one should "Keep KNOWLEDGE for the world of matter, force and function. It has got nothing to do with being."[8] Yet he himself employs this rhetoric of force and matter in *Women in Love*, mirroring the very process of dehumanization which he condemned in industry and in the war. The war, that monstrous display of collective insanity, could only confirm his suspicion of human society, driving him further along that path which Ursula pursued in search of vegetable laws "working entirely apart from the purpose of the human world," deeper into the natural, the nonhuman, in search of some life which man, with his destruc-

[8] SCAL 66.

tive will and distorted purposes, had not defiled. The dramatic increase in state control, in propaganda, in commercial activity and public hysteria engendered by the war forced Lawrence on his own road of conquest deeper into human nature; the mine shafts of his prose bored into the last virgin territory of the self.

In stressing the natural man, Lawrence slighted what Marx called "species" man—the uniquely human, the social dimension. The deeper he plunged into the impersonal reaches of the unconscious, the shallower his commentary on those social diseases which had driven him to despair. The more he stripped from his characters the contaminating ties of class, job, family and education, the less he had to say about them as creatures living in history. Of all his novels *Women in Love* contributes most to that dehumanization of modern art, defined by Ortega y Gasset and pilloried in the novel itself in the character of Loerke, for whom the work of art is an autonomous form, bearing no relation to anything outside itself. (While practicing Loerke's abstraction, in this dialectical novel Lawrence also attacks it through the words of Ursula, who insists that "The world of art is only the truth about the real world.") Wilhelm Worringer, in his *Abstraction and Empathy* of 1908, provided a generation of artists with a rationale for the impulse to abstraction. This he found exemplified in primitive art; it was marked in contemporary painting by the reduction of organic shapes to geometrical ones, and ultimately by the complete abandonment of representational modes. From the *Study* of Hardy, from the later "Introduction to These Paintings" (1929), and also from the critique of primitive carvings in the novel itself, it is clear that Lawrence strongly objected to this desire for abstraction. Yet the pressure of external events (during 1916 the newspapers were carrying lists of about 4,000 casualties per day; 20,000 men died on the first day of the Battle of the Somme) drove him also to reduce the human to an algebra of forces and substances.

The nonhuman forces unleashed in *Women in Love* are overwhelmingly destructive. When we do encounter creative forces—in the ritual love scenes of "Excurse" and "Death and Love," for example—they are so encrusted with jargon, or so fleeting, as to seem feeble in comparison with the powers of destruction. The vicious struggle between Gerald and Gudrun is more convincing,

as many readers have attested, than the mysterious harmony between Birkin and Ursula. Like Milton, who also wrote despairingly
in a time of strife, Lawrence found it easier to depict the forces
of darkness than those of light. We are led through the inferno,
skirt purgatory, but scarcely glimpse paradise. Unlike Dante, who
also explored the soul's diseases, Lawrence inherited no ideological framework strong enough to withstand the pressure of
social turmoil. T. S. Eliot, who had his own ideology to promote,
berated Lawrence as well as Blake and others for seeking to invent
private schemes of salvation. But in this respect Lawrence rather
than Eliot is the representative modern. Trapped in an era of international slaughter and domestic turmoil, Lawrence seemed
unable to reassert that faith which had informed his earlier novels
—faith in the life-renewing power of organic nature, and in the
holiness of the instincts. Nothing in the world of *Women in Love*
fully escapes the social disease, not even instinct. At such a time,
to such a man, death might seem—as it does to Ursula—the only
certain triumph of the nonhuman over the human; life might
seem, in the words of Thomas Mann, a mere fever in matter,
pathological and transient; universal annihilation might seem—
as it does to Birkin, Loerke and Gudrun—the only cure for the
spreading disease of human society. But any philosophy which
views death as the only antidote to life, which views the end of
history as the only solution to the disorders of history, is itself
diseased.

2 The War and the Psyche

Describing *Women in Love* to a correspondent in 1917, Lawrence attributed its apocalyptic mood to the war: "This actually
does contain the results in one's soul of the war: it is purely
destructive, not like *The Rainbow*, destructive-consummating."[9]

---

[9] Letter to Waldo Frank, CL 519. 27.vii.17. On the negative, nihilistic
aspects of the novel, see K. K. Ruthven, "The Savage God: Conrad and
Lawrence," *The Critical Quarterly*, X (1968), Nos. 1 and 2, pp. 39–54. For
a discussion of this aspect of Lawrence's work in general, see Jascha Kessler,
"D. H. Lawrence's Primitivism," *Texas Studies in Literature and Language*,
V (1963–4), pp. 467–88; and two articles by Kingsley Widmer: "The Primitivist Aesthetic: D. H. Lawrence," *Journal of Aesthetics*, XVII (March, 1959),
pp. 344–53 and "D. H. Lawrence and the Art of Nihilism," *Kenyon Review*,
XX (Autumn, 1958), pp. 604–16.

In *The Rainbow*, despite encroachments by the ruinous social realm upon the creative reserve of nature, nature still triumphs. Although in Skrebensky and Uncle Tom society has won a victory —the one subjugated by the army and the national ideal, the other by industry and the mechanical ideal—the victory is a meagre one. Through Ursula, Will, Anna, Tom and Lydia, the virtues of instinct achieve triumphant expression. Natural processes, whether apprehended within the self or in the external world, still overpower the feeble forces wielded by man in society.

But in *Women in Love* the balance has shifted. The very deepest psychic processes and the most intimate personal relations are affected by the social disintegration; the violent social upheaval sends tremors even into the cellars of the unconscious. Thus *Women in Love* completes a movement in Lawrence's thought, the beginnings of which we have traced in the previous two novels. In *Sons and Lovers* the acknowledged role of society is minimal; Lawrence is too preoccupied with problems of personal development to deal other than indirectly with the social context. Society enters ominously into the world of *The Rainbow*: through school, industry and commerce, through convention and opinion, through war, it invades the domain of the individual; yet social pressures remain weaker than the impersonal forces operating in the unconscious and in nature. But in *Women in Love* even the psyche is infected by the social disease: individual and society, nature and culture, are thoroughly integrated in the process of dissolution, so that public strife, conflicts within the unconscious and struggles between lovers all seem to be part of the same historical phenomenon.

As in *Sons and Lovers*, so in *Women in Love* the underlying subject is a larger historical reality. In the Foreword to the later book Lawrence wrote that

> it is a novel which took its final shape in the midst of the period of war, though it does not concern the war itself. I should wish the time to remain unfixed, so that the bitterness of the war may be taken for granted in the characters.

By focusing a cultural crisis, the war did indeed shape *Women in Love*. Only the extreme inhumanities of the war can account for the novel's profound bitterness, or for its pervading atmosphere of violence. As the letters of the period show, Lawrence recognized the connection between outer and inner violence, between social and personal disorder. "The war is dreadful," he wrote in a letter of 1914. "It is the business of the artist to follow it home to the heart of the individual fighters . . . it's at the bottom of almost every Englishman's heart—the war—the desire of war—the *will* to war."[10] Gerald is the only fighter in *Women in Love*; like Skrebensky he was an officer in the Boer War. But the desire of war, the lust for violence, lurks in every character in the novel. (All the later novels and many of the tales are haunted by ex-soldiers or active soldiers, like specters from a traumatic past.)

Whereas in *The Rainbow* Lawrence had celebrated the release of "the dark sensual or Dionysic or Aphrodisic ecstasy" within the individual—one thinks of Anna's dance in pregnancy or Ursula's violent trances in the moonlight—the war had released this frenzy on a mass scale, and the issue, as we know, was bloody. "What I did through individuals," he wrote to a correspondent in 1917, referring to *The Rainbow*, "the world has done through the war."[11] The stampeding horses signify in that earlier novel a revolt of the instincts which grew beyond all bounds in the world war. Lawrence simultaneously damned this Armageddon for its slaughter, and celebrated it for promising to sweep away the old world. The apocalyptic elements in *Women in Love*, which tempted him to call it *The Latter Days*, and the theme of disintegration which gives the book such a *fin de siècle* tone, refer simultaneously to history and to the individual psyche:

> The Prussian rule would be an external evil. The disintegrating process of the war has become an internal evil, so vast as to be almost unthinkable, so nearly overwhelming us, that we stand on the very brink of oblivion.[12]

Thus the pressure of violent historical events broke down the barrier which Lawrence had erected, in previous novels, between the personal and the social realms.

Newspapers, diaries, novels, poems and letters from the war years indicate as one would expect that the feelings of English people were numbed by the holocaust. When a single battle such

[10] Letter to Harriet Monroe, CL 295. 17.xi.14.
[11] Letter to Waldo Frank, CL 519. 27.vii.17.
[12] Letter to Cynthia Asquith, CL 375. 2.xi.15.

as that at Passchendaele could leave behind nearly 300,000 casualties in exchange for negligible military gains, death lost all proportion. In an era that introduced aerial bombardment, gas warfare, synthetic foods and materials, and unprecedented state interference in every aspect of life both private and public, only the most extreme innovation in the arts could produce much of an impact. Amidst the mass circulation newspapers (typified for Lawrence in Horatio Bottomley's *John Bull*), which frequently outdid the government in vilifying the enemy; amidst faked atrocity stories—the Germans were transforming dead soldiers into oils, pig-foods and manure—and genuine atrocity stories; amidst continual propaganda campaigns which, assisted by film, attacked sloth and drinking and pacifism, urging recruitment and thrift and jingoistic nationalism; amidst inflated rhetoric of all breeds issuing from pulpits and presses and street corners, language became a devalued currency.

Small wonder if Lawrence feared, cut off as he was in Cornwall, that like the shell-shocked Septimus Smith in Virginia Woolf's *Mrs Dalloway*, his readers had lost their ability to feel. Much of the writing in *Women in Love* exhibits a desperation which is attributable to this loss of confidence both in the medium and in the audience. As an example, consider the following exchange between Gudrun and Gerald:

> And they both felt the subterranean desire to let go, to fling away everything and lapse into a sheer unrestraint, brutal and licentious. A strange black passion surged up pure in Gudrun. She felt strong. She felt her hands so strong, as if she could tear the world asunder with them. She remembered the abandonments of Roman licence, and her heart grew hot. She knew she wanted this herself also—or something, something equivalent. Ah, if that which was unknown and suppressed in her were once let loose, what an orgiastic and satisfying event it would be. And she wanted it, she trembled slightly from the proximity of the man, who stood just behind her, suggestive of the same black licentiousness that rose in herself. She wanted it with him, this unacknowledged frenzy.

This passage illustrates a verbal extremism which recurs throughout the novel. Lawrence overstates, inflates, strives violently for effect. Like the bitter letters returning from the front (most of them intercepted by the censors), like the outraged poetry of

Siegfried Sassoon, Isaac Rosenberg and Wilfred Owen, Lawrence's wartime writings seemed designed to shock a numbed public.

Events of the war years aggravated Lawrence's sense of persecution, which verged on paranoia, and his fear of the public, which verged on hysteria. Ostracized from certain social circles for his affair with Frieda, constrained to declare himself bankrupt after refusing to pay her divorce costs, submitting to three military physical examinations, doubtless handed the white feather by girls who thereby shamed him for not serving his country (the white feather campaign was designed to rout skulkers into the army), encountering difficulties in his applications for visas and passports, having *The Rainbow* banned, himself defamed in the press, spied on by the suspicious Cornish folk and finally, in the fall of 1917, a year after finishing *Women in Love*, being ordered by the police to leave Cornwall and to report all further movements—Lawrence had more than enough fuel for his persecution complex. I refer to it as a complex rather than genuine persecution because he regarded as personal assaults the sort of treatment which was rendered to millions under the various Defense of the Realm Acts. The notorious D.O.R.A. empowered the government to shut down newspapers, requisition ships, force changes of residence and employment, imprison persons for lighting lamps near uncurtained windows, discourage drinking, and generally to manage civilian life according to the needs of war. Even the banning of *The Rainbow* —which reviewers feared would undermine morale with its "German psychology"—appears to be a natural consequence of that censorship which was liberally applied to the press, the publishers and the mails. ("A thing like *The Rainbow* has no right to exist in the wind of war. It is a greater menace to our public health than any of the epidemic diseases," wrote James Douglas in the *Star* of 22 October 1915.) Besides, *The Rainbow*, like its sequel, was *intended* to be subversive, of social as well as sexual attitudes. Lawrence also naturally attracted suspicion onto himself: the son of a miner, at a time when unrest in the unions threatened to disrupt munitions manufacture and to curtail the nation's vital coal supply; a man opposed to conscription and refusing any form of national service; a friend of prominent pacifists such as Bertrand Russell and Ottoline Morrell; married to a German whose family were distinguished military careerists under the Kaiser; writing and speaking freely about the need for a revolution to overturn the present economic system; planning an anti-war lecture series and writing novels that ridiculed the military mentality. That was indeed a suspect character.

In *Women in Love* Lawrence's sense of persecution translates into a fear and hatred of the masses. This appears in the contempt which Gerald and Gudrun feel for the miners, the distaste which Birkin and Ursula feel for the vermin-like city dwellers of "A Chair," in the scorn which all four characters show towards society, and in Birkin's misanthropy. There runs through the novel a solipsistic strain which is best articulated in the words already quoted from Gudrun—the wish that the earth might be cleared of other people, leaving the self alone in freedom. The flight of Birkin and Ursula is a negative expression of this desire: when the world refuses to leave, leave the world. Of course the stark alpine scenes provide the sort of antidote that Lawrence was always administering to his own solipsistic yearnings. (Compare "The Man Who Loved Islands," for instance, or "The Man Who Was Through with the World," or the southern Italian scenes of *The Lost Girl*.) Trapped in the barren Alps, Ursula yearns for the world again. It is the other side of Lawrence's dialectical relationship with the rest of mankind, the urge to mingle countering the urge to separate. Yet nowhere is that urge to community fainter than in *Women in Love*.

The war also confirmed in Lawrence's eyes the triumph of the mechanical principle. The organization of men into armies to slay one another and lay waste the earth was simply industrialism writ large. The ideology of capitalist industry, which regarded labor as an exchangeable commodity, and therefore treated human beings as part of the physical plant, provided a rationale for the war, in which soldiers and civilians alike were conscripted and managed and spent as if they were machinery, having been persuaded by those in power to fight for the same causes that motivated industry—empire, trade-routes, prestige. The dehumanization bred by the war had been prepared for by a century of dehumanization in industry.

In the portrait of Gerald Crich, Lawrence presents his critique both of industrialism and of the impulses which he felt lay behind the war. "Coal-Dust" opens with Gerald's torture of the mare at the railroad crossing, when he forces her to stand while the trains clank by. This brilliant piece of symbolic action exhibits the violence latent in his character, and illustrates the domineering cruelty which reappears in his relations with Minette, Gudrun and the miners. He forces his will upon the mare with "mechanical relentlessness," and she finally surrenders by pawing and trembling "mechanically." For Lawrence this mechanization of a living creature is the cardinal sin against nature, one repeated in Gerald's treatment of the miners. "In their voices," Gudrun "could hear the voluptuous resonance of darkness, the strong, dangerous underworld, mindless, inhuman. They sounded like strange machines, heavy, oiled. The voluptuousness was like that of machinery, cold and iron." The managerial class, including Gerald himself, are a part of the machine. Gudrun's friend the electrician represents the pure type: "he was really impersonal, he had the fineness of an elegant piece of machinery. . . . He was polarized by the men. Individually he detested them. In the mass they fascinated him. They were a new sort of machinery to him." As those below him are his instruments, so he is an instrument to those above. He dehumanizes the miners by responding to them as an undifferentiated *mass*—a term which bears in the novel overtones of the mob and of inert clay.

In *Women in Love* the workers have ceased to be, as they still were in *Sons and Lovers*, a body of individuals facing their common conditions in various personal ways: they now appear simply as a collective phenomenon, a brutalized herd, less than human.

> Their voices sounded out with strong intonation, and the broad dialect was curiously caressing to the blood. It seemed to envelop Gudrun in a labourer's caress, there was in the whole atmosphere, a resonance of physical men, a glamorous thickness of labour and maleness, surcharged in the air.

All the terms are generic—physical men, maleness, laborer's caress—or collective—atmosphere, envelop, glamorous thickness of labor. Whereas in *Sons and Lovers* Lawrence had been almost oblivious of society in his preoccupation with the individual, and in *The Rainbow* had eloquently defended the personal or natural against the social, in *Women in Love* he seems overwhelmed by the pressure of collective phenomena. The individualistic view of Bestwood life gives way to a collectivist view of Beldover.

This mass perspective on the workers may be seen as yet another reflection of the war. In Skrebensky the soldier this pure instrumentality was prefigured; and at the time Lawrence was writing *Women in Love* there were millions of men whom he took to be duplicates of Skrebensky entrenched in Europe and slaughtering one another. The wartime atmosphere of latent violence saturates the air of Beldover, where everyone, Gudrun and her electrician included, "had a secret sense of power, and of inexpressible destructiveness, and of fatal half-heartedness, a sort of rottenness in the will." The desire for violence may well have seemed universal at a time when the whole of society was bent on destruction. Yet while condemning industrialization and militarism, which had reduced millions of people to what seemed to him a single power-craving mass, Lawrence himself, by viewing the miners and city-dwellers as an undifferentiated herd, reinforced the process of dehumanization. In describing the workers as solely motivated by greed, for example, he was false to the experience recorded in his earlier novels, to his own past, and to the contemporary facts. Price increases were outstripping increases in wages throughout the war for much of the working class; those who kept their heads above water did so by working overtime; as in every previous war the only men to get rich were the rich, so outrageously rich in many cases that "profiteering" became a popular cry; and the miners in particular, who were not only supplying the war needs but also producing England's principal export commodity, had to fight for every concession, from the mine owners and their own union officials right up to Asquith and Lloyd George.

Suspicion of the "masses" ran deep in nineteenth-century social thought, notably that of Taine, De Maistre, Burckhardt and Nietzsche. The French Revolution and the widespread uprisings of 1830, 1848 and 1871 provoked ever greater dread of the anonymous "lower orders," a dread visible in the studies of mass psychology current during Lawrence's lifetime. Gustave Le Bon's *The Crowd* appeared in 1895, Graham Wallas' more moderate *Human Nature in Politics* in 1908, then Wilfred Trotter's *Instincts of the Herd in Peace and War* in 1916, William Mc-

111

Dougall's *The Group Mind* in 1920, and, in 1921, the first of Freud's ventures into social theory, *Group Psychology and the Analysis of the Ego.* Fear of trade union tyranny tinged with fear of revolution ripples through the work of Carlyle and Disraeli, through Dickens' *Hard Times* and George Eliot's *Felix Holt.* Wherever labor agitators appear in Lawrence's own work—in *The White Peacock, Touch and Go, Kangaroo* and several tales—they seem vicious or greedy or both. Masked as contempt for the barbarian lower orders, this fear of the masses became fashionable among Lawrence's contemporaries in English letters, including T. E. Hulme, Wyndham Lewis, T. S. Eliot, Pound and Yeats.

In *Women in Love* the "seething masses of miners" are said to accept the brutal industrial machine, indeed to relish their subjection. Gerald's ruthless system afforded the sort of freedom "they really wanted." "They were exalted by belonging to this great and superhuman system which was beyond feeling or reason, something really godlike." Something crucial to their humanity having died in them, they submit willingly to their Leader, desiring only a fatter slice of the cake—a view which looks forward to Orwell's treatment of the proles in *1984.* Lawrence's memory of the coalfields was refreshed by a brief stay in December 1915 with his sister in Derbyshire, where he found the workers hopelessly locked within the iron ring of production and wages. But once again in generalizing from this brief tour he falsifies the historical picture, and in doing so serves his own psychological needs. For the unions mounted the only massive opposition to the war; the South Wales miners and the Clydeside workers led the way in resisting increased state control; the Labour Party was wedded to socialism as an alternative to the prevailing economic and political system; periodic agitation throughout the war showed that many workers were but feebly enamored of their leaders, either industrial, military or governmental. Like Freud, who explained away revolutionary ferment as regressive disobedience to the father, Lawrence, by representing workers as motivated solely by greed, submissiveness and fear, provided a rationale for his own inaction, and for the inaction of the governing classes in general. His Freudian paradigm of politics as the interaction of an authoritarian father-figure who craves affection with subservient children who crave authority, outlined here in the relation between Gerald and his workers, is projected again on a fuller screen in *Kangaroo* and *The Plumed Serpent*.

Gerald, the "high priest" of the industrial cult, suffers from a production-compulsion which Lawrence firmly roots in social history. Having repudiated his father's sentimentally Christian and pre-industrial world-view, he finds himself like so many of his contemporaries confronted by a meaningless existence:

> He did not inherit an established order and a living idea. The whole unifying idea of mankind seemed to be dying with his father, the centralizing force that had held the whole together seemed to collapse with his father, the parts were ready to go asunder in terrible disintegration.

In the slow death of Mr Crich, in the replacement of his paternalistic system by a more ruthless industrialism, we observe the failure of that "certain moral scheme" to which Lawrence referred in his repudiation of the "old stable ego" of character. The disastrous consequences of this failure are worked out in the life of Gerald, who turns first to the mines and then to Gudrun as external bulwarks against an inner chaos. For all the characters of *Women in Love* the center no longer holds, either within the psyche, where we have found violent forces at work, or within society as a whole. Instability of the self is a symptom of social instability; this is no personal crisis, but the crisis of a civilization.

Gerald's apotheosis in "The Industrial Magnate" is presented in terms of power, control and will. The chapter is central to any understanding of the novel, whether as diagnosis of England's ills, or as a symptom of Lawrence's own. The struggles between Birkin and Hermione, Gerald and Gudrun, Ursula and Birkin; the "rottenness of will" among the miners of Beldover; the various proofs of a lust for mastery—Gerald with his mare and with Minette, Gudrun with her bullocks, Hermione with her house guests, Loerke with his model—all can be seen as by-products of the general perversion of human effort by industrial civilization. In his late essay on "Nottingham and the Mining Country," Lawrence was to describe this perversion as "the base forcing of all human energy into a competition of mere acquisition"—a competition, as he works testify, not just for things, but for land, for power, for prestige, for sexual and spiritual mastery. In "Mino" he refers to this desire for domination by its Nietzschean tag, the *Wille zur Macht*, the will to power. In Gerald it is symbolized by electricity: he has electrified his house and mines in order to defy nature; and his tyrannous relations with Minette and Gudrun are appropriately described in terms of electrical imagery. The language of force—which serves to represent conflicts within the psyche as well as between individuals—was appropriate to an era governed by force. The war only confirmed Lawrence's belief in the destructive effects of contemporary social organization, as it confirmed Freud's.[13] Destruction on a scale unknown in human history was made possible by the mechanical techniques of industry, and rendered inevitable by the instrumental attitude towards life. This conjunction of order and annihilation accounts for Lawrence's gloomy, paradoxical augury near the end of "The Industrial Magnate":

> It was the first great step in undoing, the first great phase of chaos, the substitution of the mechanical principle for the organic, the destruction of the organic purpose, the organic unity, and the subordination of every organic unit to the great mechanical purpose. It was pure organic disintegration and pure mechanical organization. This is the first and finest state of chaos.

The results of that long process of organization—what Max Weber called the complete "rationalization" of human society—was not order but chaos, not technological utopia but war.

3 *Lawrence's Precarious Social Position*

During 1914–1915 Lawrence set out in search of allies. Determined like Stephen Dedalus to forge or at least alter the consciousness of his race, he had felt from the beginning the need to ally himself with some group of people who would disseminate and carry through his ideas. This could not be the working-class—some eighty percent of the population in 1915—for to identify with the class from which he had escaped would have meant

[13] See Freud's "Thoughts for the Times on War and Death," first published in *Imago* in 1915. In *Civilization and Its Discontents* he suggests that the war be interpreted as a collective neurosis, resulting from "the pressure of civilizing trends." Cf. "Lawrence and the War," by Neil Myers, in *Criticism*, IV (Winter, 1962), pp. 44–58; and George Panichas, "D. H. Lawrence's War Letters," *Texas Studies in Literature and Language*, V (Autumn, 1963), pp. 398–409.

reversing his social trajectory. Psychologically, it would also have meant submitting again to the governance of his father. "What we must hasten to prevent is this young democratic party from getting into power," he wrote to Bertrand Russell in 1915, referring to the Labour Party. "The idea of giving power to the hands of the working class is *wrong.*"[14] Nor could he marry himself to the bourgeoisie, his mother's people—roughly another fifteen percent of the population, depending upon one's definition—for these he held responsible for the war, the industrial blight, sexual repression and the reign of Mammon.

There remained the upper class and a free-floating intelligentsia. It was to these two groups he turned in 1915, to a traditional ruling class, which was to diminish in power, and to an artistic elite that was to lose much of its privileged status during the war. His prime correspondents for 1915–1916 were Lady Ottoline Morrell and Lady Cynthia Asquith, the first a landed society hostess and the second a daughter-in-law to the prime minister. His friends and acquaintances during the same period included Edward Marsh, secretary to the prime minister; Bertrand Russell, a Cambridge don and brother to an earl; novelists Gilbert Canaan, E. M. Forster and David Garnett; man of letters John Middleton Murry; literary agent Edward Garnett; poets Harriet Monroe and Amy Lowell; plus dozens of others drawn for the most part from London's still class-bound circle of intellectuals, including a fair number from the charmed sanctuary of Bloomsbury. His eventual disillusionment with both the liberal aristocracy and the London intelligentsia is recorded in *Women in Love*. But he arrived at that state of bitter disillusion only after failing in several schemes for changing society.

Early in 1915 Lawrence met Bertrand Russell and Lady Ottoline Morrell, who were to figure in most of these schemes. He shortly began speaking of revolution in his letters to Russell:

we shall smash the frame. The land, the industries, the means of communication and the public amusement shall all be nationalised. Every man shall have his wage till the day of his death, whether he work or not, so long as he works when he is fit. . . . Then, and then only, shall we be able to *begin* living. Then we shall be able to *begin*

[14] CL 353. 15.vii.15. Lawrence's italics.

to work. Then we can examine marriage and love and all. Till then, we are fast within the hard, unliving, impervious shell.[15]

The program was that put forward by the Fabians and the Labour Party. But Lawrence lacked their constituencies. From the first his revolution was a highly personal and isolated affair, which was to have altered the conditions of the masses without venturing to touch the masses themselves. He wanted the material system rearranged on socialist principles, not so that new forms of common life might be evolved, not so that work itself might be reintegrated with other human activities, but so that the individual might be free to pursue his own goals, without being nagged by those who lacked food, shelter or clothing. The priorities outlined in the letter to Russell were soon to be reversed: "marriage and love and all" must be got right before bothering to tinker with the framework. In proportion as he lost faith in the prospect of smashing the frame by peaceful means, he looked to the war itself to demolish the old order, as indeed many of his contemporaries believed it would.

Meanwhile he talked of forming a "revolutionary party," and looked forward to recruiting supporters from among Russell's friends at Cambridge. "I feel frightfully important coming to Cambridge," he wrote on the eve of his visit, "quite momentous the occasion is to me. I don't want to be horribly impressed and intimidated, but am afraid I may be. I only care about the revolution we shall have."[16] The visit of course was disastrous. It is difficult to imagine any group in which Lawrence would have been more out of place, or which was less likely to initiate a revolution. Cambridge was quickly dropped from the scheme. He next projected a series of public lectures with Russell, which never came off. This was followed by a plan, which also never materialized, for setting forth his philosophy in a series of pamphlets. Meanwhile he was industriously expounding that philosophy in such essays as "The Reality of Peace," "Education of the People," "Democracy," *Twilight in Italy*, *The Crown*, *Le Gai Savaire*, *The Signal* and *Goats and Compasses*, most of which remained unpublished during his lifetime. *The Crown* was printed in the autumn of 1915 in the *Signature*, a little magazine which he launched together with John

[15] CL 320. 13.ii.15. Cf. CL 322, 324, 346.
[16] Letter to Russell, CL 327–8. 2.ii.15.

Middleton Murry and Katherine Mansfield. Designed as a crusading periodical—"I don't want the *Signature* to be a 'success,' I want it only to rally together just a few passionate, vital, constructive people."[17]—it ran to three issues. During that autumn he and Murry began a shortlived series of open weekly meetings, for which he also held high hopes: "this is my first try at direct approach to the public: art after all is indirect and ultimate. I want this to be more immediate."[18] But this turning in his search for a more direct access to the public also led into a blind alley.

It is not clear what Lawrence expected of any of these projects. At the very least they promised to satisfy that longing for social connection, for a role in the "world of cities and governments and the active scope of man," which haunts the Brangwen women at the opening of *The Rainbow* and which haunted Lawrence all his life. His Rananim scheme expressed the same longing. Rananim was to have been a colony designed along the lines of the communistic societies that flourished in nineteenth-century America. Peopled by the elect, the colony was to change the larger society, or at least, like the medieval monasteries that Lawrence admired, to preserve through the dark ages a germ of truth which might blossom in the fairer weather of the future. In the novel it appears in Birkin's Happy Isles, and in his yearning for a life "with some few other people—a little freedom with people." Variously imagined in real life for Florida ("we go to Florida: a new life, a new beginning: the inception of a new epoch"), the Andes, Palestine, Russia, New Mexico, Cornwall and islands off the English coast, during 1915 it took its most concrete shape in Garsington, the Oxfordshire estate of Lady Ottoline Morrell. This was a gathering place for artists, pacifists and discontented intellectuals in general —"it is *so* remote, so perfectly a small world to itself, where one *can* get away from the temporal things to consider the big things"[19]—and here Lawrence imagined gathering with Russell, the Murrys, Lady Ottoline and a few others, if not to change the world, at least, like the refugees in Boccaccio, to last out the plague.

This scheme also soured, as the other pilgrims proved too in-

[17] Letter to Cynthia Asquith, CL 370. 14.x.15.
[18] Letter to W. E. Hopkin, CL 368. 14.ix.15.
[19] Letter to Ottoline Morrell, CL 350. 20.vi.15.

dependent of mind. Lawrence broke with Russell in 1915, with the Murrys and Lady Ottoline in 1916. The degree of his disillusion is apparent in *Women in Love*, where Garsington reappears as Breadalby, Lady Ottoline as Hermione and Russell as Sir Joshua. Among them, we are told,

> The talk was very often political or sociological, and interesting, curiously anarchistic. There was an accumulation of powerful force in the room, powerful and destructive . . . this ruthless mental pressure, this powerful, consuming, destructive mentality that emanated from Joshua and Hermione and Birkin and dominated the rest.

It is a measure of Lawrence's distance from Birkin and from his own past that he can show the cranky hero still closely identified with this decaying remnant of the old world. In breaking with Hermione, a sepulchral hostess presiding over a cemetery, Birkin renounces class pretensions and social aspirations, as well as Hemione's domineering, parasitic love. Lawrence had made the break in his own life by the end of 1916, when *Women in Love* was completed. "It is no use adhering to that old advanced crowd —Cambridge, Lowes Dickinson, Bertie Russell, young reformers, Socialists, Fabians—they are our disease, not our hope."[20] By the following spring he had abandoned society altogether: "It is impossible to believe in any existing body, they are all part of the same evil game, labor, capital, aristocrat, they are the trunk, limbs, and head of one body of destructive evil."[21]

In that period of bitterness Lawrence withdrew emotionally from all social involvement, as he had withdrawn physically in the spring of 1916 when he moved to Cornwall. The years 1915–16 mark a watershed in Lawrence's work, because before then he could still imagine some social embodiment for his ideas, and after that he could not. The later works are sapped by that disillusion.

Women in Love records the transition between the two periods. Birkin is still visited by messianic impulses. Ursula twits the "Salvator Mundi" in him. The Halliday party at the Pompadour, reading out his very Lawrentian letter on the dissolution of man, call him another Jesus. But he has become a messiah without a people. He repudiates the elite of wealth and station at Breadalby, the artistic elite in London, and the elite of power at Shortlands. The

[20] Letter to Cynthia Asquith, CL 491. 11.xii.16.
[21] Letter to Mrs S. A. Hopkin, CL 511. 7.v.17.

potentialities of the old landed class are embalmed in Hermione, who is surrounded by a coterie of intellectuals and politicians whom Birkin views as puppets, lifeless and futile. For Lawrence the original of Hermione stood at the top of the social scale, a messenger from the old England, but equally futile. He remarked in a letter that Lady Ottoline Morrell's Garsington stood for "the past, the falling, perishing, crumbling past, so great, so magnificent." The passing of the old plutocracy is symbolized in the death of Mr Crich, who is succeeded by his son the technocrat, one of the social types fostered by the war. The savage treatment of the London bohemia in "Crème de Menthe," "Totem" and "Gudrun in the Pompadour" also reflects the animus of a recent convert, saved from absorption into that same artistic milieu. Gudrun views the café as the "central whirlpool of disintegration and dissolution;" it is a world, in Lawrence's eyes, populated by "halfmen," perverts, parasites. The spell of Shortlands, finally, is less easily broken—as witness Birkin's continued longing for some connection with Gerald, whose power fascinates him as much as his physique. As witness also Lawrence's romance with heroic leaders in his next three novels. Birkin roundly criticizes Gerald's production-compulsion, seeing it for what it is, a surrogate religion, masking an inner vacancy and expressing a desire for mastery over others. But that very mastery allures Birkin, as it did Lawrence; in the end Ursula cannot solace her lover for the loss of Gerald.

Like Lawrence himself, having quit the liberal aristocratic circle and the intelligentsia, Birkin is set adrift. His middle-class background (he has been to Oxford, rubs shoulders with the plutocracy, possesses four hundred a year) apparently leaves him no other avenue to social involvement. Like most of Lawrence's figures he becomes an outsider, not simply *déclassé*, as George Beardsall, Paul Morel and the Brangwen sisters were, but a drifter, rootless, the first of the vagabonds who wander bitter and troubled through the later novels.

Birkin turns to Ursula for consolation against the loss of society. Radical isolation is incorporated into his love ethic, which treats the partners in love as monads that act out their ritual in the absence of all other selves. As soon as he feels confident of her love—seeing her as one wheel, and Gerald as possibly the other, of the chariot which he will ride to what he calls "completeness of being"—he immediately decides that he and Ursula must drop their jobs, must cut themselves off from all social responsibilities whatsoever. The four hundred pound annuity which conveniently makes this possible—roughly four times the income of a prosperous working-class family at that time—also makes it impracticable as a general solution. The overwhelming majority of Englishmen lacked the means to retreat into isolation, and during wartime lacked the freedom. *Women in Love*, insofar as it proferred a love ethic, was pitched at the same elite to whom Lawrence continually appealed in his letters, the elite of the educated and the affluent.

The members of this elite in the novel are doomed to impotence and despair. The "great dark void" which harrows Gerald echoes at the center of each soul in the novel. Against the "terrible void," the "deficiency of being" within her, Hermione "piled up her own defences of aesthetic knowledge, and culture, and world-visions." Suffering the same anxiety, Gudrun accumulates knick-knack art and lovers; Gerald conquers coal and mistresses; Birkin and Ursula nurture their frail love. The incessant talk is one symptom of their parlous condition. By comparison with the earlier novels there is far more dialogue in *Women in Love*. The protagonists are much more conscious of their condition but less able to do anything about it than were their counterparts in *The Rainbow* and *Sons and Lovers*. And they are correspondingly more frustrated. In all the succeeding novels Lawrence was to insist upon the correlation of articulateness and impotence, an insistence which would take the form, in *Lady Chatterley's Lover*, of a radical opposition between talking and living.

When Catherine Carswell asked Lawrence why he had chosen such sophisticated, spoiled, apparently abnormal characters for *Women in Love*, "he replied that it was only through such people that one could discover whither the general run of mankind, the great unconscious mass, was tending."[22] The truer answer is that these were the types of people he knew (Gerald was a synthesis of several types), and they *were* doomed by the war, either to

[22] *The Savage Pilgrimage*, rev. ed. (London, 1951), p. 42. In his study of the novel F. R. Leavis treats the characters of *Women in Love* as considerably more representative of the condition of England than I am able to treat them. See *D. H. Lawrence: Novelist* (London, 1955; New York, 1956), Chapter, 4.

change drastically or to disappear. The landed aristocracy, hard hit by the increased death duties, were forced to consolidate their possessions while suffering a decrease in their political influence. The intellectuals were divided over pacifism, socialism and Bolshevism; the war decimated their ranks; and the spiralling rise in prices ate away at the fixed incomes on which many of them depended. The liberal hegemony in England was passing. Squeezed on the one side by a Tory reaction and on the other by the rise of a mass Labour Party, the Liberals were also doomed as a political grouping, a doom sealed in Lawrence's eyes, and in reality, by the ousting of Herbert Asquith as Prime Minister at the end of 1916 in favor of Lloyd George. Insofar as Lawrence felt any political identification at all, it lay with the genteel, intellectual, outmoded set that surrounded Lady Cynthia Asquith's father-in-law. Only the technocrat among Lawrence's social types was to thrive after the war, and Gerald was the one person whom he destroyed. Having drawn most of his characters from social groups that were in disarray, if not dissolution, it is not surprising that Lawrence should paint a picture of disintegration. But from that bleak picture it is not valid to conclude, as his remark to Catherine Carswell would suggest and as the novel itself implies, that the general run of mankind was downhill.

Judging from his money worries during the war, Lawrence would have been glad of Birkin's four hundred pounds—roughly the amount which sustained Virginia Woolf through her lean years. The banning of *The Rainbow* at the end of 1915 cost him the royalties for that book, which would have supported him perhaps two years, and cast a pall over the sales of his other works. Even while writing *Women in Love* he feared that no publisher would touch the book, and indeed none would for over four years:

> already it is beyond all hope of ever being published, because of the things it says. And more than that, it is beyond all possibility even to offer it to a world, a putrescent mankind like ours. I feel I cannot *touch* humanity, even in thought, it is abhorrent to me.[23]

[23] Letter to Barbara Low, CL 449. 1.v.16. Christopher Caudwell offers a useful, if schematic, account of the impact of commodity relations on literature in "D. H. Lawrence: A Study of the Bourgeois Artist," in *Studies in a Dying Culture* (London, 1938; reprinted New York, 1958), pp. 44–72.

Not until 1923 was his financial position reasonably secure, and then only after he had moved to the richer publishing market of America. Birkin's four hundred pounds would have freed Lawrence from the publishers whom he mistrusted, the reviewers whom he scorned and the readers whom, in some moods, he despised. Being a writer he was physically free of his public, could live anywhere he wished, but at the same time he was economically dependent on his readers. One way of interpreting the bitterness and violence in *Women in Love* is to see it as *resistance* against the market, a refusal to make the novel a pleasurable and profitable commodity. Yet in the end, if Lawrence was to survive as a writer, he had no other choice, and his letters after 1919 to his publisher Martin Secker indicate how hard he worked to produce marketable books. *Women in Love* struggles against becoming a public commodity even while it becomes one. Inclined at the same time to offend his audience and to woo it, to despise it and to save it, Lawrence was torn by the contradictions inherent in the literary trade and in the messianic role.

The radically individualistic doctrine which he elaborated in his subsequent writings served in part as a rationale for the isolation into which he gravitated during the war. In an early draft of his essay "The Spirit of Place," for example, written sometime during 1917–18, his own condition appears masked as a description of Celtic Christianity: "Its first principle was individualistic, separatist, almost anti-social, a recoil of the individual into a mystic isolation, quite the contrary of the European religious principle, which was the fusing into a whole."[24] We encounter this dichotomy—absolute merging vs. absolute separation—repeatedly in the later works. Lawrence increasingly despaired of the third possibility, namely, a dialectical relationship with other persons and with communities. Birkin proposes something resembling this third possibility to Ursula—a balanced polarity, in which each partner maintains his identity in relation to the other—but he is driven by his insecurity to try to dominate her, and thereby sins

---

[24] *The Symbolic Meaning*, pp. 21–2. On the effects of the split between social and personal dimensions in the novel, see the fine study by Mark Schorer, "Women in Love and Death," *Hudson Review*, VI (Spring, 1953); reprinted in *The World We Imagine* (New York, 1968; London, 1969), pp. 107–21.

against his own love ethic. Lawrence's central figures continue to seek out that third possibility, with growing desperation. At best they achieve isolation in pairs.

In summary, it is apparent that Lawrence's social pessimism in the novel was a function of his precarious social position. His love ethic, in its stress on monadic isolation, reflected his own alienated condition. The animus which colors his satirical portraits was bred of his real life entanglement with the social groups to which these portraits correspond. Had he not tried to make himself a part of these artistic and aristocratic circles in 1915, had he not looked upon them as recruiting ground for disciples, he would not have satirized them with so much relish or rancor.

4 *Homosexual vs. Heterosexual Impulses*

The "Prologue" to *Women in Love*, suppressed by Lawrence and not finally published until 1963,[25] depicts Birkin as fiercely divided between heterosexual and homosexual desires, with the latter gaining the upper hand:

> although he was always drawn to women, feeling more at home with a woman than with a man, yet it was for men that he felt the hot, flushing, roused attraction which a man is supposed to feel for the other sex . . . the male physique had a fascination for him, and for the female physique he felt only a fondness, a sort of sacred love, as for a sister. . . . So he went on, month after month, year after year, divided against himself, striving for the day when the beauty of men should not be so acutely attractive to him, when the beauty of woman should move him instead. . . . His deep dread was that it would always be so, that he would never be free. His life would have been one long torture of struggle against his own innate desire, his own innate being. But to be so divided against oneself, this is terrible, a nullification of all being.

Repressing his homosexual desires ("This was the one and only secret he kept to himself, this secret of his passionate and sudden, spasmodic affinity for men he saw. He kept this secret even from himself."), he tries to force himself to love women.

[25] *Texas Quarterly*, Spring 1963, with a Note by George Ford. My interpretation of the male friendship theme in Lawrence should be balanced by Mark Spilka's argument in Chapter 7 of *The Love Ethic*.

In the "Prologue" this struggle between homosexual and hetero-sexual impulses takes the form of a choice between Gerald and Hermione:

> The incapacity to love, the incapacity to desire any woman, posi-tively, with body and soul, this was a real torture. . . . He did not love Hermione, he did not desire her. But he wanted to force him-self to love her and to desire her. He was consumed by sexual desire, and he wanted to be fulfilled . . . he *would* have this physical fulfilment, he would have the sexuality.

Turning from the woman, Birkin seeks release through Gerald:

> he plunged on triumphant into intimacy with Gerald Crich exclud-ing the woman, tormenting her. . . . Birkin felt a passion of desire for Gerald Crich, for the clumsier, cruder intelligence and the limited soul, and for the striving, unlightened body of his friend.

This desertion infuriates and disgusts Hermione, who is said to have been "revolted" by this "guttering prostration," this "low, degraded heat, servile," this "fawning on a coarse, unsusceptible being." Disguised in her response is an outraged moral judgment, which perhaps reflects Lawrence's fear of the public response to the inclinations he was describing in Birkin:

> To Hermione, it was insupportable degradation that Rupert Birkin should maintain this correspondence, prostituting his mind and his understanding to the coarser stupidity of the other man. She felt confusion gathering upon her, she was unanchored on the edge of madness. Why did he do it? Why was he, whom she knew as her leader, starlike and pure, why was he the lowest betrayer and the ugliest of blasphemers?

Purity vs. degradation, holiness vs. blasphemy—these are the radical Dostoevskian contrasts which recur in the relationship between Birkin and Ursula, stemming from their unnamed acts of love (in "Continental"). Here they stem from Birkin's homosexuality, a source which the published novel only partly reveals.

By suppressing the "Prologue" Lawrence makes Hermione's vicious assault on Birkin, near the end of "Breadalby," appear to be the incomprehensible outburst of irrational forces:

Her whole mind was a chaos, darkness breaking in upon it, and herself struggling to gain control with her will, as a swimmer struggles with the swirling water. . . . Terrible shocks ran over her body, like shocks of electricity, as if many volts of electricity suddenly struck her down. . . . Then swiftly, in a flame that drenched down her body like fluid lightning and gave her a perfect, unutterable consummation, unutterable satisfaction, she brought down the ball of jewel stone with all her force, crash on his head.

The real source of her rage—the jealousy over Birkin's love for Gerald, which drove her to "the edge of madness"—is concealed beneath Lawrence's celebrated imagery of the unconscious. The word "convulsive," which is applied to Hermione at least a dozen times, and which appears, along with "shuddering," "possessed" or "rhapsodic" almost every time she appears, like a Homeric epithet, suggests the ungovernable violence latent within her. Of course she is a domineering woman. But in "Breadalby" she is also a woman whose lover has spurned her in favor of a man.

By excising (as George H. Ford points out in his Note which accompanies the first publication of the "Prologue") most of the explicitly sexual descriptions of the love between Birkin and Gerald, Lawrence also mystifies their relationship. In the published version of the novel Gerald still appears to Birkin as "manly," "beautiful," "attractive," exactly as the men appear to Birkin in the "Prologue." And Birkin is similarly "roused" by the other man. In the novel they are said to share a dark, unspoken knowledge, which in the "Prologue" is simply the awareness of Birkin's physical love for Gerald. Thus in the "Prologue" we read that "They scarcely knew each other, yet here was this strange, unacknowledged, inflammable intimacy between them." And in the novel we encounter passages such as the following, which occurs at the end of "Shortlands":

It was always the same between them; always their talk brought them into a deadly nearness of contact, a strange, perilous intimacy which was either hate or love, or both. . . . Yet the heart of each burned for the other. They burned with each other, inwardly. This they would never admit . . . they were not going to be so unmanly and unnatural as to allow any heart-burning between them. They had not the faintest belief in deep relationship between men and men, and their disbelief prevented any development of their powerful but suppressed friendliness.

125

Again the evaluative words creep in—"unmanly," "unnatural"—to signal that Lawrence is not simply talking of friendship or comradeship, because if he were he would not need to cloak it in such evasive, portentous terms.

The nearest their sexual love comes to acknowledgement in *Women in Love* is in the controversial naked wrestling scene of "Gladiatorial." Even without the information provided by the "Prologue," this scene appears explicitly sexual, with the two men "fusing," "penetrating," "joining." "Often, in the white interlaced knot of violent living being that swayed silently, there was no head to be seen, only the swift, tight limbs, the solid white backs, the physical junction of two bodies clinched into oneness." At the climax the two wrestlers/lovers lose consciousness; Birkin wakes briefly to find himself prostrate upon the body of Gerald, dozes, then wakes again, realizing that still "he was leaning with all his weight on the soft body of the other man. It startled him, because he thought he had withdrawn." Before drawing apart they exchange an affectionate handclasp, which Birkin is to recall in the last chapter when he confronts the frozen body of Gerald for the last time. Returning after their bout to "normal consciousness"—the state to which Paul and Clara return after their illicit lovemaking in *Sons and Lovers*, Ursula and Skrebensky after theirs in *The Rainbow*, Connie and Mellors after theirs in *Lady Chatterley's Lover*— the two men engage in a strained discussion in which they try to persuade themselves that such physical intimacy between men is healthy and "sane." " 'I don't know why one should have to justify oneself,' " says Birkin—in the course of justifying himself. Judging from his suppression of the "Prologue" and his excisions in the text, Lawrence himself clearly felt that defense was necessary. Behind the notion of *Blutbrüderschaft* lurks the less mysterious reality of homosexual love which he was unwilling or unable to acknowledge.

Certain of Birkin's feelings towards men which appear in the "Prologue" are transposed in the novel into the experience of Gudrun. She becomes in many respects his alter ego, a female version of himself. Like Birkin she is rootless and cynical. He "moved about a great deal, his life seemed uncertain, without any definite rhythm, any organic meaning," while she also "was one of life's outcasts, one of the drifting lives that have no root." Like

Lawrence she is an artist, alienated from her Midlands background, fascinated by the crowds of workers yet repelled by them.
Like Birkin and Lawrence both, she is at once attracted and dis-
gusted by the London bohemia. And of course she shares with
Birkin a love for Gerald. Walking in the streets of Beldover is a
sensuous delight to her, amidst "a resonance of physical men, a
glamorous thickness of labour and maleness." According to the
"Prologue," these are Birkin's feelings: "In the street it was the
men who roused him by their flesh and their manly, vigorous
movement, quite apart from all individual character, whilst he
studied the women as sisters." Attracted by the crowd of miners,
by the electrician, by the colliers at their bath, by Gerald, by
Loerke, by Leitner, Gudrun is scarcely more vulnerable to a passion
for men than is Birkin in the "Prologue":

> every now and again, would come over him the same passionate
> desire to have near him some man he saw, to exchange intimacy,
> to unburden himself of love to this new beloved. It might be any
> man, a policeman who suddenly looked up at him, as he inquired
> the way, or a soldier who sat next to him in a railway carriage.

Just as Gudrun is charmed on the one hand by the dark, sensual,
herd-like miners, and on the other by the northern, crystalline,
aloof Gerald, so Birkin's men divide themselves into two classes
in the "Prologue": the

> white-skinned, keen limbed men with eyes like blue-flashing ice and
> hair like crystals of winter sunshine, the northmen, inhuman as
> sharp-crying gulls, distinct like splinters of ice, like crystals,
> isolated, individual; and the men with dark eyes that one can enter
> and plunge into, bathe in, as in a liquid darkness, dark-skinned,
> supple, night-smelling men, who are the living substance of the
> viscous, universal heavy darkness.

In "Moony" Lawrence erects this division into a metaphysical
opposition between the "African" way and the "Arctic" way, the
former promising ruin through an excessive cultivation of the
senses, the latter through an excessive cultivation of the mind.
The first way also corresponds to Lawrence's fear of engulfment,
the second to his fear of isolation. Choosing the third way of
dialectical relationship with Ursula, Birkin at the same time exor-
cises the demons of his homosexual desire.

Transferred from Birkin to Gudrun, these homosexual desires appear to be heterosexual. But they clearly retain for Lawrence some of the negative emotional charge which they carry in the "Prologue." Thus the love between Gerald and Gudrun is treated from the beginning as corrupt, depraved, decadent, obscene— exactly as Hermione treated the relationship between Gerald and Birkin. The hyperbole which dogs Gerald and Gudrun through the novel continually evokes something diseased but unstated in their relationship. After the tussle with Bismarck in "Rabbit," for example, "Gudrun looked at Gerald with strange, darkened eyes, strained with underworld knowledge, almost supplicating, like those of a creature which is at his mercy, yet which is his ulti- mate victor. He did not know what to say to her. He felt the mutual hellish recognition." Their shared sadism accounts only in part for the language of corruption which envelops them. Bearer of Birkin's repressed desires, the figure of Gudrun must also bear the fear and shame which Lawrence attached to those desires.

On the surface *Women in Love* compares two forms of hetero- sexual love; but on a deeper level it records a struggle between heterosexual and homosexual love. Birkin is divided between the self who loves Ursula, and the self, compounded with Gudrun, who loves Gerald. Lawrence ratifies the love for Ursula and condemns the love for Gerald, thus accomplishing in the novel what Birkin strove but failed to do in the "Prologue":

> He could never acquiesce to his own feelings, to his own passion. He could never grant that it should be so, that it was well for him to feel this keen desire to have and to possess the bodies of such men, the passion to bathe in the very substance of such men, the substance of living, eternal light, like eternal snow, and the flux of heavy, rank-smelling darkness. He wanted to cast out these desires, he wanted not to know them. Yet a man can no more slay a living desire in him, than he can prevent his body from feeling heat and cold. . . . So he went on, month after month, year after year, divided against himself, striving for the day when the beauty of men should not be so acutely attractive to him, when the beauty of woman should move him instead.

The final choice is made in the Alps. Gudrun is attracted away from Gerald by Loerke (also a homosexual, living with his young male "love-companion"), thus confirming her depravity. Once again Loerke bears an extraordinary negative emotional charge, appearing as a "noxious insect," a "mud-child," an "obscene monster of the darkness" living in the "sewer stream," a creature depraved, licentious, evil. At one moment an abstract sculptor, at another moment a social realist and yet again a Futurist, Loerke serves Lawrence as a general dumping-ground for grievances, chief among them being the animus against homosexuality. (Halliday, together with his apartment full of young men, shared the same fate in "Crème de Menthe" and "Totem.") It is at this point near the middle of "Continental," Gudrun having deserted Gerald, that Birkin undertakes those notoriously obscure "shameful" acts with Ursula, which ratify his love for the woman, and liberate him from the spell of the man. Afterwards hostility forms between the two men, and Ursula entices Birkin away from the Alps, thus leaving the depraved form of love alone in the mountains to fester and die.

Not even by destroying Gerald can Lawrence fully release Birkin from his love for the other man. On the last page of the novel Birkin still yearns for "eternal union with a man," and Ursula reacts as Hermione had reacted, with jealousy and mistrust, calling it a "perversity." The uncertainty of his grasp upon male identity is evident, for example, in "Mino," where he champions the bullying tomcat; asserting male dominance, he belies his own sexual insecurity. In "Woman to Woman," Hermione warns Ursula against Birkin, saying he is sensitive, spiritual, weak, unvirile; and she informs her obscurely that he is very unstable, subject to violent oscillations in love. Indeed in the "Prologue," "sick, helpless" Birkin swings back and forth in affection between Hermione and Gerald. In "Excurse," the chapter that follows "Woman to Woman," Ursula launches into a bitter tirade which, nominally prompted by jealousy of Hermione, reflects some deeper discontent:

'You love the sham spirituality, it's your food. And why? Because of the dirt underneath. Do you think I don't know the foulness of your sex life—and hers?—I do. And it's that foulness you want, you liar. . . . What you are is a foul, deathly thing, obscene, that's what you are, obscene and perverse. You, and love! You may well say, you don't want love. No, you want *yourself*, and dirt and death—that's what you want. You are so *perverse*, so death-eating.'

Behind this language of perversion, foulness and obscenity, which spreads throughout the novel, lie the feelings of guilt and dread of public reaction evident in the "Prologue." The aura of decadence which attaches to Birkin's homosexuality is confused with the decadence of particular social classes, and with the decline of an entire culture.

Considering the state of public opinion at the time *Women in Love* was written, Lawrence's fear of treating homosexuality directly is neither surprising nor dishonorable. In *The Rainbow* Ursula's homosexual love for Winifred Inger is gingerly presented in a chapter entitled "Shame," and is then supplanted by the heterosexual love for Skrebensky. Clement Shorter, whose review in the *Sphere* (23 October 1915) was used as evidence for the prosecution in banning the novel, picks out "Shame" for special condemnation. Already smeared in the press, Lawrence was doubtless reluctant to enter the ring again over *Women in Love*, which in any event purveyed more heterosexual love than the public could stomach. A short time earlier, in 1913, E. M. Forster wrote a novel called *Maurice* celebrating homosexual love, but he chose never to publish it during his lifetime. Homosexuality flourished in Bloomsbury—for example in the writings of Lytton Strachey —but remained underground. The example of Oscar Wilde, imprisoned and broken, was still a fresh memory for that generation of writers. During the war years Proust continued work on his great novel, quietly giving female names to his male lovers. Even Gide, the European pioneer in dignifying homosexuality, after two decades of indirection and camouflage, from *The Immoralist* of 1902 onward, only confessed his homosexuality publicly in his autobiography of 1926. Ten years after the completion of *Women in Love*, Gide's daring still created a public scandal, despite Freud's revelations of latent homosexual impulses in all men and women.

Lawrence's own homosexual impulses are evident not only in *The Rainbow* and *Women in Love*, but in well-known scenes from *The White Peacock, Aaron's Rod* and *The Plumed Serpent*; in his tumultuous relations with John Middleton Murry and his bucolic relations with the Cornish farmer William Hocking; in his habitual celebration of male loins and phallus, and his comparative neglect of the female body. The dark, sensual men who appear in clumps throughout his works, as miners or peasants or Indians, provoke in him radically ambivalent emotions of attraction and loathing; they embody at once his homosexual desire, and the disgust, even terror which this desire evokes in him. We noted in the chapter on *Sons and Lovers* that Lawrence was attracted by the handsome young men at the army medical examination, but in the next moment he feared sinking into the "sticky male mass." Thus his increasing dread of the "mass," the "mob," the herd may be in part a defense mechanism against those homosexual desires recorded in the "Prologue," where Birkin hungers for "the men with dark eyes that one can enter and plunge into, bathe in, as in a liquid darkness." Lawrence's response to the war also contains an element of sexual insecurity. In the autobiographical "Nightmare" chapter of *Kangaroo* the hero's opposition to the war is not based on political or moral principles, but on a fear of losing his "manly isolation," of being "swept away with the ghastly masses of other men." Dreading "loss of manhood," he thinks of Oscar Wilde in prison. His anger and humiliation surpass all rational bounds during the physical exam, when he must submit his naked body to the eyes and hands of other men: "because they had handled his private parts, and looked into them, their eyes should burst and their hands should wither and their hearts should rot." Like many savage, murky passages in *Women in Love*, this text registers a concentration of psychic energy which the event itself does not explain. However, viewed as a cathexis of Lawrence's frustrated homosexual desires and his coincident feeling of guilt, such outbursts become comprehensible.

Lacking an acceptable father-figure, dominated by an aggressive mother, married to an aggressive wife, deeply inhibited in his earliest sexual relations, frail of body—it is not surprising that there should have been a strong homosexual element in Lawrence's make-up. The factors recorded in *Sons and Lovers* which made him a social outcast also confused his sexual identity. For Paul Morel all women appeared as mother, and hence as forbidden objects of sexual love; so for Birkin in the "Prologue" all women appear as "sisters," they all seem "kin," and hence also forbidden; only men

131

seem attractive. Like both of his autobiographical projections, Lawrence struggled to *force* himself to love women, and this desperate effort accounts for much of the stridency in his advocacy of heterosexual love. Under the stress of the war, the failure of his social ambitions and the turbulence of his relations with Frieda, Lawrence succumbed temporarily and guardedly to the homosexual impulses which dogged him throughout his career, but which he could never publicly honor. His wartime delusions of persecution, his deep ambivalence toward the male "herd," his overt obsession with heterosexuality, his touches of megalomania and even certain articles of his metaphysic may all be viewed as components of what Freud called a reaction formation, a complex of psychic mechanisms designed to protect him against his homosexual desires. Likewise much of what is obscure in *Women in Love*—the mysterious rages, the luxuriant talk of corruption, the hyperbolic denunciations, the confusion of love among all the major characters—may be partly explained as symptoms of the frustration or masking of homosexual impulses.

If Freud is right in claiming that every human being oscillates throughout his life between homosexual and heterosexual inclinations, and that "frustration or disappointment in the one direction is apt to drive him over into the other,"[26] then Lawrence's bitter wartime trials with Frieda (abundantly documented by the gossips, the friendly and the curious) make this outbreak of homosexual feeling more easily intelligible. According to Freud such an outbreak may also be prompted by frustration of the societal instinct, and it is often accompanied by delusions of persecution. Thus Lawrence's paranoia and his social frustration may both be associated with his sexual indeterminacy, the first as symptom, the second as partial cause.

5 Personal and Social Disorders

Women in Love bears the violent imprint of its historical

---

[26] "Psychoanalytic Notes upon an Autobiographical Account of a Case of Paranoia (Dementia Paranoidea)," *Collected Papers* (New York, 1959), Vol. III, pp. 429–30. (Vol. 12, 1958, of the London Standard Edition of the Complete Psychological Works of Sigmund Freud.) This famous case-study of Dr Schreber offers many parallels with the condition of Lawrence during the war years.

moment. The fragmented, episodic form of the novel mirrors the surrounding moral and political chaos; it registers an ideological interregnum. The beliefs which sustained Victorian fictions having crumbled, the form of Victorian fiction—the communal narrator, the historical perspective, the assured moral commentary—no longer sufficed. In *Women in Love* Lawrence offers neither the communal narrator of Jane Austen or George Eliot, nor the limited point-of-view figures of James; rather he offers a prophetic, dissident narrator who defines himself *against* the community. The monadic isolation of the individual which is characteristic of an advanced, highly bureaucratized capitalist society is reflected in James by the idiosyncracy of the lonely observer, and in Lawrence by the increasing stridency of the alienated oracle. The surface structure of *Women in Love* is that of the chronicle, a history written without causal connections. But in its depths it records the working-out of passional laws, instinctual relations. By divorcing these relations from their context, Lawrence sought to withdraw from the social level at precisely that historical moment when the state laid unprecedented claim to control of the individual. As the possibilities for living narrowed, in Lawrence's view, so he narrowed the scope of his fiction.

As in the case of Lawrence's other novels, so in my study of *Women in Love* I have been concerned to trace the social and psychological coordinates of his leading ideas and attitudes. Such an exercise discourages us from any longer reading the novel as a reliable diagnosis of cultural ills, as unerring social history, or as prophecy. *Women in Love* reveals a synthesizing and symbolizing intelligence of astonishing powers; but it also displays a narrowing of vision which temporarily rendered all but extraordinary souls opaque. It captures the sheer feel of being-in-the-flesh with a vividness that is unrivalled outside of Lawrence's own works; but for the most part it neglects the experience of being-in-society. True, it exhibits a mind at work with a genius for language, but a mind which also frequently resorts to stridency and jargon in the attempt to exorcize both personal and social demons. *Women in Love* remains a compelling record of a profound historical crisis, but its value as a diagnosis is compromised by the distorting effects of the crisis in Lawrence's own life, with its attendant anxieties, hatreds and ambitions. Of course the same reservations

133

must be made against *Remembrance of Things Past, A Portrait of the Artist as a Young Man* and *The Magic Mountain*, all of which overlap *Women in Love* in time and theme, all of which fuse cultural and personal crises. We should not expect Lawrence to be a prophet, a revolutionary strategist or an unerring social historian, any more than we expect these exalted services from Proust, Joyce or Mann. *Women in Love* should be read, then, not as diagnosis, not as blueprint for renewed human relations, but as the anguished response to a world-wide trauma by an isolated and frustrated man, albeit a man of genius, a man at once compassionate and contemptuous towards his fellows, a man seized in turn by revolutionary hope and misanthropic despair.

Although at the end of the novel Birkin speaks bravely of "the creative spirit" replacing man as it had replaced the mastodon, experience of the war prevented Birkin's creator from ever again believing that the power of nature would triumph over the power of society. In *The Lost Girl, Aaron's Rod* and *St Mawr*, as in *Women in Love*, the quarrel with society is resolved by flight; in *The Plumed Serpent* by reversion to a pre-industrial order; in *Lady Chatterley's Lover* by retreat to a fast-diminishing reserve of nature; in *The Man Who Died* by myth.

Writing *Sons and Lovers* Lawrence could still largely ignore the social existence of his characters, could remain blind to the historical forces shaping their lives. In that novel his focus remained individualistic; he explained the condition of his characters psychologically rather than historically. Society had advanced too far into the world of *The Rainbow*, however, to be any longer ignored. Yet nature still seemed to provide a sanctuary from the ravages of the mechanical social order, more than a sanctuary, perhaps even a staging area from which counterattacks could be launched. Events soon destroyed the naïveté manifest in *Sons and Lovers*, forcing him to recognize the impact of social existence on individual lives. And in the end, the natural world invoked in *The Rainbow* proved no defense against war. Only in *The Plumed Serpent* did nature recover the prominence it had for Lawrence in those two earlier novels, and there its presence is hostile. But meanwhile the characters of *Women in Love* are exposed, without sanctuary, without possibility of retreat into organic nature, to the destructive forces of history. Into their plight Lawrence wove his own. Pressed from all sides and harrowed by the war, divorced from all social groups, divided by his own androgynous impulses, Lawrence fused his private disorders with the public one to produce a novel which in part succumbs to those disorders and in part triumphs over them.

4

The Plumed Serpent: The Politics of Nature

Defeated in his wartime hopes for a radical change in English society, Lawrence settled for a change of place. In the autumn of 1919 he and Frieda set out from England in search of some charmed territory which had escaped the murderous influence of European civilization. Five years later, after glimpsing in Sicily, Italy, Ceylon and Australia the primitive modes of life which he sought to recover, Lawrence arrived in the American Southwest, where the Indian and the desert fulfilled his vision of a state of nature more completely than any other place or people ever would.

Lawrence was one of the last European writers to romanticize America. As early as 1915 he had planned to go there, had even ventured to apply for a passport, but wartime restrictions and *The Rainbow* litigation shackled him to England. At that time he still thought of the new world primarily as a refuge from the old, where he could "start a new school, a new germ of a new creation." By 1917, however, America also represented his only hope for survival as a writer, since his two most recent novels could not be sold in Britain, and his others scarcely earned enough to keep him alive. In that year he wrote to his agent that his prime reason for desiring to emigrate to the United States was the necessity of securing a market. From the early twenties on, as he complained to his English publisher, he was to depend upon the new world for his livelihood: "England makes me about £120 a year, if I got no more than that I should have to whistle my way across the globe. Therefore America must have the first consideration. On the English crust I could but starve, now as ever."[1] The England of Shaw, Wells, Bennett and Galsworthy would not support Lawrence. America meant an income, as well as landscape.

The country he imagined was that of Fenimore Cooper, Hawthorne and Whitman, not the rich, brash, automated democracy of Henry Ford and Woodrow Wilson. Judging from his letters he detested every American city he ever visited, and despised what passed for the American way of life. It was the land rather than the people that drew him. The wild pre-human landscape of Old and New Mexico seemed to hold out promise for the renewal of society by negating all social relations and institutions, as he knew them in Europe:

> I must say I am glad to be out here in the Southwest of America—there is the pristine something, unbroken, unbreakable, and not to be got under even by us awful whites with our machines—for which I thank whatever gods there be.[2]

Just as Ursula in *The Rainbow* had been fascinated by "the strange laws of the vegetable" world because she glimpsed in them "something working entirely apart from the purpose of the human world," so Lawrence admired in this desert landscape a savage power which man had failed either to comprehend or control. Complaining of America's barbaric state, Henry James had emigrated to England, where he was joined first by a trickle, and later by a flood, of artistic expatriates, among them Eliot and Pound, who echoed his complaint. And for precisely the same reason Lawrence emigrated from England to America: the European veneer was spread more thinly there. In "The Evening Land," one of several poems which he dedicated to America, he asked himself:

> And I, who am half in love with you,
> What am I in love with?
> My own imaginings?

Doubtless the answer to that question is yes. His pristine, aboriginal America disappeared with Cooper. Having resisted the forces of civilization, the desert spaces of the American Southwest proved all the less resistant to his imagination.

[1] *Letters from D. H. Lawrence to Martin Secker, 1911–1930* (Bridgefoot, Iver, 1970), p. 50. 19.ix.22.

[2] Letter to Harriet Monroe, CL 786. 8.iv.24.

Here between 1923 and 1925 Lawrence conceived and wrote his religious romance, *The Plumed Serpent*. Following immediately on the *Studies in Classic American Literature* (1923), owing a particular debt to Cooper's wilderness landscapes and noble savages, Hawthorne's moral allegories, Melville's South Seas idylls and Whitman's mystic celebrations of the American continent, *The Plumed Serpent* shows marked similarities with what Richard Chase has defined as the romance tradition in American fiction.[3] Lawrence's novel shares with the American romance a tendency to melodrama; indulgence in the picturesque and heroic; a setting on what is, from the European perspective, the border of the civilized world; characters who are two-dimensional (Kate being the only exception); an easy movement toward mythic, allegorical or symbolic forms; the tolerance of radical contradictions in character and theme; and a story which encounters little resistance from reality. Unlike the traditional realistic European novel—the sort epitomized by *Middlemarch* or *Anna Karenina*—Lawrence's Mexican romance withdraws from the sphere of shared action and speech into the private recesses of fantasy. Conflicts which could not be resolved realistically within the stubborn English environment of *Sons and Lovers*, *The Rainbow* or *Women in Love*, could be resolved mythically in an alien setting.

The Plumed Serpent marks at once the climax and the failure of Lawrence's attempt to discover a social expression for his private vision. It was his one concerted attempt to project an alternative society in which men could be free together as well as individually, a society in which the self could develop naturally in relation and in commitment to others, within the whole life of a community. Beneath the novel's primitivist trappings, beneath its ceremonial embellishments, beneath the flummery of its hero-worship, there is a movement, crippled though it may be, for a reconciliation between nature and culture. Thus it temporarily arrests the movement which we traced through *The Rainbow* and *Women in Love*, where nature was divorced from society, and it reasserts, without in fact validating, Lawrence's faith in the possibility of creating a humane community, a faith which by the writing of *Women in Love* he had all but lost.

[3] *The American Novel and Its Tradition* (Garden City, New York, 1957; London, 1958).

The novels which immediately succeeded *Women in Love* were remarkable neither for their ideas nor their art. Ursula and Birkin were followed on that cruel and fruitless route south by Alvina Houghton in *The Lost Girl*, by Aaron Sisson and Rawdon Lilly in *Aaron's Rod*, and by Lovat Somers in *Kangaroo*. All of them refugees, not so much seeking a new world as fleeing the old one, they act out loss rather than discovery. Somers and Lilly share Birkin's messianic aspirations, but they are equally lacking in disciples. As Lawrence ventured further afield in search of a location for his ideal society, he became ever more estranged from the European audience which he sought to reform, and therefore more impotent. Speaking through the figure of Somers in *Kangaroo*, Lawrence tells us that

> He felt broken off from his fellow-men. He felt broken off from the England he had belonged to. The ties were gone. He was loose like a single timber of some wrecked ship, drifting over the face of the earth. Without a people, without a land.

Distance from Europe did not relieve him of the sense of mission, however, a fact which shows up clearly in the essays that he wrote in defense of the novel during the early twenties, demanding public commitment and moral responsibility on the part of the artist, while attacking what he took to be the solipsistic self-consciousness of Proust and Joyce. Once again he allied himself with the British moralists—with Shelley and Carlyle, Ruskin and Arnold—rather than with the moderns. Fully a decade earlier than the leftist writers of the 1930s, long before the struggle between fascism and socialism obscured every other political fact, Lawrence perceived the heavy social burden which literature would be called upon to bear between the wars.

Like George Orwell, Christopher Caudwell and the other British writers who marched off to fight for the republicans in Spain in 1937, Lawrence, between the end of the World War and his arrival in Mexico, came to feel that in an era so beset with ills writing must give way to action. His sense of impotence and isolation as a writer shows up in the contemporary letters, in the character of Lilly, and even more clearly in Somers, who complains, " 'I want to do something with living people, somewhere, somehow, while I live on the earth. I write, but I write alone. And I live alone. Without any connexion whatever with the rest of men.' " During the war this mood of frustrated impotence had driven him in search of allies; by the 1920s the only allies remaining to him were the ones he invented himself. Thus while his own social writings had no apparent impact, those of Somers in *Kangaroo* influence the fictional leaders of rival fascist and socialist parties in Australia. And in *The Plumed Serpent* Lawrentian doctrine enjoys a fictional social existence in the Quetzalcoatl movement, a revival of the ancient gods of Mexico.

The religion of Quetzalcoatl incarnates that change of perspective which Lawrence had been urging upon his readers from the beginning: renewed respect for the instincts and a recovery of desire; an attitude of husbandry toward the earth; a feeling of kinship toward the cosmos; reverence for sex; and the substitution of organic for mechanical rhythms in communal life. But when translated into action this doctrine assumes an anti-democratic, hierarchic, authoritarian political shape which, especially in view of its date, is alarming. The social pyramid culminates in a cult of the hero, in which we can detect the lineaments of Lawrence's recurrent anxieties: his fear of the masses, his dread of social impotence and his sexual insecurity. Kate Leslie, heroine of the novel, provides the ballast for Lawrence's fantasy balloon, observing all these activities with the jaundiced eyes of a European refugee, eager to discover a new life, yet skeptical. The drama of her indecision in face of the primitivist revival shares the center of the novel with the revival itself.

There are thus four levels to sort out: the religious romance, the political doctrine, the hero principle, and Kate's radical ambivalence.

1 *The Religious Romance*

The Mexico of 1923, still seething from the shock of revolution, offered fertile soil for Lawrence's political and religious imaginings. During the previous one hundred years the country had suffered a succession of rebellions, coups and civil wars, interrupted only by brief periods of stability under military dictators. The longest reign, that of Porfirio Diaz, was ended in 1911 by a popular revolt which issued in the radical constitution of 1917. Providing for land reform, restrictions on foreign investment, nationalization of all subsoil resources and democratization of the political process, this constitution held out the mirage of radical social change while withholding the substance, thus focusing that popular discontent which convulsed the nation throughout the period of Lawrence's stay. Presidents Obregon and Calles, who governed from 1920–24 and 1924–28 respectively, redistributed some of the land, nationalized some of the resources, expanded education, supported the unions and placed restrictions on the churches. Their reformist activities, and particularly their quarrels with the Catholic Church, lay behind the character of President Montes, the newly-elected ruler of Mexico in *The Plumed Serpent*.

Social turmoil was familiarly linked in Lawrence's mind with hopes of the millenium. By 1918 it seemed to him that only "a quite bloody, merciless, almost anarchistic revolution . . . a fearful chaos of smashing up" would renovate England.[4] For a time after the October Revolution he had been hopeful of drastic changes in Russia; then after 1919, when Mussolini's blackshirts and the red-scarved communists took to the streets in Milan and Rome, Italy seemed to him to promise a new birth; and then in the early 1920s his hopes temporarily settled upon Germany, which threatened to "become manly again, and a bit dangerous in a manly way . . . the old fierceness coming back."[5] Seizing upon fascist or communist revolutions impartially, Lawrence eagerly greeted every tremor as sign of the rebirth of the natural man. Now in Mexico he found himself in the middle of a social revolution; observing the ferment at close range, he wrote of the Mexicans that "If they only had a new faith they might be a new, young, beautiful people."[6]

The new faith which he offers in *The Plumed Serpent* is actually an old one—a revival of Aztec religion under the messianic leadership of Don Ramon. The survival of paganism in a Christian land clearly fascinated Lawrence; like antique wood beneath dead varnish it might be restored, and with it, he imagined, might be recovered the unspoiled forms of primitive life. The very opening sentence of the novel yokes Easter and a bull fight, the Christian and pagan rites co-existing in an uneasy truce which Ramon's religious movement is to upset in favor of paganism. Thus in the

[4] Letter to Mark Gertler, CL 542. 21.ii.18.
[5] Letter to Koteliansky, CL 777. 9.ii.24.
[6] Letter to Baroness von Richthofen, CL 744. 31.v.23.

chapter called "Auto da Fe" the old idols of Christianity are carried out of the church, to be ritually burnt on an island in the holy lake, and the new idols of the Quetzalcoatl cult are borne in. For the old wedding ceremony there is a new one, as there is a new form of the eucharist. In order for the common people to accept the cult of Quetzalcoatl, Don Ramon repeatedly insists, they must have "manifestations," and much of the novel is devoted to their manufacture.

Far and away the most prominent "manifestations" are the hymns and sermons, which are written in Lawrence's most thoroughgoing Biblical style. Throughout his career, of course, he was prone to lapse into his Biblical manner on occasions demanding solemnity or profundity. Replete with Biblical quotations, parodies and metaphors, with Biblical rhythms and poses, with Biblical characters who serve him as archetypes of human predicaments, his writings amply bear out the testimony in *Apocalypse* that because as a child he had had the Bible poured every day into his "helpless consciousness," it "became an influence which affected all the processes of emotion and thought." Aside from the Apocalyptic imagery and the abundant Christian symbols, his prose betrays a habit of formulaic repetition, a preference for short verse-like paragraphing, a flair for aphorism, a love of illustrative parables, and a sustained prophetic tone. Collectively, these stylistic features evoke the Biblical cosmology without adhering to its letter. Irritated by this facet of Lawrence's style, T. S. Eliot accused him of "using the terminology of Christian faith to set forth some philosophy or religion which is fundamentally non-Christian or anti-Christian,"[7] a charge which may well have been prompted by the outrageous example of *The Plumed Serpent*.

For the anti-Christian hymns and sermons of Don Ramon could not have been written without copious borrowings from the King James Version. The use of the second person singular, the archaic inversion of normal subject-verb order, the syntactic parellelism (*my flower on earth is the jasmine flower, and in heaven the flower Hesperus*), the short verse paragraphs, the formulaic repetitions, the familiar vocative phrases (*I tell you . . . and I tell you*

---

[7] In a review of John Middleton Murry's *Son of Woman*, in *Criterion*, X (July, 1931), p. 770.

truly), and the outright parodies produce a style which is unmistakably Biblical in its derivation. Consider these parallel passages:

I always am, says his sleep . . . the sleep that is dreamless breathes *I Am!* . . . In the dreamless Now, *I Am.* . . .	And God said unto Moses, I AM THAT I AM: and he said, Thus shalt thou say unto the children of Israel, I AM hath sent me unto you (Exodus 3:14).
I tell you . . . he shall be proud, and perfect even as the Morningstar is perfect.	Be ye therefore perfect even as your Father which is in heaven is perfect. (Mt. 5:48).
Do not look with the eyes of yesterday, nor like yesterday listen.	For now we see through a glass darkly; but then face to face (I Cor. 13:12).
Neither heaven nor earth shall swallow you up at the last, but you shall pass into the place beyond both, into the bright star that is lonely yet feels itself never alone.	Neither death, nor life, nor angels, nor principalities, nor powers, nor things present, nor things to come, nor height, nor depth, nor any other creature, shall be able to separate us from the love of God (Romans 8:38).
Nought is possessible, neither gold, nor land nor love, nor life, nor peace, nor even sorrow nor death, nor yet salvation.	

By so closely imitating the style of the Old and New Testaments, in particular the evangelical language of St. Paul, Lawrence reproduces on the verbal level the Christian/pagan confrontation that occurs on the dramatic level in the encounters between Ramon and Carlota, and between Ramon and the bishop.

The novel's ritual speech is addressed simultaneously to two different audiences, one inside and one outside the novel. Criticisms can be advanced against it from both perspectives. To begin with the peasants, although we are told that the hymns and sermons move them deeply, we are shown no reason why this should be so. On the contrary, the pagan doctrine is couched in an alien, artificial language which appears to have little connection with their lives. The chief priest, Don Ramon, is a wealthy *patron* of European descent, living comfortably on his hacienda amidst a desert of poverty, and is thus divided from them both by class and race. The chief evangelist, Don Cipriano, is another in a long line of military tyrants—a career not calculated to endear him to the peasants. As for the audience outside the novel, if we remain unpersuaded by the ritual language it is partly because we do not share the theological or political assumptions on which it is based, but also partly because we recall the coherence and eloquence of the Biblical tradition which such language evokes, and we are reluctant to accept a contrived and fragmentary alternative.

The form of the novel itself, with its elaborate ceremonials and incantations, reflects Lawrence's belief—shared with the surrealists and supported by Jung and Freud—that ritual and mythic forms have the power to by-pass reason and work directly upon the unconscious. Already at the time of reading Jane Harrison's *Art and Ritual* in 1913, he was fascinated by the links between art and the elementary forms of religion. From *Sons and Lovers* onward, as Mark Spilka has shown in *The Love Ethic of D. H. Lawrence* (Bloomington, Ind., and London, 1955), ritual plays an important structural part in Lawrence's fiction. In *The Plumed Serpent* it becomes the message as well as the medium: the novel deals with the recovery of our religious sense by acting upon that sense. The sermons and hymns parcel out the universe into metaphors of flowers and animals and stars, just as the new cult parcels out the day into the watches of rabbit, hawk, turkey-buzzard and deer. Here is a sample of that procedure:

> In the place of the west
> In peace, beyond the lashing of the sun's bright tail,
> In the stillness where waters are born
> Slept I, Quetzalcoatl.
>
> .   .   .
>
> I bound the bright fangs of the Sun
> And held him while Jesus passed
> Into the lidless shade,
> Into the eyes of the Father,
> Into the womb of refreshment.
>
> And the breath blew upon me again.
> So I took the sandals of the Saviour
> And started down the long slope
> Past the mount of the sun.
> Till I saw beneath me

White breast-tips of my Mexico
My bride.
Jesus the Crucified
Sleeps in the healing waters
The long sleep.
Sleep, sleep, my brother, sleep.
My bride between the seas
Is combing her dark hair,
Saying to herself: Quetzalcoatl.

Thus Quetzalcoatl steps into the sandals of Jesus, voyaging in an anthropomorphic universe, bound for a female Mexico. In a letter of 1923 to Frederick Carter regarding the latter's work on the mythology of the heavens, Lawrence advised him that "the sum of all your work would be to translate so that the thing lives again."[8] This is precisely what he himself set out to do, through the hymns and sermons as well as the astonishingly vivid landscapes: bring the cosmos back to life.

"The novel," wrote Georg Lukács, "is the epic of a world that has been abandoned by God." And indeed this seems generally true of the modern novel—the works of Kafka, Mann and Beckett spring to mind. But in this as in so many other respects, Lawrence harks back to the Romantics, perceiving a divinity in natural things —as in this passage near the close of *The Plumed Serpent*:

> The ink-black ass foal did not understand standing up. It rocked on its four loose legs, and wondered. Then it hobbled a few steps, to smell at some green, growing maize. It smelled and smelled and smelled, as if all the dark aeons were stirring awake in its nostrils.
>
> After bethinking itself for a time, the ass-foal walked uncertainly towards the mother. She was a well-liking grey-and-brown she-ass, rather glossy and self-assured. The ass-foal straight found the udder, and was drinking.
>
> Glancing up, Kate met again the peon's eyes, with their black, full flame of life heavy with knowledge and with a curious reassurance. The black foal, the mother, the drinking, the new life, the mystery of the shadowy battlefield of creation; and the adoration of the full-breasted, glorious woman beyond him: all this seemed in the primitive black eyes of the man.

Son of an industrial age in which nature had become for the first time simply a dead reservoir of matter and energy, Lawrence

[8] CL 748. 26.vii.23.

sought throughout his writings to restore wonder to all those creatures and creations which exist independently of our designs. At the heart of the Quetzalcoatl cult, beneath the ceremonial antics, he urges a renewed reverence for the natural world, for each other, and for our own bodies.

Reverence for one's body involves a ratification of all desires— another article of faith which Lawrence shared with the surrealists. "I shall accept all my desires and repudiate none," he wrote in *The Reality of Peace*, echoing Whitman.[9] This will mean, in *Kangaroo* and *The Plumed Serpent*, accepting savage desires along with benign ones, thereby licensing murder so long as the blood urges it. Thus Somers treats political murders as the vindication of instinct; and after killing several men, albeit in self-defense, Ramon appears to Kate as the pure expression of animal impulse:

> His brow was like a boy's, very pure and primitive, and the eyes underneath had a certain primitive gleaming look of virginity. As men must have been, in the first awful days, with that strange beauty that goes with pristine rudimentariness.

Such a glorification of instinct has vicious political implications which are sufficiently obvious, and to which I shall return in the following section. For the present I wish to stress the connection which Lawrence makes between primitive man and the purity of desire.

The primitive in Lawrence stands for those modes of thought, feeling and action which modern society has repressed, just as desire represents that residue of freedom in which the body eludes the dictatorship of consciousness. *The Plumed Serpent* acts out, in the Freudian sense, a return of the repressed, which Kate finds both exciting and frightening: "This strange dumb people of Mexico was opening its voice at last. It was as if a stone had been rolled off them all, and she heard their voice for the first time, deep, wild, with a certain exultance and menace." Although her feelings toward the revival remain deeply divided, she finally accepts the idea which Lawrence had been reciting throughout most of his career, that if we are to survive as a civilization we must recapture the wisdom of primitive religions, we must recover the nonrepressive freedom of primitive life-styles. The pagan

[9] PI 680.

religions, he declared, had kept men in touch with the living universe; and for a time during the middle ages—in the monasteries which fascinated him, and which influenced his utopian visions of an organic community—Catholicism still maintained the correspondence between natural and human worlds; but Protestantism broke this connection, and thereby frustrated "the eternal human need of living in ritual adjustment to the cosmos in its revolutions, in eternal submission to the greater laws."[10]

Of course, as twentieth century anthropology has shown, most primitive cultures are highly repressive, enforcing rigid codes of behavior upon all members of the community. Drawing on many of the same authorities (notably Frazer) whom Lawrence had read, Freud stressed the constraints which primitive societies impose upon natural impulses. Wyndham Lewis and T. S. Eliot both accused Lawrence of romanticizing the savage, and their charge was justified; but they failed to acknowledge that for Lawrence, as for the Romantics, invocation of primitive social models was a defense against contemporary social abuses. In his critique of modern Europe the primitive appears as a supplement for the modern, not as a substitute. Thus Skrebensky returns from the Boer War with a sheen of African mystery about him, and manages temporarily to seduce Ursula into believing he will fulfill her repressed desires; Birkin uses the African totem to represent the purely physical counterpart to Europe's mental culture; aboriginal Celts haunt the stories from Cornwall with memories of ancient religions. In *The Ladybird* Count Dionys, an Egyptian prototype of Cipriano, serves as foil to a crippled war-veteran who represents modern Europe. In *The Lost Girl*, *St Mawr*, and *The Woman Who Rode Away* the primitive contrast is provided by Indians. And of course scattered throughout the novels, from *The White Peacock* onwards, there are numerous peasants, gardeners, gamekeepers and grooms who have resisted the forces of modernization. In each case the primitive functions in dialectical opposition to the modern, just as for Lawrence the uncorrupted child functions in opposition to the psychically crippled adult.

Read symbolically, therefore, *The Plumed Serpent* is a protest against a repressive, alienated culture; read as a program for social change, it is nonsense. Lawrence was aware, not only from

[10] *A Propos of "Lady Chatterley's Lover"*, PII 509.

147

his extensive reading in anthropology but also from his study of Indian culture in New Mexico, that collective ritual arises out of and sustains communal life, but does not produce it. Any ideology bearing as little relation to social structure as the Quetzalcoatl cult bears to Mexican society in *The Plumed Serpent* would surely fail to promote the revolution that Lawrence desired. Nor is there any more promise in the elaborate ceremonials. "The ideal, the religion, must now be *lived, practised*," he wrote in a letter of 1915; and what he had in mind was clearly a revival of old communal rituals, such as the Indian dances and songs.[11] But ritual ceremonies, like mythology, arise out of corporate life rather than generate it.

All the ceremonies, costumes, earthly pantheons, hymns and sermons—indeed "manifestations" of any sort—would seem to be incompatible with the very nature of Lawrence's religious vision. For his God, like the God of the Old Testament, is transcendent, never to be limited to one place or one rite. His terms for the life force invariably appear cloaked by such modifiers as *dark, inscrutable, undefinable, indescribable, ineffable, mysterious, invisible, hidden*. This divine force can be glimpsed in nature or in the depths of the self, but it cannot be made fully articulate, for to articulate is to rationalize, and to rationalize, in Lawrence's scheme, is to destroy. At one point Ramon advises Kate that her countrymen should also reinstate their old religions, should "substantiate their own mysteries . . . as we have tried to substantiate Quetzalcoatl." Doubtless, after years of invoking the dark god Lawrence felt a need to substantiate his own mysteries. But his religious vision derived much of its force from its sheerly negative quality: his dark god dwelt in the realm of the repressed, it stood for all that society had denied, all that Christianity had ignored. When what was hidden becomes manifest in ritual, and what was forbidden becomes an obligation, the mystery vanishes.

2 *The Politics of Nature*

In his *Reflections on Violence* of 1908, Georges Sorel argued that all descriptions of society, even those such as Marxism that

[11] Letter to Lady Ottoline Morrell, CL 311. 1.ii.15. See also his series of letters to Rolf Gardiner, who actually constructed such a community in southern England.

claim to be scientific, are in effect political myths which command irrational faith from their adherents and serve as the basis for social action. In his Mexican novel Lawrence offers us such a political myth, one which summarizes the plan for social reconstruction which he had been urging for a decade: a theocratic state arranged hierarchically, with a vast lower class of workers who have no responsibility for government and little education; a select class of supreme legislators; and finally a heroic leader whose task it is to interpret the divine will, and whose privilege it is to exact unswerving obedience from his subjects.

Lawrence began elaborating this political scheme during 1915 in letters to Cynthia Asquith and Bertrand Russell, attacking democracy and popular education at a time when Russell himself, in letters and pamphlets, was advocating expanded education for workers and increased democratic control. Both men reacted strongly to the war, attributing it to opposite causes: Russell to a lack of democracy, Lawrence to an excess. Democracy, Lawrence complained, had given the rabble power but not wisdom; it had reduced the sensitive and creative classes to the humble level of the proletariat; it had enshrined the instincts of the herd. Lawrence's animus against socialism, which advanced the claim for democracy in its most uncompromising form, was already evident in *The White Peacock*, where the socialists are depicted as creatures driven by greed and vindictiveness—a portrait which survives unchanged into *The Plumed Serpent*. In *Women in Love* Birkin elaborates Lawrence's critique by charging that democracy adds to its justified demand for material equality a pernicious demand for spiritual equality, thus tyrannizing over the individual, forcing him to conform to collective standards of thought and behavior. This attack on democracy recurs, with slight variations, throughout the writings of 1915–1925, notably in "Democracy," "Education of the People," *Studies in Classic American Literature, Fantasia of the Unconscious, Reflections on the Death of a Porcupine, Aaron's Rod* and *Kangaroo*.

Writing to Lady Cynthia Asquith in 1915, Lawrence outlined what was to remain his plan for salvation of the world from democracy:

> Let us have done with this foolish form of government, and this idea of democratic control. Let us submit to the knowledge that

149

there are aristocrats and plebeians born, not made. Some amongst us are born fit to govern, and some are born only fit to be governed. Some are born to be artisans and labourers, some to be lords and governors. But it is not a question of tradition or heritage. It is a question of the incontrovertible soul. If we have right spirit, even the most stupid of us will know how to choose our governors, and in that way we shall give the nucleus of our classes.[12]

Essentially this is a restatement of the medieval doctrine that social classes are ordained by God, that every man is born naturally into one of these stations, and that any attempt to change positions in the hierarchy is to meddle with the natural order and to defy God. In light of Lawrence's religious upbringing it may also be viewed as the translation of Calvinism into political terms, producing a theory of social predestination.

The social consequences of this plan are spelled out more explicitly in the essays which Lawrence wrote late in 1918 as a summary of his judgement on the causes of the war, and perhaps also as an attempt to establish his reputation in educational circles preliminary to a resumption of teaching. Collected under the title "Education of the People," these essays recommend a system of graduated training—a minimum for the naturally unconscious, a maximum for the naturally conscious—that would produce, he concluded,

distinct classes of society. The basis is the great class of workers. From this class will rise also the masters of industry, and, probably, the leading soldiers. Second comes the clerkly caste, which will include elementary teachers and minor professionals, and which will produce the local government bodies. Thirdly we have the class of the higher professions, legal, medical, scholastic: and this class will produce the chief legislators. Finally, there is the small class of the supreme judges: not merely legal judges, but judges of the destiny of the nation.[13]

Substituting divine election for popular election, his Platonic scheme would thus enforce as a fact of nature the crippling social

[12] CL 361. 16.viii. 15.
[13] "Education of the People," PI 607. In *A Modern Utopia* (1905) and other novels, some of which Lawrence surely read, H. G. Wells envisioned a similar Platonic hierarchy, ruled over by a technocratic elite. Aldous Huxley, of course, was to satirize this scheme in *Brave New World*.

divisions which already existed in English society, and in particular that division between manual and intellectual labor which we found so deeply embedded, and so cancerous, in the life of *Sons and Lovers.* In *The Plumed Serpent* Ramon even goes so far as to suggest an international consortium of the supreme judges of the several lands, to rule the earth in place of the current financial and political barons—an idea which Lawrence had put forward in his essay on "Aristocracy."

All mankind, we are told in *Kangaroo*, is divided into two categories, the irresponsible and the the responsible, otherwise known as the proletariat and the ruling class, and the first must yield absolute authority to the second. In *Fantasia of the Unconscious* Lawrence describes the proper relation between the two classes:

> The leaders must stand for life, and they must not ask the simple followers to point out the direction. When the leaders assume responsibility they relieve the followers forever of the burden of finding a way. Relieved of this hateful incubus of responsibility for general affairs, the populace can again become free and happy and spontaneous, leaving matters to their superiors.[14]

As in apologies for slavery, the freedmen are reputed to have been happier under their old masters. For a theory designed to better accommodate the luxuriant variety of human nature, his scheme is remarkably lacking in distinctions, the only significant division falling between those fit to be sheep, and those fit to be shepherds.

While on his way to Australia Lawrence wrote to his New Mexican hostess, Mabel Dodge Luhan, a letter in which he set forth, in terms that recur throughout the period 1915–1925, the rationale for his power elite:

> I don't believe either in liberty or democracy. I believe in actual, sacred, inspired authority: divine right of natural kings: I believe in the divine right of natural aristocracy, the right, the sacred duty to wield undisputed authority.[15]

These natural aristocrats reappear under various guises as educators, inspectors, judges, legislators, patricians, life-priests, prophets, heroes, "adepts in the dark mystery of living, fearing

[14] Op. cit., p. 78.
[15] CL 700. 10.iv.22.

nothing but life itself, and subject to nothing but their own reverence for the incalculable life-gesture."[16]

We see, then, that in this middle period Lawrence shifted from a Protestant to a Catholic view of the relation between man and God. In the early works every man was his own priest, apprehending the movements of the creative impulse within himself; but in the works written during the decade that followed 1915, it appears that priests must intercede between the common man and God, for only the elect can discover and embody the divine will. In the works subsequent to 1925, as we shall see in the next chapter, Lawrence reverted to his earlier position.

The potential for tyranny implicit in the notion of embodied will is evident. When Cipriano takes it upon himself to execute prisoners in *The Plumed Serpent*, Kate is temporarily horrified; but she eventually persuades herself that he acted not from individual will—in which case he must be condemned for murder— but from the divine will, which knows no higher authority: "Why should I judge him? He is of the gods." Like the fictional Carthage of Flaubert in *Salammbô*, Lawrence's fictional Mexico allowed him to indulge a bloodlust for which his own society provided no outlet. "The moment the divine power manifests itself," he says in an essay entitled "Blessed Are the Powerful," "it is right."[17] Thus a man with a charge—from God, from nature, from "the people"— may be permitted atrocities which would otherwise be censured. The examples of Mussolini, Stalin and Hitler are too recent and too bitter to bear rehearsal. In the name of the Cross, the Fatherland, Manifest Destiny, Free Trade, White Man's Burden and other embodied abstractions, most of history's cruelties have been perpetrated. Lawrence devoted much of his *Movements in European History* to the celebration of such crusades, on the theory that the divine life impulse is most nakedly revealed where irrational forces operate most powerfully.

Like many politically conservative thinkers, Lawrence buttressed his reactionary social order with appeals to nature, which in his thought is functionally equivalent to God. Democracy, he

[16] "Education of the People," PI 607.

[17] Op. cit., PII 442. The leadership theme recurs throughout *Reflections on the Death of a Porcupine*, of which "Blessed Are the Powerful" is one essay.

asserts again and again, embodies the mechanical principle, aristocracy the organic:

> As the leaves of a tree accumulate towards blossom, so will the great bulk of mankind at all time accumulate towards its leaders. We don't want to turn every leaf of an apple tree into a flower. And so why should we want to turn every individual human being into a unit of complete expression. . . ? The people is an organic whole, rising from the roots, through trunk and branch and leaf, to the perfect blossom. This is the tree of human life. The supreme blossom utters the whole tree, supremely.[18]

This falls only a hairsbreadth short of claiming, with Nietzsche, that the blossom is the tree's reason for being. When applied to the individual the organic metaphor had expressed for Lawrence the continuity between the unconscious roots, the trunk of the sensual body, and the blossoms of the creative spirit. In transposing this metaphor to society, however, he assigned completely different individuals to the various levels of the tree—the unconscious drones to the roots, the masters of industry and soldiers to the trunk, the clerks and doctors to the branches, and finally the supreme judges to the blossoms. Although the hierarchic principle is latent in the organic metaphor, nothing constrains a writer to translate it from the individual to society. Shelley, Godwin and the young Wordsworth (the older Wordsworth suggests comparisons with the older Lawrence) used similar language, without drawing Lawrence's political conclusions. In other words, the terms which served Lawrence from the beginning as the central categories of his thought—organic principle, nature, life-impulse, dark power—lent themselves to a reactionary political philosophy, but left the choice of that philosophy to Lawrence himself.

The manner in which the natural elite will be made known remains necessarily obscure. At times Lawrence says that we will recognize the divinity in certain men by instinct; we will feel power radiating from them like electricity; we will perceive it in the middle of their forehead; we will behold it, as in the case of Ramon and Cipriano, in their eyes. Birkin in *Women in Love*, Lilly in *Aaron's Rod*, Count Dionys in *The Ladybird*, Kangaroo in the novel which is named after him—all lay claim to this mysterious lordship, which others perceive or not, according to the vigor of

[18] "Education of the People," PI 609–10.

their instincts. Once again Lawrence appears to be guilty of falsely generalizing from his own social rise: if he could escape the working class, then it lay within the power of every divinely gifted man to escape. But that is to ignore the limiting influence of environment, work, and class expectations.

In the essays collected in *Reflections on the Death of a Porcupine* (1925), where Lawrence addressed himself directly to the political issues broached in *The Plumed Serpent*, the doctrine of natural election appears nakedly for what it is, a resurrection of Social Darwinism:

> Life moves in circles of power and of vividness, and each circle of life only maintains its orbit upon the subjection of some lower circle. If the lower cycles of life are not *mastered*, there can be no higher cycle.

> In nature, one creature devours another, and this is an essential part of all existence and of all being. It is not something to lament over, nor something to try to reform. . . . As far as existence goes, that life-species is the highest which can devour, or destroy, or subjugate every other life-species against which it is pitted in contest.

This trial by nature, Lawrence goes on to explain, not only distinguishes between man and beast, but between man and man:

> Vitality depends upon the clue of the Holy Ghost inside a creature, a man, a nation, a race. When the clue goes, the vitality goes. And the Holy Ghost seeks for ever a new incarnation, and subordinates the old to the new. You will know that any creature or race is still alive with the Holy Ghost, when it can subordinate the lower creatures or races, and assimilate them into a new incarnation.[19]

Pushed to its logical extreme, natural election becomes natural selection. Having begun in *Sons and Lovers* with an attack on the *status quo*, Lawrence contrives by 1925 to furnish it a defense. For if the possession of power implies the right to power, then the industrial magnates, the dictators, the demagogues may be shot but not reproached. Apologists for the British Empire employed the same arguments to justify the subjugation of dark peoples by white. "While the white man keeps the impetus of his own proud onward march," reflects Kate, "the dark races will yield

[19] Reprinted in PII, 467–8 and 471.

and serve, perforce. But let the white man once have a misgiving about his own leadership, and the dark races will at once attack him, to pull him down into the old gulfs."

In his attempt to transfer responsibility for the shape of political systems back from man to nature, or from man to God, Lawrence surrendered all rational basis for criticizing the systems that actually existed. That in itself would be evidence enough to demonstrate the bankruptcy of his politics of nature. But the fundamental objection to his view remains that levied by John Stuart Mill against an earlier generation of Social Darwinists:

> however offensive the proposition may appear to many religious persons, they should be willing to look in the face the undeniable fact, that the order of nature, insofar as unmodified by man, is such as no being, whose attributes are justice and benevolence, would have made, with the intention that his rational creatures should follow it as an example.[20]

Whoever or whatever created nature, man is the creator of society, and although he may learn from natural orders he is not compelled to imitate their hierarchies, their waste, their competition for survival, or their injustice.

3 Origins of the Hero Principle

Movements in European History paints Lawrence's elitist politics onto a vast canvas. The book was conceived in that mood of snobbish misanthropy which tainted so much of his work between 1915 and 1925: "The chief feeling is, that men were always alike, and always will be, and one must view the species with contempt first and foremost, and find a few individuals, if possible . . . to *rule* the species."[21] The resulting history is heroic in the old style: Lawrence's sympathies lie with the Roman Emperors, the Byzantine hierarchs, the German warlords, while the remainder of mankind appears merely as raw material for the designs of generals and popes and kings. The final chapter of the book, devoted to the unification of Germany (a country in whose barbarian past Lawrence discerned hopes for a rebirth of the natural man), concludes with a sinister invocation of a world-historical leader:

[20] *Nature* (written 1851–8, and originally published in 1873).
[21] Letter to Cecil Gray, CL 560. 3.vii.18. This text, which went through several editions, was intended for school-children.

a great united Europe of productive working-people, all materially equal, will never be able to continue and remain firm unless it unites also round one great chosen figure, some hero who can lead a great war, as well as administer a wide peace. It all depends on the will of the people. But the will of the people must concentrate in one figure, who is also supreme over the will of the people. He must be chosen, but at the same time responsible to God alone. Here is a problem of which a stormy future will have to evolve the solution.[22]

Written in 1919, only three years before Mussolini's march on Rome, only four years before Hitler's putsch in Munich, this is the most chilling expression of Lawrence's cult of the hero, a cult whose origins can be traced back to his social frustration, his sexual insecurity and his fear of the masses.

Throughout Lawrence's writings we meet characters who fulfil, or at least lay claim to, the messianic role which Gerald Crich described in *Women in Love*: "a man who will give new values to things, give us new truths, a new attitude to life"—in short, a Nietzschean revaluator of all values, a culture hero. Birkin himself is not so much a messiah as an evangelist, since he is too isolated to muster a following, yet he is convinced of the need for a hero. Rawdon Lilly of *Aaron's Rod* carries Birkin's alienation a stage further, being even more isolated, and even more convinced of the necessity for the weak to submit "to the heroic soul in a greater man"—a conviction which leads him at one point to toy with the idea of reviving slavery. In *Kangaroo* the "mystery of lordship" is incarnate in the proto-fascist Diggers movement, which is presided over by the benevolent despot Kangaroo, and which is organized according to the principles of authority and subservience that Lawrence was to describe even more glowingly in the account of Cipriano's army in *The Plumed Serpent*. But far and away the most striking of these messianic heroes is the authorial personality of Lawrence himself, that oracular presence which emanates from all of the works. His claim to be a culture hero is everywhere implicit. When he sets himself up as teacher in "Education of the People," for example, and then writes that in the redeemed society educators "will be the priests of life, deep in the wisdom of life . . . the life-priests of the new era," we are

[22] Originally published by Oxford University Press in 1921. I quote here from the illustrated edition, Oxford, 1925, p. 344.

clearly required to consider him a candidate for that future office. And when he declares elsewhere that a "saviour" is anyone who "can establish . . . a new connection between mankind and the circumambient universe," or that "the hero is he who touches and transmits the life of the universe," we recognize in these definitions an account of Lawrence's own efforts as novelist and essayist. The debt to Carlyle's conception of the artist as hero is evident, as is the even more profound debt to the Romantic definition of the artist as cultural revolutionary—among the saviors Lawrence names Rousseau, Wordsworth, Byron and Shelley.

His list of saviors also includes St Paul, Savanarola, Luther, Cromwell, Napoleon and Lincoln, all of whom exemplify what Max Weber called charismatic authority. Such unifying leaders arise, according to Weber, amidst historical crises for which prevailing legal, political or ideological systems offer no solution. The possibility of furnishing this sort of leadership for his own troubled times appealed to Lawrence; the times themselves seemed to cry out for a hero. His experiments with authoritarian ideas must be understood first of all, therefore, as a response to that sense of cultural crisis which gripped him during the war, and which is so sharply engraved into *Women in Love*. Of course it is no accident that Weber formulated his theory of charisma in the same period of crisis, or that so many of his contemporaries—Pareto, Durkheim, Sorel, Mosca, Freud—should have concerned themselves with the problem of authority. Throughout Lawrence's career the principles of liberal democracy were under attack from both left and right. On the left, Lenin was modifying Marx's theory of the dictatorship of the proletariat in order to provide for dictatorship by the vanguard. The Futurists and some of the Fabians were calling for a government by experts. Shaw, in the twenties, was admiring the efficiency of the dictators. On the right, men such as Pareto, Mosca and Hulme were recommending rule by an elite as the only means of avoiding the Scylla of liberal democracy and the Charybdis of revolutionary socialism. And finally the conservative writers—Wyndham Lewis, Eliot, Yeats, Pound, Gottfried Benn, Gabriele D'Annunzio, Céline—were showing sympathy with the principles of autocracy, and in several cases with the autocrats themselves. During the entire period of Lawrence's stay in Italy immediately after the war, from November of 1919 until

February of 1922, the fascists and communists battled in the press, in the Chamber of Deputies and in the streets. It was at the end of 1922 that Mussolini marched on Rome, and at the beginning of 1923 that he was granted dictatorial powers. From his mother-in-law Lawrence was meanwhile hearing reports of similar struggles between revolutionary and counter-revolutionary forces in Germany, and from Koteliansky about the battles in Russia. "More and more I feel that meditation and the inner life are not my aim," he restlessly informed a correspondent on the eve of his journey to the new world, "meditation and the inner life are not my aim, but some sort of action."[23] Authoritarian models were ready to hand.

But why did he use them? In the first place, as a means of compensating for his social impotence. Although isolated, unrecognized and powerless, the natural aristocrat should by rights be a ruler of men. Like Cinderella his royalty is hidden, but royalty nonetheless. Although denied actual power in society, being swelled by the divine afflatus the hero can lay claim to an importance which his real social position would not justify. Like an Old Testament prophet he is spurned by his people but beloved of God. In *The Ghost Dance*, his monumental study on the origins of religion, Weston LaBarre has identified a recurrent priestly figure, very similar to the Lawrentian natural aristocrat, which he calls a vatic personality or shaman: "The shaman was the intermediary between his group and the supernatural unknown, the intermediary between man's needs and anxieties, and the world he lives in and only partly knows."[24] Like Weber's charismatic leader, LaBarre's shaman emerges into prominence at times of cultural crisis: "When old 'cultural' means fail to provide social equilibrium (in times of tribal clash, acculturation, or failure of culture to defend peace of mind), we seem invariably to witness the rise of these vatic 'personalities' to compose the difficulties."[25] In LaBarre's analysis the shaman is commonly a man who is unable to fulfil the responsibilities defined for the male in his culture—the hunt, war, heavy labor, procreation—and who therefore takes on masculine power as a prophet, becoming the collector and trans-

[23] Letter to E. H. Brewster, CL 681. 2.i.22.
[24] I quote here from the 1972 Delta paper edition, p. 138.
[26] Ibid, p. 329. See in general Chpt. XI, "Culture and Culture Heroes."

mitter of supernatural male power: "the shaman may be seen as the individual most threatened by the uncertainties of life, and perhaps also the most unable to meet them on practical secular grounds or in ordinary male terms."[26]

We can observe corresponding circumstances in Lawrence's case. His frailty as a child prevented him from undertaking the arduous work assigned to men of his class in the mining community. The education which enabled him to escape that community also unsuited him for every sort of work which his father would have considered proper to a man. He was rejected for war duty three times, and on each occasion was reminded that his body was not acceptable. No doubt his opposition to the war was genuine, but his paranoid response to the physical examinations suggests outrage against the knowledge that he could not have fought if he had wanted. In his writings he professed a desire for those warlike activities—slaughtering enemies, leading revolutions, sacrificing victims—which he shunned in the flesh. One feels a certain vicarious awe in the description of political murders in *Kangaroo* and *The Plumed Serpent*. And finally, he was never able to father children in a woman who was extremely bitter about losing the children from her first marriage whom she had given up in order to marry him. Indeed, during much of the time with which *The Plumed Serpent* deals, illness prevented him from engaging in sexual intercourse at all. In terms of the working-class peer group through which the world was mediated to him as a child—and his respect for the compact, supple, powerful body of the miner lingers with him to the end—and in terms of the middle-class or even aristocratic conceptions of masculinity which he acquired from his mother, from his spell in London and from his reading, Lawrence fell short of full manhood. The roles of manual worker, soldier, steady breadwinner, father and even, for stretches of time, lover, were beyond him. To compensate he invented shamans, and became one himself—a priest of the phallic god, a transmitter of supernatural male power.

These same facts help account for that sexual insecurity—already evident in *The White Peacock*, grown acute in *Sons and Lovers*—which Lawrence exhibited throughout his writing career. This sexual insecurity, in turn, offers a second explanation for his

[26] Ibid, p. 138.

attraction to authoritarian political models. Forceful social action was a crucial part of his notion of male identity; social inaction was equivalent to emasculation. Thus he argued in an essay on Hawthorne that Dimmesdale becomes the hapless tool of Hester in *The Scarlet Letter* because he is unable "to conquer society with a new spirit and a new idea." Similarly in *The Rainbow*, Will Brangwen fails as a man in Anna's eyes because he refuses social involvement. In *Aaron's Rod* both Aaron and Lilly flee their wives in a desperate attempt to assert themselves as men, while in *Kangaroo*, closer than any of the other novels to a transcription of Lawrence's own experience, Harriet ridicules her husband's claims to a role in society, and Somers duly shuns every chance for action. Struggles similar to these led in 1923 to a prolonged separation between Lawrence and Frieda, and during that year he was at work upon *The Plumed Serpent*, writing into it a doctrine of male supremacy.

In an essay written somewhat later, and significantly entitled "Matriarchy," Lawrence blames women for the social frustration of men. Since woman is dominant in every other department of life—sex, the home, the family—he argued, denial of the public realm to a man emasculates him. The fictions are littered with men, lacking any public base for the assertion of their masculinity, who are dominated in their private relations with women: old man Morel, Paul Morel, Will Brangwen, Skrebensky, Gerald Crich, Aaron Sisson, Rawdon Lilly, Rico in *St Mawr*, Basil in *The Ladybird*, and, most graphic example of all, Clifford Chatterley. Hepburn in *The Captain's Doll* only escapes emasculation by destroying his wife, as does Ramon in *The Plumed Serpent*. The emasculating women suffer appropriately horrible fates: the woman in *The Fox* has a tree fall on her; the one in *The Captain's Doll* falls out of a window; the heroine of "None of That" is raped and murdered by a gang of thugs; the heroine of "The Woman Who Rode Away" is stripped of her identity and ritually stabbed to death; and in *The Plumed Serpent* Carlota suffers a stroke and while dying must listen to the egotistic rantings of Cipriano.

The powerful dread of emasculation is particularly striking in the Mexican novel. The authoritarian social structure imposed by the cult of Quetzalcoatl is reproduced in sexual relations; the women are subservient to the men, the men to the priest, and the priest to the dark god. Teresa's slavish submission to Ramon parallels the submission of the soldiers to Cipriano, and provides Kate with a model for her own surrender. Like the anonymous heroine of "The Woman Who Rode Away," who is taught to yield "her kind of womanhood, intensely personal and individual," her mistaken concern for the "individual independence of woman," in deference to "the ancient fierce human male," Kate becomes resigned, at least for a time, to "the death of her individual self." One characteristically obscure passage near the end of Chapter XXVI even suggests that she abandons her claim to sexual satisfaction, consenting to accept whatever pleasures Cipriano in his wisdom sees fit to provide. In fulfillment of Lawrence's repeated call for the liberation of the male through social action, the flamboyant public efforts of Ramon and Cipriano impress Kate with the mystery of masculine independence: "She felt, for the first time in her life, a pang almost like fear, of men who were passing beyond what she knew, beyond her depth." Ramon in particular, making up for the defeats of Somers and Lilly and the others, gives "her a feeling of helplessness, a woman's utter helplessness with a man who goes out to the beyond." The shaman can only be male.

Hence Lawrence was driven by his sexual insecurity to associate masculinity with the power ideal. Writing to his mother-in-law late in 1923, near the end of his separation from Frieda, he complained that "Frieda doesn't understand that a man must be a hero these days and not only a husband: husband also but more."[27] Cut off from all possibility of social action, he could only become a hero in fiction. Wilhelm Reich showed in *The Mass Psychology of Fascism* that the authoritarian structure of the fascist state was mirrored in the authoritarian structure of the lower-middle-class and peasant families.[28] The hierarchic submission of wife and children to the father, according to Reich, created a psychological set which was ideally suited to the accommodation of a fascist ideology. Proceeding along the same psychological path but in the reverse direction, Lawrence embraced an

[27] Letter to Baroness von Richtofen, CL 763. 10.xi.23.
[28] Third edition, New York, 1970; London, 1972. See Chapter II, "The Authoritarian Ideology of the Family in the Mass Psychology of Fascism."

authoritarian model for the state because it assured male dominance in marriage.

There is a third factor, intimately linked to his social frustration and sexual insecurity, which helped shape his political
doctrine, and that is his fear of the masses. Evidence of this fear
crops up in all of the novels from *The Rainbow* onwards. In that
earlier novel Ursula is terrified by the "power of the mob," while
in *Women in Love* the terror is concentrated for Birkin in the
"seething masses of miners." Alvina Houghton in *The Lost Girl*,
Lilly in *Aaron's Rod* and Somers in *Kangaroo* are all haunted by
the same specter. Nor is Kate spared, for during the war, we are
told, she contracted "The terror of the rabble that, mongrel-like,
wanted to break the free *spirit* in individual men and women . . .
the cold, collective lust of millions of people, to break the spirit
in the outstanding individuals." The quest for safety from con-
tamination by the herd reaches a terrifying climax in "The Reality
of Peace," where Lawrence invokes Death as the great savior,
which like the plagues of Egypt will slaughter the bulk of mankind, leaving himself and the chosen remnant free. During the war,
as we have seen, his fear of falling back into the working class
was compounded by his dread of the mass authority which he
encountered in the guise of conscription, censorship, militant
public opinion, warring armies and police. Equating the democratic
principle with mob rule—an equation which recurs with hallucinatory force in the "Nightmare" chapter of *Kangaroo*—Lawrence seized upon the authoritarian model as an alternative to
democracy.

Like many of his contemporaries he anticipated that a bloody
struggle between capital and labor would follow the war, and
like most other British intellectuals he dreaded a victory by
the herd-like proletariat. In his eyes this meant victory by the
Labour Party, whose rise to power he was already lamenting in
1915, when he informed Bertrand Russell that "The idea of giving
power to the hands of the working class is *wrong*."[29] In the play
Touch and Go which he wrote as the war was drawing to a close,
he deals explicitly with the conflict between capital and labor,
pitting the stalwart mine owner against the brutal mob of colliers,
then mythically resolving the situation by means of a Lawrentian

[29] Letter to Russell, CL 353. 15.vii.15.

mediator who offers them an obscure "new state of things" that would not be founded on money or the competition for power. Meanwhile real events were intensifying his fear of working-class hegemony. Concerted union action in 1920 prevented British entry into the war in Poland against Russia, thus demonstrating for the first time the power of the general strike, and promising increased solidarity among the workers of different nations. In 1921 unemployment was running at 2 millions, and was not to fall below one million before Lawrence's death, thus giving colour to the rumours of revolution which circulated in England throughout the early and mid-twenties. During these same years, of course, the bogey of Bolshevism haunted Europe—and haunted Lawrence himself, to judge from the frequency with which he refers to it. He detected Bolshevik—or at least socialist—tendencies in Sicily, Italy, Germany, Australia and Mexico. And then in 1924, confirming his wartime fears, the first Labour government took office in England. Although Ramsay MacDonald proved to be an eminently restrained Prime Minister, and although Labour was soon turned out of power, the precedent was established: the working class could elect a government.

Whether or not the working class actually conquered power in England—or even in Russia, for that matter—is immaterial; what is important is that Lawrence read events in this light, and constructed his political model accordingly. Marx, Shaw, President Wilson and the trade union leaders, he argued in *Fantasia of the Unconscious*, had corrupted the workers by bringing them to self-consciousness, pumping them with ideas of class and rights, destroying their natural spontaneity. The solution was to take back political control from the working man in exchange for a gift of "living, spontaneous, original being":

> I would like him to give me back the responsibility for general affairs, a responsibility which he can't acquit, and which saps his life. I would like him to give me back the responsibility for the future. I would like him to give me back the responsibility for thought, for direction. I wish we could take hope and belief together. I would undertake my share of the responsibility, if he gave me his belief.[30]

[30] Op. cit., p. 104.

In other words Lawrence was claiming for himself the role played by the industrial magnate in his earlier novels, and was proposing for working men the status of miners. The theocratic order which he sketched in *The Plumed Serpent*— for a Mexico governed both inside the novel and out by a Labour president—mirrors the industrial despotism which he had formerly condemned. The social paradigm which informs the cult of Quetzalcoatl is the contrast between unconscious masses of miners and the strong-willed, priest-like manager: Cipriano is a translation of Gerald Crich into a military uniform, Ramon his translation into priestly gowns.

The doctrine of natural aristocracy masks class prejudice and class fear. The only person who is unequivocally a member of the elect is Lawrence himself; the only ones who are unequivocally excluded from rule are the working people, his father's people, the people whom he had escaped and whom he wanted to believe were naturally unconscious, spontaneous and powerless. The cult of the hero also masks a need for sexual supremacy; and the mystique of the shaman, the mediator between man and God, betrays a profound desire for a role in society that is becoming to a man.

4 *The Pattern of Ambivalence*

Once these criticisms of Lawrence's politics during 1915–1925 have been made, they must be modified with respect to *The Plumed Serpent*. For long stretches of that novel he seems to discard one half of the dialectic between the primitive and the modern, as if he were seriously proposing an alternative model for society. Such a proposal can be attacked from several quarters, and has been. It may be adjudged unsound sociologically, since the religion has no social base, either in Lawrence's England or in the Mexico of the novel; pragmatically, since, if it is a serious attempt to suggest a reform, then one must agree with Orwell that such primitivism "is a species of defeatism, because that is not the direction in which the world is moving;"[31] politically, as I have argued, because of the authoritarian model which it embodies; and anthropologically, because it implies a view of the "state of nature" which the findings of Darwin, Freud and their respective

[31] "Inside the Whale," *Selected Essays* (Harmondsworth, 1957), p. 26.

followers have made it extremely difficult to maintain. If taken seriously, such thoroughgoing primitivism would represent a retreat from history, an evasion of Lawrence's self-proclaimed responsibility to make men see and feel in a fundamentally new way.

Yet for much of *The Plumed Serpent* the dialectic is in fact preserved, the political doctrine and the religious romance are implicitly criticized, because the primitive world is filtered to us through the very European consciousness of Kate and of the narrator. We see Mexican landscape and culture as something foreign, never comprehended, having a life of its own which Kate and the narrator, as outsiders, can never fully penetrate. Like Adela Quested and Mrs Moore in *A Passage to India*—a novel which Lawrence read while at work upon *The Plumed Serpent*, and which resembles his Mexican romance in its confrontation with alien modes of life—Kate is an exile from the old society yet a stranger in the new, and it is her frequent comparisons between the two cultures, her attempts to reconcile the one with the other, that create the psychological interest of the novel. Our attention is focused as much upon her reaction to the cult as upon the cult itself.

Her responses to the native Mexicans are almost always ambivalent, registering affinity as well as difference:

> In a sense they were like parasites, they wanted to live on her life, and pull her down, pull her down. Again, they were so generous with her, so good and gentle, she felt they were wonderful. And then once more she came up against that unconscious, heavy, reptilian indifference in them, indifference and resistance.

Likewise her response to the primitivist revival:

> Kate was at once attracted and repelled. She was attracted, almost fascinated by the strange *nuclear* power of the men in the circle. It was like a darkly glowing, vivid nucleus of new life. Repellent the strange heaviness, the sinking of the spirit into the earth, like dark water. Repellent the silent, dense opposition to the pale-faced spiritual direction.

This expression of ambivalence is sustained in Kate's observations throughout the novel, because the contradictions which she seems to find in the natives themselves in fact only mirror her own deeply divided feelings towards the primitive.

So long as her point of view predominates, then, we are aware of a modern European consciousness sympathetically engaged with a pre-modern and non-European culture, fascinated by that earlier mode of life without pretending to identify herself with it. Through her eyes we see the primitivist revival as something to be measured against our own social forms, but not as something in which we or she could ever truly participate. A psychological and historical gulf permanently separates her from the natives. That is why she habitually sees the peasant world as *distant* or *alien*, why even in the last chapter, as she watches a bull being loaded onto a boat, at a moment when she seems most completely reconciled to Mexican life, the native tableau appears to her at the same time "near, yet . . . strange and remote":

> She was aware of a duality in herself, and she suffered from it. She could not definitely commit herself, either to the old way of life, or to the new. She reacted from both. The old was a prison, and she loathed it. But in the new way she was not her own mistress at all, and her egoistic will recoiled.

She can never overcome her ambivalence, for it is a reflection of her own divided nature: part modern consciousness and part primitive unconscious, part social being and part radical individual, mental as well as physical creature, member of culture and equally member of nature. In short, her ambivalence is another expression of that painful and irresolvable dualism with which Lawrence was preoccupied throughout his life: the desire for social commitment and the fear of commitment; the desire for community and the fear of anonymity. So long as her point of view predominates, therefore, we are treated to the balanced, ambivalent response of Lawrence himself, as revealed in *Mornings in Mexico, Studies in Classic American Literature* and the various New Mexico essays reprinted in *Phoenix*—in particular that compact and elegant piece, "Indians and an Englishman." In her simultaneous recognition of affinity and difference, in her desire to reincorporate the past without herself ceasing to live in the present, Kate obeys Lawrence's conviction, expressed in regard to Melville's own primitive experiments, that "we must make a great swerve in our on-

ward-going life-course now, to gather up again the savage mysteries. But this does not mean going back on ourselves."[32]

However, when Lawrence abandons Kate's point of view, as he
does for long stretches between Chapters XI and XXV, he seems
to lose all critical perspective on his material, to repress the negative side of his own response to primitive America. Only by gain-
saying the character of Kate as it has been built up over the first
two hundred pages of the novel can Lawrence pretend to integrate
her into the Quetzalcoatl pantheon, or have her acquiesce in
Cipriano's ritual murders. To do so he must ignore her radical
ambivalence, which has been so intricately and convincingly established in those early chapters. As a European, able to perceive in
the primitive the savage as well as the child, the ugly as well as the
beautiful, Kate cannot wholly submit to the religious movement.
As a self-conscious individual, she cannot wholly submit either to
the consciousness of the group or to the will of Ramon. Her trans-
mutation into Malintzi is no more convincing than the translation
of the hostile Mexican landscape into the landscape of Ramon's
myth.

More is at stake here than continuity of character. Kate is
Lawrence's refugee from the urban-industrial world, she is the
test case for the experiment of reconciling individual and communal existence. Yet her redemption, such as it is, is wholly personal; it follows the pattern of sexual initiation and deepening
emotional commitment with which the other novels have made us
familiar. It depends not in the least upon the Quetzalcoatl revival,
nor does it relate to the nascent religious community. While
Ramon's doctrine demands absorption of the self into the whole,
Kate remains staunchly an individual. Within the religious order,
only Ramon, and to a lesser extent Cipriano, retain the right to full
individuality. They are the guardians of a hierarchical, theocratic,
totalitarian social order (by the end of the novel all other ideologies have been outlawed), a form of society, as we have seen, which
Lawrence advocated from wartime onwards; and such a society
accords to the ruling priests alone the right to free and full
development of the self—a right which, in his saner moments,
Lawrence demanded for everyone.

Far from being an organic outgrowth of the peasant life which

[32] "Herman Melville's *Typee* and *Omoo*," SCAL 130–1.

167

it is designed to transform, Ramon's religion is an artificial blend of Christian language, Aztec mythology, Nietzschean or Carlylean devotion to the hero, and Cambridge anthropology. Far from being an expression of actual social relations, far from being the issue of inward prompting, it is a sham imposed from without. "I know there has to be a return to the older vision of life," he wrote in a letter of 1924,

> But not for the sake of unison. And not done from the *will*. It needs some welling up of religious sources that have been shut down in us: a great *yielding*, rather than an act of will.[33]

Whether we speak of Ramon as character or of Lawrence as author, it is clear that the religious revival is an act of will. Rather than yielding to a spontaneous popular movement, Ramon synthesizes a religion and Cipriano with his army sets out to make it popular. What was to have been natural turns out to be artificial. Unlike Tolstoy, whose political vision was given historical force by the rising peasant class, Lawrence was unable to identify his own hopes with any real social group, and so the religious and political doctrines advanced in *The Plumed Serpent* appear in a kind of limbo: not fully endorsed by the heroine or the narrator, not grounded in the actual history of Mexico or Europe, yet earnest and disturbing.

5 *Authoritarianism and Radical Individualism*

Lawrence is able to present his theocratic order uncritically only by switching from the perspective of Kate to that of Ramon—by switching, that is, from the viewpoint of the individual who suspects the claims of all communities, to the view point of the high priest who will remain the one truly free individual in the new society. In other words, the vision of a theocratic social order is merely another expression of the individualistic ethic which Lawrence proposed in more and more extreme forms, from *Sons and Lovers* through *Women in Love* and *Kangaroo*, as the only defense against the demands of an increasingly repressive society. The claims for absolute freedom, for unfettered pursuit of the soul's desires, have been smuggled into the theocracy for the benefit of the priests. The individual's supreme responsibility to obey his

[33] Letter to Rolf Gardiner, CL 796. 4.vii.24.

inward natural promptings has become the priest's duty to interpret God to the masses, and to see that the masses obey. Just as
Lawrence's individualistic perspective prevented him from seeing
the connections between Paul Morel and his society in *Sons and
Lovers*, so it prevents him, for most of *The Plumed Serpent*, from
seeing, or at any rate admitting, the lack of connection between
Don Ramon and his society. The blindness is the same in both
cases. I believe that Lawrence later recognized this intimate kinship between his radically individualistic perspective and his fascination with the absolute leader or priest; this seems to be what he
had in mind, for example, when he wrote to Trigant Burrow, two
years after finishing *The Plumed Serpent*, that "The hero illusion
starts with the individualist illusion."[34] To retain his integrity the
atomic individual must be isolated from society, and to retain his
the hero must be elevated above society. Either way he is insulated
from the demands of communal existence.

By advocating an authoritarian order, Lawrence was only translating the absolute claim for freedom of the inividual into a
political form. This explains his contradictory remarks on authority: when imposed upon the Lawrentian hero by the masses,
authority is evil; when imposed by the hero upon the masses, it is
good. Thus Lilly in *Aaron's Rod* can switch adroitly from arguments in favor of lordship to one in favor of sacred individuality,
and then again to one in favor of slavery. Thus Kate can appear to
sacrifice her ego upon joining the Quetzalcoatl pantheon, because
she regains it again in becoming a goddess. The seeming contradiction in Lawrence's thought is rooted in a deeper contradiction
in bourgeois ideology. For that ideology affirms individual liberty,
on the one hand, and the rights of property on the other; it forbids
one man to dominate another, and yet by enshrining property
rights it permits, even encourages, domination mediated by wealth.
Lawrence proposes a form of domination mediated by "nature":
the individual is sacred, yet he must submit to "natural" authority. The natural rights to which Thomas Paine and the framers of
revolutionary constitutions in France and America appealed were
the property of all men; those to which Lawrence appealed were
the property of a few.

Defenders of Lawrence, as of Yeats, Eliot or Pound, often argue

[34] CL 989. 13.vii.27.

that we must distinguish the mythic visions of a writer from the political shapes they take. On these grounds, Mary Freeman, L. D. Clark, Eugene Goodheart, Keith Sagar and M. Jarret-Kerr, among others, have eloquently defended him against political criticism. Thus in *The Plumed Serpent*, one might argue, Lawrence is imagining a reintegration of the self, or a rediscovery of the religious faculty, not a revival of some neo-fascist pre-Columbian state. But men's imaginings about nature, personality and society *do* take political shapes, which often mirror personal anxieties and desires. If we are to be guided by literary visions, we must know their sources and their consequences. By 1928, having written in the meantime the very different and humane romance of *Lady Chatterley's Lover*, Lawrence himself was to repudiate what he referred to in a letter as "the whole business of leaders and followers."[35] But that there was such a business to repudiate is important; it reflects Lawrence's troubled social position and his anxieties; and it colors our reading of his fiction.

In the end, *The Plumed Serpent* fails to resolve that seminal conflict, which we have encountered again and again in Lawrence's novels, between the claims of nature and the claims of culture, between private urges and social pressures, between the desire for isolate selfhood and the desire for communal life. "This is the tragedy, and only this," he wrote in his study of Hardy:

> it is nothing more metaphysical than the division of a man against himself in such a way: first, that he is a member of the community, and must, upon his honour, in no way move to disintegrate the community, either in its moral or its practical form; second, that the convention of the community is a prison to his natural, in-dividual desire, a desire that compels him, whether he feel justified or not, to break the bounds of the community, lands him outside the pale, there to stand alone.[36]

---

[35] Letter to Rolf Gardiner, Huxley ed. *Letters*, pp. 712–3. 4.iii.28. In a frequently cited letter, written later in the same month to Witter Bynner, Lawrence formally renounced the hero principle: "The hero is obsolete, and the leader of men is a back number. After all, at the back of the hero is the militant ideal: and the militant ideal, or the ideal militant, seems to me also a cold egg, . . . the leader-cum-follower relationship is a bore. And the new relationship will be some sort of tenderness . . ." (CL 1045, 13.iii.28).

[36] Op. cit., PI 411.

It is not difficult to find autobiographical evidence for translating this sense of "tragedy" into Freudian terms of conflict between ego, id and superego—take for example Lawrence's recollection of his childhood in *Assorted Articles*:

> The boy that had excited sexual thoughts and feelings was the living, warm-hearted, passionate me. The boy that in the morning remembered these feelings with such fear, shame and rage was the social mental me . . . the two were divided against one another.[37]

But a translation into Freudian terms is unnecessary, for Lawrence presents us with a direct experience of this conflict, which he sees as a permanent feature of man's existence, aggravated at this juncture of our history by the increasing mechanization and depersonalization of our society. "There must be brotherly love," he wrote during the war years,

> a wholeness of humanity. But there must also be pure, separate individuality, separate and proud. . . . In the duality lies fulfilment. Man must act in concert with man, creatively and happily. This is greatest happiness. But man must also act separately and distinctly, apart from every other man, single and self-responsible and proud . . . moving for himself without reference to his neighbour.[38]

Needless to say he never found a community that would fulfil both halves of the duality. Nor could he construct one—although he tried to do so in *The Plumed Serpent*—that would convince either his audience, or his heroine, or, one feels, himself. Having deified nature, having made its demands absolute, no compromise with culture was really possible. "That a feeling is bestowed on us by Nature," wrote J. S. Mill, "does not necessarily legitimate all its promptings."[39] But for Lawrence, if the feeling were genuinely bestowed by nature, then its fulfilment became not only a legitimate right but a holy duty. The distance divorcing the second view from the first was the distance separating Lawrence from commitment to social existence.

[37] "The State of Funk," PII 568.
[38] "Love," PI 155–6. Compare Aldous Huxley's sensitive comments on Lawrence's search for community, in his Introduction to the *Letters* (1932), reprinted in H. T. Moore's edition, CL 1261–2.
[39] From the Everyman edition of *Utilitarianism* (London, 1962), p. 38.

5

Lady Chatterley's Lover: Eros and Civilization

In August and September of 1926 Lawrence paid a final visit to his home terrain among the collieries in Nottingham and Derby. What he witnessed on that trip—the disfigurement of his fields, the decay of his villages, the misery and hopelessness of his people—moved him to write his last, gentlest and most compassionate novel, *Lady Chatterley's Lover.*

Times had always been hard in the mining communities, but they grew harsher in the years following the war, and by the autumn of 1926 they had grown cruel. In May of that year the unions had staged a General Strike in support of the miners, who were refusing to accept the coalowners' terms of reduced wages and longer hours. Spokesmen for the propertied class and for the Conservative Government, notably Winston Churchill, declared that class warfare had begun, and that the workers must be forced to yield what Churchill was to demand again of the Germans—unconditional surrender. After little over a week the General Strike ended peacefully and indecisively, but the realities of class conflict and the possibilities of civil war had been exposed with a nakedness which disturbed many Englishmen, including Lawrence, who wrote from Italy of his fears: "Myself, I'm scared of a class war in England. It would be the beginning of the end of all things."[1] The example of Russia was still fresh. Disillusioned with the Bolsheviks, tempered in his bitterness against civilization, Lawrence no longer relished the prospect of revolution; it was likelier to lead to the death of England than to renewal.

[1] Letter to S. S. Koteliansky, CL 912. 17.v.26.

172

The coalowners were apparently persuaded that a class war was inevitable, and accordingly prepared their forces to smash the unions and beggar the miners. They were aided from the outset by Baldwin's Government, which passed legislation permitting longer working hours, which endorsed the owners' attempt to ruin the national miners union, and which acted to restrict the payment of poor relief. In August, as a show of strength and without provocation from the miners, the Government dispatched thousands of police into the colliery districts. The *Manchester Guardian, Daily Herald* and *New Statesman* agreed with the miners and with subsequent historians in viewing Baldwin as a mouthpiece of the coalowners. So the lines were clearly drawn: on the one side the workers; on the other side the capitalists and the Government.

Feeling themselves abandoned by the other unions, fighting for their dignity and their livelihood, the miners doggedly continued their strike through the summer and into the autumn. Already by the end of May strike funds had been exhausted in Nottingham and Derby, where according to the *New Statesman* distress was particularly acute. Relief from the national union failed in July. Once their own savings had been spent miners were forced to seek poor relief, and some were driven into the workhouse. The hardship spread throughout the industrial districts as unemployment, already severe before the strike, mounted for lack of coal. By the time Lawrence visited the Midlands in September the suffering was widespread. "This strike has done a lot of damage," he wrote from Derby, "and there is a lot of misery—families living on bread and margarine and potatoes—nothing more. The women have turned into fierce communists—you would hardly believe your eyes. It feels a different place—not pleasant at all."[2] Concerted efforts by British Communists on behalf of the unemployed, added to rumors that the strike was being subsidized by the Russians, lent color to the Bolshevik scare which the Government and the coalowners were concerned to promote.

Finally starved into surrender at the beginning of December, the miners returned to work at lower wages for more hours in the pit. They were in debt, their union was shattered, their jobs were prey to trade slumps and machinery. The people who had

[2] Letter to Koteliansky, CL 937. 15.ix.26.

surrounded Lawrence during his youth were to wait over a decade for relief; the villages and fields might wait forever.

In an essay entitled "Return to Bestwood," written shortly after his visit, Lawrence spoke with sadness of the strike, the policemen, the class bitterness, the hunger and hopelessness. Insofar as he belonged anywhere, he belonged to those colliery families and that gutted countryside. Despite his physical escape from the working class the ties of feeling and consciousness remained intact. Like Gudrun in *Women in Love* who mingles nostalgically with the miners, like Lovat Somers in *Kangaroo* who "seemed to be drifting away, drifting back to the common people, becoming a working man, of the lower classes," upon his return to the Midlands Lawrence identified once again with the plight of those people whom he had travelled around the world to avoid:

> I feel I hardly know any more the people I come from, the colliers of the Erewash Valley district. . . . At the same time, they have, I think, an underneath ache and heaviness very much like my own. It must be so, because when I see them, I feel it so strongly. They are the only people who move me strongly, and with whom I feel myself connected in deeper destiny. It is they who are, in some peculiar way, 'home' to me. I shrink away from them, and I have an acute nostalgia for them. And now, this last time, I feel a doom over the country, and a shadow of despair over the hearts of the men, which leaves me no rest. Because the same doom is over me, wherever I go, and the same despair touches my heart.[3]

Still trusting against all odds in nature and in man, Lawrence responded to their plight with a promise of renewal:

> One is driven back to search one's own soul, for a way out into a new destiny. . . . I know we must take up the responsibility for the future, now. A great change is coming, and must come. What we need is some glimmer of a vision of a world that shall be, beyond the change.[4]

The vision he offered, born of anguish, was *Lady Chatterley's Lover.*

1 The Myth of Eros and the Social Crisis

As soon as he returned to Italy in October of 1926, with impres-

[3] "Return to Bestwood," PII 264.
[4] Ibid., 264–5.

sions of the colliery districts fresh and bitter in his memory, Lawrence began the novel which was to be his last and most notorious. A first draft was completed by early December, a second apparently by February of 1927, and a third by the following winter. All three versions have been published, the earliest as *The First Lady Chatterley* in 1944, the second as *John Thomas and Lady Jane* in 1972, and the third, familiar version as *Lady Chatterley's Lover* in 1928. For ease of reference I shall refer to them as I, II and III.

The anguish which he felt over the fate of his people aches like a wound through all three versions of the novel. "I was at my sister's in September," he wrote soon after his return to Italy, "and we drove round—I saw the miners—and pickets—and policemen—it was like a spear through one's heart."[5] Connie Chatterley retraces Lawrence's drive through the colliery district, seeing the idle miners, the poverty, the dingy towns, the delapidated houses, the angry wives, the pinched and despairing faces, and everywhere the hatred of her class:

> It was something she dreaded coldly and fatally, the working-out of this new, unconscious, cold, reptilian sort of hate that was rising between the colliers of the under-earth, the iron-workers of the great furnaces, and the educated, owning class to which she belonged.

In all three versions Clifford represents the propertied class. Inspired by fear and loathing of the colliers who support his existence, ruthless in his operation of the mines, spiritually crippled and sexually impotent, he becomes, like Gerald Crich in *Women in Love*, a slave of the industrial machine which he sought to master. Opposite him stands Ivy Bolton, chronicler of Tevershall, district nurse, widow of a miner, a woman endowed with the gusto, the sensuality and the generosity of soul, but also with the envy of her betters, the love of gossip and the desire to get on which Lawrence invariably associated with the working people. Connie and the gamekeeper stand a little apart from their respective classes. Connie is a lady, propertied, educated and travelled, but she despises the sterile, parasitic upper class to which she belongs. The gamekeeper comes of collier stock, but he has re-

[5] Letter to Rolf Gardiner, CL 952. 3.xii.26.

treated from the mining villages into the wood, where he carries on a silent war with lords and laborers alike.

Between these two outcasts, who are separated by wealth, status and culture, Lawrence imagines a union of tenderness and sensuality that overturns all social barriers. Where class divisions and industrial labor had made objects of people, love restores humanity. In each of its three versions *Lady Chatterley's Lover* is a gesture of faith in what one character calls the "democracy of touch," the common humanity which for Lawrence resided in the shared life of the flesh. "How ghastly, now, is this division into upper and lower classes!" he proclaims in version II, "How resolve them back into a onèness?" His answer, implicit in all three drafts of the novel, is summarized in that second version by Connie: "It was touch that one needed: some sort of touch between her class and the under class."

From the very beginning of his career Lawrence had insisted upon the subversive nature of sexuality. The lovemaking of Paul and Clara next to the flooded River Trent in *Sons and Lovers*, or of Ursula and Skrebensky upon the dark hillside in *The Rainbow*, prefigures the furtive lovemaking between rebels in Zamyatin's *We* and Orwell's *Nineteen Eighty-four*, where coitus has become a political act, defying the totalitarian claims of the state. In *The White Peacock* and "Daughters of the Vicar" passion draws together a laborer's son and a daughter of the middle or upper class, a theme which Lawrence was to enact in his own life, and which he was to rehearse in novel after novel, story after story, but most poignantly of all in *Lady Chatterley's Lover*: ". . . if the lady marries the gamekeeper . . . it is not class spite, but in spite of class."[6] Desire recognizes no class boundaries, it respects none of the political and economic barricades which men have erected to parcel out the earth. The classless future which we glimpse from time to time in Lawrence's writings can only be reached, he tells us in this novel, through love rather than strife, through a restored reverence for our bodies rather than sharpened hatred, through a recovery of desire rather than civil war. Poor in health, keenly aware of his own approaching death, he restated his myth of Eros in a last attempt to persuade men that through sexuality they could renew not only themselves, but their world.

[6] *À Propos of "Lady Chatterley's Lover,"* PII 514.

176

The Virgin and the Gypsy, a tale which immediately precedes Lawrence's visit to the Midlands, embodies this myth of erotic renewal—a woman from the higher classes is reborn through the love of a lower-class renegade—but it lacks the overt social message of *Lady Chatterley's Lover*. Only in the work written after that tour of savagely divided England does the erotic myth become political. In his apology for *Lady Chatterley* Lawrence explained his fable of love by reference to this social division:

> The so-called "cultured" classes are the first to develop "personality" and individualism, and the first to fall into this state of unconscious menace and fear. The working classes retain the old blood-warmth of oneness and togetherness some decades longer. Then they lose it too. And then class-consciousness becomes rampant, and class-hate. Class-hate and class-consciousness are only a sign that the old togetherness, the old blood-warmth has collapsed, and every man is really aware of himself in apartness. Then we have these hostile groupings of men for the sake of opposition, strife. Civil strife becomes a necessary condition of self-assertion.[7]

It is easy to object that Lawrence has the bull by the tail: that the division of mankind into competing classes has been responsible for the death of brotherhood, rather than the other way round. But his theory about the origins of class conflict is less important than his recipe for its abolition, which he offers as the central fable in *Lady Chatterley's Lover*. The gamekeeper, representative of the laboring millions, the downtrodden, the silent and suffering lower orders, meets the titled representative of the ruling class in a hut in the magical wood. Their love bridges the gulf between them. With their story Lawrence sent his last message of hope to England, where it waited thirty years for publication.

The gulf between Connie and her lover yawns widest in version I, where Parkin, as the gamekeeper is there called, seems a purely physical creature. In her eyes he represents the missing physical half of Clifford, but lacks the educated consciousness which she values in the ruling class:

> Apparently it was impossible to have a whole man in any man. Her two men were two halves. And she did not want to forfeit either half, to forego either man. . . . Of two things she was con-

[7] Ibid., PII 513.

177

vinced: that she would *never* try to 'elevate' him, to bring him towards her own level of life: and that she could no more abandon her own way of life than he could his.

Despite Lawrence's efforts, Connie remains trapped in this impasse. Parkin never overcomes his bitterness towards her class, nor can she ever fully overcome her revulsion against his class, or her fear of being pulled down and humiliated by the common mob. With the gamekeeper she can share only her body, but not the educated conversation, art, ballet, books, spacious housing or gracious living to which she has grown accustomed.

Matching her in fierce attachment to his own origins, Parkin refuses to climb out of the working class on the ladder of her money. Unlike the later gamekeepers, he speaks only in the dialect and makes no pretense to book learning. After he is forced to leave Clifford's employ he moves to Sheffield, where he works in the steel-mill and lives with a working family. Near the end of the novel when Connie visits him for tea at his lodgings she is embarrassed by the alien manners, speech and attitudes of her working-class hosts. Her lover remains surly and bloody-minded over the class issue, stressing the radically opposed interests which pit the laborers against the owners. In Parkin's unrelenting bitterness and anger Lawrence registered the effects of that 1926 strike, which followed on years of frustration and hardship among working people. Feeling responsible for his fellow laborers, Parkin once again refuses to be rescued from their fate by Connie's money. So fully does he identify with the needs of his class that he becomes local secretary of the Communist League.

Thus matters stand at the end of version I, Parkin working in Sheffield and Connie dreaming of life with him on a farm or in a "suburban villa with nine or ten rooms." Nothing binds them together but sensual pleasure, which even the prophet of Eros considered too slender a cord to withstand the strains of marriage. The class barrier between them becomes more rather than less obvious as the novel unfolds. When Lawrence moves Parkin out of the magic wood into industrial Sheffield, the mythic union between the potent common man and the sleeping lady seems less plausible. The gamekeeper stubbornly adheres to the realities of power, education and wealth, in defiance of the social myth which governs the novel.

178

Unable to bridge the gulf which divides the lovers in *The First Lady Chatterley*, Lawrence promptly rewrote the novel, jacking Parkin a few notches higher on the social scale. The gamekeeper in version II is not the son of a miner but of a professional cricketer (as was H. G. Wells), and is thus marked out by birth as well as by temperament from the tribes of miners. Still unlettered, Parkin has learned to speak "standard" English, but his natural speech is once again the dialect. He remains taciturn, venturing but rare remarks on sex or society, yet his thought seems more complex, in part because Lawrence presents it in greater detail. In *John Thomas and Lady Jane* Parkin has become less of the opaque, mysterious gypsy, but has not yet become the garrulous Lawrentian spokesman of *Lady Chatterley's Lover*.

Resenting the upper class less bitterly in this version, Parkin is not so troubling to Connie, who finds him somewhat more of a gentleman, somewhat less tightly bound to the working class. Her visit for tea at Sheffield is less of an ordeal. Parkin identifies more closely with her, less closely with his working-class hosts, and not at all with his fellow workers. His unlikely career as a Communist League Secretary has been abandoned between versions I and II, and his angry political outbursts have been muted. If he cannot make a go of it at the steel works, he tells Connie, he will accept her money. In fact he soon quits the steel-mill and plans to seek work on a farm. Lawrence's retreat from history has begun.

Both Connie and Parkin thus appear in *John Thomas* as more thorough renegades from their respective social classes. They meet beyond the pale, where they are less trammeled by the fears and ignorance which divided their counterparts in the earlier version. But it becomes correspondingly more difficult to apply their story to the mass of people who remain bound within the real conditions of a class society. Echoing Lawrence himself, Connie brushes aside the differences of power, education and wealth which separate her from Parkin by deciding that "the proletariat is a state of mind," rather than a social class opposed to her own. Among the proletariat she would include her husband, along with almost all the aristocrats and the bulk of the workers, everyone in fact who is cold-hearted, materialistic, barren. Among the very few who remain warm-hearted and passionate, she includes herself and Parkin. By a sleight-of-hand which one observes repeatedly in Lawrence's work, social categories are translated into psychological ones. Connie resurrects in a more benign form his notion of the natural arristocracy, the instinctual elite, which stands outside all class boundaries. But her sister Hilda will not let her evade the issue so deftly, for she reminds Connie that Clifford still gives the orders and Parkin still obeys, that power and privilege reside in Wragby. Parkin's sexual virility does not alter the fact that he is socially impotent.

Between *John Thomas and Lady Jane* and *Lady Chatterley's Lover*, Parkin is transformed into Mellors, who has all the credentials of a gentleman except genteel birth. An officer in the army, educated, travelled, Mellors is very much a man of the world. He uses dialect only as a shield, since in the military he had grown accustomed to upper-class speech together with upper-class manners. His return to the working class was thus willed and artificial, and for that reason only temporary. Dwelling alone in the wood, damning all factions—the materialistic and narrow-minded working-class equally with the parasitic and sterile propertied class—Mellors becomes an outsider. He becomes in fact a natural aristocrat, combining warmth and vitality with educated consciousness. If there is a cultural gap between this gamekeeper and his lady, the lady is the inferior party. He is perfectly presentable in educated company, proving himself in a club luncheon with Connie's titled father, acquitting himself well in the arty circles of London to which his lady introduces him. Connie meanwhile has become much more the modern woman, engaging in sociological talk, hobnobbing with cultivated bores, and enjoying several love-affairs before the encounter with Mellors, whose working-class origins pique her interest rather than her fears.

Unlike Parkin, who has been victimized by the ruling class, Mellors has benefitted from their patronage. He is no longer the threatening representative of an oppressed class; for Connie he is no longer, as Parkin had been, a strong reminder of her class guilt. Where Parkin is for doing away with the bosses, Mellors is for doing away with industry. When driven from the forest, Mellors does not retreat to working-class Sheffield, but to arty London, and thence to a farm. The harsh, gritty industrial world which intrudes into versions I and II has been all but excluded from III, where the pastoral mood remains dominant throughout. The aura of fairy-tale, the romance of the magical forest, which only tinged the earlier versions, becomes prominent in *Lady Chatterley's Lover.* As the stubborn class barriers between the lady and her gamekeeper are eliminated by making Mellors a gentleman in disguise, so the ugly facts of life in an industrial class society are pushed further away by making a fairy-tale of their story.

2 Fiction vs. Life

As Lawrence mutes the social message in *Lady Chatterley's Lover,* he accents the sexual message. The descriptions of coitus become much more explicit in the final version, the use of four-letter words more systematic and tendentious. Sex becomes the obsessive topic of conversation between all parties in the book. The gamekeeper emerges as a Lawrentian spokesman, theorizing and dogmatizing about love. Where Parkin fucks in unthinking silence, Mellors forces sex into speech and consciousness. By comparison with the preceding drafts, *Lady Chatterley's Lover* reads less like a political fable and more like a sexual tract.

The fairy-tale aura notwithstanding, in many respects Lawrence's final novel marks a return to conventional realism. It has a simple unified plot, which is at least of Roman vintage: a servant absconds with his master's wife. Its setting of woods, mining village and stately home is described in the best nineteenth-century manner. Unlike their counterparts in the earlier novels, characters here resemble the old stable egos that Lawrence scorned in the work of contemporaries such as Galsworthy or Bennett; they are coherent personalities, chiefly defined by their social positions; their motives are rarely obscure, they dwell almost wholly in daylight. There are few of those dizzy plunges, so common in the other novels, into the verbal and psychological depths. Over the conventional story and conventional characters broods an omniscient, moralizing, confidently articulate—in short, a nineteenth-century—narrator. No other Lawrence novel seems so thoroughly managed and penetrated by the narrator's consciousness, no previous novel seems to offer so little that is opaque to his ironic vision.

Certainly there were distinguished precedents for Lawrence's portrayal of a frustrated bourgeois or aristocratic wife, bored by her husband, oppressed by the sterility of her life, seeking renewal

through the love of another man: stripped to these sparse outlines, Lady Chatterley's plight is that of Stendhal's Mme. de
Rênal, Flaubert's Emma Bovary or Tolstoy's Anna Karenina. Lawrence outraged his contemporaries, and for thirty years after his
death continued to offend the courts of England, by spelling out
what had long since been implicit in realistic fiction. By introduc-
ing the taboo words into polite literature he merely pushed to its
logical conclusion the venerable tradition of imitating vulgar
speech—a tradition which includes Chaucer's bawdy pilgrims,
Shakespeare's vagabonds, Dickens' Coketown workers and Hardy's
rustics. Likewise his detailed accounts of sexual relations merely
extended the techniques of realism into the last prohibited
area.

But for that very reason *Lady Chatterley's Lover* posed in
acute form Lawrence's besetting dilemma: by translating the most
delicate shades of sexual experience into the language of conventional fiction, had he betrayed the fragile life which he set out to
defend? Had he delivered up to the curators of the museum of
mind the last wild, free creature, to be stuffed and mounted along-
side all the other victims of consciousness? In the last version of
the novel, where the sexual descriptions become painstakingly
thorough, where the taboo words dance methodical attendance
upon the acts of love, where the gamekeeper and aristocrats
theorize copiously about sex, Lawrence appears to question the
very act of writing. Over and over in the novel he stresses the dis-
continuity between fiction and life, between language and experience. These dichotomies had plagued him throughout his career,
and forced him, as we have seen, to push outward the boundaries
of language, to expand the domain of fiction; in *Sons and Lovers*
by intensifying psychological analysis of character; in *The Rainbow* by stressing the physical stratum in human experience; in
Women in Love by reducing the socially-defined ego to material
terms; in *The Plumed Serpent* by evoking the religious dimension.
In every case he was skirting the same contradiction: using the
tools of consciousness to define and defend the unconscious. But
never before had the contradiction appeared so starkly as in *Lady
Chatterley's Lover*. Lawrence could no longer ignore the question: had he cheapened sex—the one domain of freedom left to
man in an insane society—by pretending to diminish it into

words? Had he substituted talk for action? Had he exchanged life for language?

3 The Mistrust of Language

After one of the typically longwinded and vacuous evenings of conversation at Wragby, Connie inwardly complains of this incessant "Talk, talk, talk! What hell it was, the continual rattle of it!" And well she might complain, for the barren discussions among Clifford's circle demonstrate the sterility of the life of the mind when it is cut off from the life of the body. They talk abstractly, ineffectually and endlessly about topics of the day—Bolshevism, industrialism, materialism, "the sexual problem," "the mental life." Lawrence had ridiculed such arid talk before, had mocked the intellectualist life-style as he knew or imagined it in Bloomsbury, in the Bohemia of London, in Mabel Dodge's New Mexico menagerie of artists, in Bertrand Russell's Cambridge. The effete intellectuals of *Aaron's Rod* assemble at Shottle House and carry on their aimless conversations in a chapter contemptuously entitled "Talk." Hermione, who in *Women in Love* presides over discussions which are every whit as lifeless and bootless as those at Wragby, is the most disturbing portrait of the "mental lifer."

Compared to Hermione, the denizens of Wragby are mere straw men, but they suffer much the same ailment—the divorce of talking from living. Tommy Dukes strikes the keynote: "Oh, intellectually I believe in . . ."—conceding in the next breath that there is no bridge between his beliefs and his life. "God!" he exclaims, "when one can only talk!" By spouting Lawrentian orthodoxy while shunning the life of the body, Dukes demonstrates the possibility of enjoying sex exclusively in the head. Indeed there is a striking family resemblance between this career soldier and previous Lawrentian spokesmen, men who are at once the most intellectual and the most violently anti-intellectual characters in their respective novels: Lovat Somers in *Kangaroo*, Rawdon Lilly in *Aaron's Rod*, Don Ramon in *The Plumed Serpent*, Birkin in *Women in Love*, even Paul Morel in *Sons and Lovers*.

Clifford of course is the prime specimen of the divorce between body and mind, a divorce which in his case corresponds to a passion for words, whether spoken or written. His craving for conversation, his subjugation to the wireless, his hunger for Mrs Bolton's Tevershall chronicles, his own compulsive writing—all are symptoms of his purely mental life. His fiction in particular seems to be a reflection of his sterile existence: "there was no touch, no actual contact. It was as if the whole thing took place in a vacuum." As a writer he "was really clever at that slightly humorous analysis of people and motives which leaves everything in bits at the end . . . it was all nothing, a wonderful display of nothingness." Lawrence treats his obsession with "infinite small analysis of people and motives" and his passion for aesthetic form as two sides of the same coin. Clifford shares these vices with two of his favorits authors, Proust and Racine. Of Proust Connie remarks that "he doesn't have feelings, he only has streams of words about feelings," a logorrhea which evidently appeals to Clifford. Racine appeals to him, on the other hand, by virtue of his formalism: "one gets all one wants out of Racine. Emotions that are ordered and given shapes are more important than disorderly emotions." As his various essays on the novel attest, Lawrence considered the Proustian psychological analysis and the Racinian aesthetic formalism to be separate expressions of the same desire to dominate life, to hold experience inferior to the artistic form which is impressed upon it. Including Flaubert, Mann and Joyce within the scope of his critique, he accused the formalists and the analysts alike of exalting the ego, and of substituting art for life.

Connie's friend Duncan Forbes paints nudes which appear as tubes and valves, thus emphasizing his own personality by abstracting from his human subject. Hence Mellors finds his paintings sentimental and self-important, much as Lawrence found the writings of Joyce, Dorothy Richardson, Flaubert and Mann. Ursula applies a similar critique to Loerke's decadent sculpture in *Women in Love*, and Kate to the industrial murals in *The Plumed Serpent*. In such art, according to Lawrence, form has become autonomous, to be valued in its own right without human reference. We find Clifford correspondingly anxious that the *form* of his marriage be maintained, regardless of its barren human content, just as Gerald in *Women in Love* insisted that social forms be preserved, regardless of the pain they caused or the lies they concealed. Both men also crave the power to dominate men and materials through the industrial system.

Thus Clifford displays all those ills which Lawrence associated with the mental life: insistence on social forms, fascination with science, lust for domination, acquisitiveness, devotion to industry, physical impotence, and substitution of art for life. Clifford stands for rather than justifies this equation of mentalism in art, society, science, industry and so on. Like a figure in chess he can only move in certain directions; his significance is defined by the rules of the game rather than by his individual character. In short, he is a type, quite proper in fable or romance, but unconvincing in a realistic novel.[8] Indeed all the characters in *Lady Chatterley's Lover*, including Connie and Mrs Bolton, are more palpably ciphers in an argument, figures in a symbolic algebra, than were any of the major characters in the previous novels. By their sharp outlines and lucid interactions they suggest Jonsonian humours or the figures in a morality play, rather than the complex and unfathomable characters in Lawrence's great earlier novels.

Connie herself drifts through the early pages of the book like a listless character from one of Clifford's stories:

> she . . . was a figure somebody had read about, picking primroses that were only shadows or memories, or words. No substance to her or anything . . . no touch, no contact! Only this life with Clifford, this endless spinning of webs of yarn, of the minutiae of consciousness.

Her own life seems to her devoid of meaning, betraying the insubstantiality of words:

> all the brilliant words seemed like dead leaves, crumpling up and turning to powder, meaning really nothing, blown away on any gust of wind. . . . It was words, just so many words. The only reality was nothingness, and over it a hypocrisy of words.

We learn in the first chapter that as a student in Dresden, experimenting in love with German youths, she had cared only about talk; love had been but a distasteful and secondary accompaniment. Yet when in a later chapter Tommy Dukes proposes exactly

---

[8] Many critics have remarked Clifford's transparency as a character, and several have defended him against Lawrence's charges. See: Eliseo Vivas, *D. H. Lawrence: The Failure and the Triumph of Art* (London, 1961, Bloomington, Ind., 1964), pp. 123–5; Katherine Anne Porter, "A Wreath for the Gamekeeper," *Encounter*, XIV (Feb. 1960), pp. 76–7; and David Holbrook, *The Quest for Love* (London, 1964; University, Alabama, 1965), pp. 281–2.

the same dichotomy between love and talk, and declares himself
in favor of the latter, Connie bitterly protests, for she has been
exposed too long to the interminable conversations of Wragby,
has trekked with her husband through too many deserts of fictional
prose, to feel nourished any longer on a diet of words:

> How she hated words, always coming between her and life: they
> did the ravishing, if anything did: ready-made words and phrases,
> sucking all the life-sap out of living things. . . . She wanted to be
> clear of Clifford, and especially of his consciousness, his words, his
> obsession with himself, his endless treadmill obsession with himself,
> and his own words.

She clearly recognizes the connection between Clifford's intense
consciousness, his obsession with words and his omnivorous ego-
tism: he is the king of the realm of mind and his scepter is
language.

This poverty of life and speech among the Wragby circle is at
least in part a symptom of that general cataclysm which the opening of the novel recalls, that crisis in consciousness and society
which for Lawrence was focused by the Great War. The festering
after-effects of war appear in the novel as a deep bruise, organic
and psychic, which cankers the souls of the survivors. For writers
such as Edmund Blunden, Robert Graves, Siegfried Sassoon and
Wilfred Owen, who experienced the conflict directly, the very
language which had served to incite and camouflage the insanities
of war seemed to have been debased. For Hemingway, reflecting
upon the holocaust in A Farewell to Arms, "Abstract words such
as glory, honor, courage, or hallow were obscene beside the concrete names of villages, the numbers of roads, the names of
rivers. . . ." For Connie also everything seemed covered with "a
hypocrisy of words," and the words themselves appeared tainted:

> All the great words, it seemed to Connie, were cancelled for her
> generation: love, joy, happiness, home, mother, father, husband, all
> these great, dynamic words were half dead now, and dying from
> day to day. . . . Frayed! It was as if the very material you were
> made of was cheap stuff, and was fraying out to nothing.

Language had been devalued. For Lawrence the most grievous
casualty was the language of sex. We had lost the ability to talk
honestly and reverently about the mysterious life of our bodies.

The Wragby circle can manage only crude or sneering references to "this sex thing," "the sex game," "the male and female business." One lady expostulates warmly that "a woman needn't be dragged down by her *functions*." Clifford considers that "sex was an accident, or an adjunct, one of the curious, obsolete, organic processes which persisted in its own clumsiness." Their conversation reflects the barrenness of their sexual lives. Viewed in contrast, Mellors' talk of the body, together with his use of the Derbyshire dialect, often pompous or awkward, but always frank and reverent, signifies a revolt against the life and mentality of Wragby, as surely as his triumph over the squire's wife signifies a revolt against social forms, against consciousness, against the governing class, against industry and materialism and all the related terms of Lawrence's dialectic.

Wragby, then, is at once a real and an unreal world. With its ties to industry, government, publishing, and the greater society, it seems a much more substantial universe than the idyllic Sherwood Forest retreat presided over by Mellors. But at the same time it seems a thin confection of words, not simply because Lawrence like any novelist has *written* his world, but because the inhabitants and friends of Wragby have spun around themselves a chrysalis of talk, theories and fictions as a shelter against life. It seems evident that in his last years Lawrence himself was haunted by questions about the purpose and effects of his own fiction. Had he substituted words for the thing itself? Had he simply provided his readers with a surrogate for living? Were his efforts to act directly through prose upon the feelings of his audience only another tyranny of mind over body? Were his novels, poems, plays, essays, letters and tales merely an intricate cocoon of words? Were his fictions in any sense *real*? Only such questioning on Lawrence's part can account for the degree of self-satire involved in the portraits of Rawdon Lilly in *Aaron's Rod*, Lovat Somers in *Kangaroo*, Don Ramon in *The Plumed Serpent*, and Clifford Chatterley, all of them rather disillusioned and ineffectual writers, unable to come to terms with their wives or their society; or for the persistence and hyperbole with which he proclaimed the value of fiction, in that remarkable series of late essays on the novel, including "Why the Novel Matters," "Morality and the Novel," "John Galsworthy," "The Novel," "The

Novel and the Feelings," *A Propos of "Lady Chatterley's Lover"* and "Pornography and Obscenity." His most eloquent and most famous defence, of course, appears in *Lady Chatterley's Lover*, where he distinguishes between that art which feeds off life like a parasite, and that which nourishes; between that which dulls and that which renews man's sensitive awareness; between that which abides by convention and that which pursues the free reckless course of life itself. But even here it seems to me that Lawrence has been provoked into self-defence, for the distinction between life-giving and life-denying art are wilful and simplistic; they will surely not enable us to sort Proust, Flaubert, Racine, Mann and Joyce into one pile, and Lawrence (with perhaps Hardy, Verga, Cooper, Melville and Whitman) into the other.

Lawrence's questioning of his vocation as a writer appears most clearly in the portrait of Clifford. Only in the third version of *Lady Chatterley's Lover*, the wordiest and most tract-like of all three drafts, does Clifford appear as a writer, one who is condemned for triviality. In the very draft in which Lawrence indulges in detailed analysis of sexual experiences he also satirizes a writer whose stories are built upon such analysis. Secure within his estate, which is surrounded by hungry and desperate villages of working people, Clifford explores the psyche of cultivated characters:

> He, as a private individual, had been catering with his stories for the populace of pleasure. And he had caught on. But beneath the populace of pleasure lay the populace of work, grim, grimy, and rather terrible. They too had to have their providers. And it was a much grimmer business, providing for the populace of work, than for the populace of pleasure. While he was doing his stories, and 'getting on' in the world, Tevershall was going to the wall.

This is also the story of Lawrence's own career, as he was brutally reminded by his trip to the Midlands. While he was spinning his fictions for middle-class readers, while he was getting on in the world, Tevershall, his own people, were going to the wall. *The First Lady Chatterley* was begun in a spirit of anguished concern over the condition of the "populace of work," but with each revision Lawrence recoiled further towards the "populace of pleasure." The underlying class critique was watered down. The working-class

Parkin became the gentleman Mellors. The demand for a social revolution was exchanged for the hope of a private peace.

In Clifford, then, Lawrence beheld a distorted image of himself. After finishing *The Plumed Serpent* he repeatedly swore to friends and publishers alike that he would never write another novel. He would paint, he would sing, he would simply be. Yet the vision of his people's misery had driven him to write another novel, not once but three times, and with each draft he despaired more completely of ever touching that misery with his art. "I myself am in a state of despair about the Word either written or spoken seriously," he confessed in a letter of November 1927.[9] Yet a few days later he was to begin *Lady Chatterley's Lover*. His doubt is borne by Connie, whose rejection of the artifice and talk of Wragby involves a challenge to the novel form in which she appears; for her mistrust of language is so deep that it implicates all literary art, not just the decadent variety for which Clifford stands. Hence escape from this sterile realm where the word reigns will mean for Connie a move, literally and symbolically, into the kingdom of silence.

4 *Meanings of Silence*

Connie has walked many times through her husband's forest, and she has even had a few fleeting glimpses of the taciturn gamekeeper, but the woods only become a *refuge* for her in her flight from Wragby after she has seen Mellors washing himself at his cottage. The introduction to this scene in chapter six is therefore very important, for it marks one of the turning points in the novel:

> The air was soft and dead, as if all the world were slowly dying. Grey and clammy and silent, even from the shuffling of the collieries, for the pits were working short time, and today they were stopped altogether. The end of all things!
>
> In the woods all was utterly inert and motionless, only great drops fell from the bare boughs, with a hollow little crash. For the rest, among the old trees was depth within depth of grey, hopeless inertia, silence, nothingness.
>
> Connie walked dimly on. From the old wood came an ancient melancholy, somehow soothing to her, better than the harsh in-

[9] Letter to Aldous Huxley, CL 1020. 14.xi.27.

sentience of the outer world. She liked the *inwardness* of the remnant of forest, the unspeaking reticence of the old trees. They seemed a very power of silence, and yet a vital presence. They, too, were waiting: obstinately, stoically waiting, and giving off a potency of silence. Perhaps they were only waiting for the end; to be cut down, cleared away, the end of the forest, for them the end of all things. But perhaps their strong and aristocratic silence, the silence of strong trees, meant something else.

As she came out of the wood on the north side, the keeper's cottage, a rather dark, brown stone cottage, with gables and a handsome chimney, looked uninhabited, it was so silent and alone. But a thread of smoke rose from the chimney, and the little railed-in garden in the front of the house was dug and kept very tidy.

The forest is the kingdom of silence. She flees the verbal prison of Wragby, which has dominated the novel up to this point, and finds solace, even hope, in "the unspeaking reticence of the old trees."

At first the woods seem to her as dead as the outer world, where silence means the arrest of industry; but in the third paragraph she begins to suspect that the stillness of the forest disguises growth. In this passage the realistic and the fabulous intersect: on a naturalistic plane, the trees are only potential industrial timber, mine props, temporarily reprieved, a pathetic remnant of the defeated past; but on the plane of fable they offer sanctuary, they stand for the enduring forces of regeneration, they shelter the potent dark prince who will restore Connie to life. The keeper's cottage partakes of the general silence and isolation of the forest, and is likewise ambiguous: it appears to be abandoned, lifeless, yet it trails a thread of smoke connoting warmth and life; realistically it is a poor and ramshackle place, but fabulously—using that word in its root sense—it lodges the dark prince, it is a frail ark that just might weather the flood. The whole pageant of *Lady Chatterley* is acted out simultaneously on these two planes of realism and fable. If the novel seems at times schematic and unpersuasive, it is because Lawrence has aroused expectations appropriate to a realistic novel when he is in fact rendering a myth.[10]

[10] The interaction between realism and myth in Lawrence's late work has been remarked but not developed by Mark Schorer in "Fiction with a Great Burden," *Kenyon Review*, XIV (Winter, 1952), 167–8 and by Keith Sagar, *The Art of D. H. Lawrence* (Cambridge, 1966), 196–7. Ian Gregor has dis-

The forest, Connie's sanctuary from the sterile verbal world of Wragby, is consistently described as silent and still:

> It was a grey still afternoon, with . . . all the trees making a silent effort to open their buds. . . . The wood was silent, still and secret . . . full of the mystery of eggs and half-open buds, half-unsheathed flowers. . . . The fine rain blew very softly, filmily, but the wind made no noise. Nothing made any sound. The trees stood like powerful beings, dim, twilit, silent and alive. How alive everything was!

In the forest, silence and stillness are coupled with potency and vitality, just as language at Wragby is coupled with sterility and death. Thus we uncover once again that scheme of oppositions which structures all the novels:

NATURE	forest	working class	body	silence
CULTURE	Wragby	ruling class	mind	language

Although Mellors talks rather a lot in the latter half of the novel—a fact with which we must deal presently—he is nevertheless typically described as silent and still, like the forest he inhabits:

> He straightened himself and saluted, watching her in silence. . . . He resented the intrusion; he cherished his solitude as his only and last freedom in life. . . . Silently, patiently, he was recoiling away from her even now.

Like ancient trees, he is endowed with the "power of silence;" indeed, the word is so often associated with him that it seems to become an attribute, like darkness, or sensual richness. His stillness partakes of the forest silence. The same power of life animates both. Ignoring for a moment his occasional fits of garrulity, there is one version of Mellors who resembles Parkin in being

cussed the matter at greater length in the volume he co-authored with Brian Nicholas, *The Moral and the Story* (London, 1962), 217–48. Among the many accounts of the mythic element in Lawrence's thought and art, see in particular Philip Rieff, "The Therapeutic as Mythmaker: Lawrence's True Christian Philosophy," in *The Triumph of the Therapeutic* (London and New York, 1966), 189–231.

a man of few words. He says yessir to his master, fends off his mistress with the vernacular, and otherwise meditates silently in the forest. During his first few meetings with Lady Chatterley, including several bouts of lovemaking, he grudges only a few words, mostly monosyllables; and thus provides a most eloquent contrast to Wragby, to Clifford's logorrhea, to the verbose lovemaking of Michaelis. Like Parkin, this taciturn version of Mellors remains a half-man, perhaps preferable to the half represented by Clifford, but nevertheless no final compromise between body and mind. He stands for that which has been excluded from Wragby, that which has been ostracized from educated society; he does not stand for the whole. The fable version of Mellors, then, fulfills the role of the repressed, the inarticulate, the physical, the natural.

(The avoidance of proper names in the conversation between Connie and Mellors is another form of silence. "I've never called him by any name: nor he me," Connie suddenly realizes, "which is curious, when you come to think of it." It is curious in realistic fiction, but common in fable. In that whole series of late tales beginning with the formula "There was a man (or woman) who . . . ," the names of central characters are used rarely or not at all— *The Woman Who Rode Away*, *The Man Who Died*, *The Virgin and the Gipsy*, "The Man Who Loved Islands," "The Undying Man," and "The Man Who Was Through with the World." Names attach to coherent social personalities; figures of parable represent universal types, or Everyman.)

But there is another version of Mellors, who expatiates on the values of warm-hearted sensuality, attacks industrial society, modestly points out the direction which future civilization should take, descants upon the body, thinks disconcertingly articulate thoughts while in the throes of sexual passion, and generally acts as guide through the labyrinth of Lawrence's thematic concerns. One suspects when listening to this Mellors that Tommy Dukes has been smuggled into the forest and fitted out with a new suit of virility. This is the Mellors whose bedside reading embraces studies of Bolshevism, the atom, geology and India; who ventures opinions on almost every topic ever broached in the discussions at Wragby. In part he may be accounted for as merely another of those redundant Lawrentian spokesmen who harp upon themes

192

which the novels have independently dramatized. But I think he should also be seen as a half-hearted and unsuccessful attempt to redeem Parkin, the silent and sensual one, from his purely physical existence. Grafting Tommy Dukes—who is all talk and no life—onto Parkin—who is all life and no talk—should produce the perfect hybrid, the intellectual Mellors, who is supposed to incorporate the best of both strains by harmonizing the mental and the physical. But this version of the gamekeeper must be subject to some of the criticisms levelled against Clifford and his cronies. His opinions may be different from theirs, but they are nonetheless opinions; his sex life may be less tempestuous, but it is only slightly less theoretical; like them he habitually translates life into thought and speech. By the criteria set up within the novel itself, this vocal Mellors can only with difficulty be distinguished from the decadent Wragby circle.

These two sides of Mellors are reflected, to a certain extent, in the two dialects he uses—that of Derbyshire and that of "standard" English. The first is the language of emotion, the speech—as Dorothy Van Ghent has observed—of "physical tenderness;"[11] the second is the language of abstraction, of social relations. The first binds him to his working-class origins, the second to his middle-class connections formed through the army. We observed the same dichotomy in the speech and background of Lawrence himself, who, like Paul Morel in *Sons and Lovers*, favored the cultivated language of his mother, while spurning his father's dialect and way of life. Derbyshire is appropriate to the forest, but "standard" English belongs to Wragby. Yet the novel itself is written in this "standard" English, in the language of abstraction and reflection, so that it is the Derbyshire dialect that stands out as the exception—and as artificial, since Mellors uses it for calculated reasons. The very language which the gamekeeper repudiates is the medium in which the novel is written; the rebellion against conceptual language is couched in terms which are themselves conceptual. The taciturn figure from myth speaks broad Derbyshire, sparingly; but the garrulous Lawrentian spokesman rambles on in "standard" English.

This conflict between the desire to theorize, to make explicit, to articulate, and the desire to defend the inarticulate, to *be* with-

[11] *The English Novel: Form and Function* (New York, 1953), p. 255.

out knowing, appears in all of Lawrence's work. And in *Lady Chatterley's Lover* it has other expressions than the ambivalence of Mellors. Consider for example, the following passage:

> And this time his being within her was all soft and iridescent, such as no consciousness could seize. Her whole self quivered unconscious and alive, like plasm. She could not know what it was. She could not remember what it had been. Only that it had been more lovely than anything ever could be. Only that. And afterwards she was utterly still, utterly unknowing, she was not aware for how long. And he was still with her, in an unfathomable silence along with her. And of this, they would never speak.
>
> When awareness of the outside began to come back, she clung to his breast, murmuring 'My love! My love!' And he held her silently. And she curled on his breast, perfect.
>
> But his silence was fathomless. His hand held her like flowers, so still and strange. 'Where are you?' she whispered to him. 'Where are you? Speak to me! Say something to me!'
>
> He kissed her softly, murmuring: 'Ay, my lass!'
>
> 'You love me, don't you?' she murmured.
>
> 'Ay, tha knows!' he said.
>
> 'But tell me!' she pleaded.
>
> 'Ay! Ay! 'asn't ter felt it?' he said dimly, but softly and surely.

Like Miriam in *Sons and Lovers*, Connie is made to appear the one demanding that feelings be translated into words; but Mellors, like Paul Morel, generally does the talking. In fact this is the only love-encounter in which the feelings of either or both are not reported with elaborate detail. In other words, even while maintaining, as he does here, that sexual experience is "such as no consciousness could seize," Lawrence is engaged throughout the novel in effecting precisely that seizure.

Rendered in these public forms, sexuality is stripped of the religious dimension which it had preserved in the earlier novels, thereby appearing diminished, artificially isolated from the rest of life. For Lawrence's contemporaries this naturalistic or "hygienic"—to borrow a descriptive term from F. R. Leavis—treatment of sex, if still shocking, must have been less disturbing than the corresponding treatment in his earlier novels. Here was Mr Lawrence's vaunted beast at long last! Exposed to the light of day it was rather a domesticated creature, not at all likely to devour or reform the world. The scheme of sexual renewal is mythic, and read as a fable the novel has the cogency of myth. But the insistent realism of the sexual descriptions prevents us from reading *Lady Chatterley* simply as a fable. Yet read as realism the novel appears either trivial or simply wrong-headed— trivial if it merely recounts in graphic detail the sexual escapades of a frustrated lady and a potent gamekeeper;[12] wrong-headed if their sexual experience is supposed to be normative, or to provide a blue-print for social change and personal salvation. In place of the debased idealistic language, in place of the great words which have become meaningless for Connie, Lawrence proposes a language of the body; but there is no transition between this language and society, for experiences of the body are purely private. Whether or not Lawrence really shared the Romantic belief that sexual love can serve to transform the larger world, this final version of his novel provides few clues to the connections between personal and social regeneration.

On the plane of fable, then, Mellors' taciturnity contrasts with Clifford's verbosity, the silence of the forest with the noise of Wragby. But silence is ambiguous: it may signify non-mental modes of being, or simply non-being. When the trees are silent, they continue to grow; but silent collieries are lifeless. The old priests in *The Woman Who Rode Away*, "who were going through some ceremony near the fire, in silence, intense Indian silence," symbolize the repressed natural dimension which the anonymous heroine is seeking. Theirs is a positive silence. But Lawrence was aware of the dangers attendant upon the total rejection of language, for that must result in the death of the mind and retreat from human society. The hermit hero of "The Man Who Was Through with the World"[13] extends his hatred of man-

---

[12] According to Aldous Huxley, this is precisely the impression created by the stage version of the novel: *Letters of Aldous Huxley*, ed. Grover Smith (London and New York, 1969), pp. 455–6. This would seem inevitable and significant, since the play version would depend wholly upon dialogue, losing the narrative, which fulfils such a crucial part in *Lady Chatterley*, eliminating the natural descriptions, minimizing the symbolic contrast between Wragby and Sherwood Forest.

[13] Uncollected. It appears with an introduction by John R. Elliott, Jr., in *Essays in Criticism,* July 1959, 213–21.

kind to include man's language, and therefore ceases reading, ceases even thinking. In "The Man Who Loved Islands" this decision is pushed to its logical conclusion, and the solipsist hero —who has obliterated every trace of the written word, has ended all spoken intercourse with humans, has stopped the very lambs from bleating, has even lost the capacity to think—is annihilated. Theirs is a negative silence which leads to death, or signifies non-being, the "eternal silence of these infinite spaces" that terrified Pascal.

The silence of Parkin and of the taciturn Mellors is positive, it partakes of the primeval forest. Their potency is associated with their reticence, as Clifford's impotence is linked with his wordiness. But their silence also signifies defeat by the world of man. In each successive version of the novel the gamekeeper becomes more of a recluse, until finally for Mellors "The hut was a sort of little sanctuary. . . . He felt if he could not be alone, and if he could not be left alone, he would die. His recoil away from the outer world was complete; his last refuge was this wood; to hide himself there!" Connie is impressed by his "solitary aloneness . . . like a soul that recoils away, away from all human contact." This side of Mellors expresses an isolationist impulse which is present, to a greater or lesser degree, in all of Lawrence's works, but particularly in *St Mawr*, *The Man Who Died*, *The Woman Who Rode Away*, "The Man Who Loved Islands," "The Man Who Was Through with the World" and, as we have seen, in *Women in Love*. Thus his silence also corresponds in part to a rejection of human society, whereas the talk at Wragby, however vapid, affirms social intercourse. Trapped once again within the contradictions of his art, Lawrence writes a novel in praise of silence, spins words about his despair of the Word, sends messages to the world about his world-weariness.

In these various ways, then, Lawrence enforces the opposition between word and experience, bearing out his complaint that "We have no language for the feelings."[14] Wordsworth had voiced the same complaint at the end of the eighteenth century, insisting in his "Preface" that literature must recover "the genuine language of passion," that it must deal with "the real language of men in a state of vivid sensation." In A Propos of "Lady Chatterley's

[14] "The Novel and the Feelings," PI 757.

Lover" Lawrence defends his use of the taboo words in a similar fashion, claiming in essence that they are "the real language of men in a state of vivid sensation." He argues that we must "make a balance between the consciousness of the body's sensations and experiences, and these sensations and experiences themselves," which we can at least partially accomplish by using "the so-called obscene words, because these are a natural part of the mind's consciousness of the body."[15] Yet in *Lady Chatterley* itself he questions the assumption, implicit in Wordsworth's remarks, that there actually is a "genuine language of passion," capable of bodying forth the deepest experiences within the self. For as we have seen, he associates the extremes of physical experience with silence. This runs contrary to the Romantic belief that highly-charged emotion finds direct expression in poetry, that feeling translates naturally into language. Thus Shelley claims, in "A Defense of Poetry," that the very form of poetry

> springs from the nature itself of language, which is a more direct representation of the actions and passions of our internal being, and is susceptible of more various and delicate combinations, than colour, form, or motion, and is more plastic and obedient to the control of that faculty of which it is the creation.

Despite the fact that Lawrence created through his fiction "a more direct representation of the actions and passions of our internal being," certainly of our physical being, than any of his predecessors in the English novel, he was perpetually conscious of how much inner experience lay beyond the scope, not merely of his own art, but of all language.

In *Lady Chatterley's Lover* he partially transcended the opposition between those who love and those who talk by making love itself a form of speech. The idea is proposed in chapter four by Tommy Dukes—that ambiguous impotent spokesman: [16]

---

[15] Op. cit., PII 490.

[16] Dukes would seem to have been justified as a human being by Lawrence in *À Propos*, with the remark that "Even if we can't act sexually, to our complete satisfaction, let us at least think sexually, complete and clear" (PII 490). Perhaps in that remark, and in the character of Dukes, Lawrence reflected upon the failing powers of his own consumptive body.

'It's an amusing idea, Charley,' said Dukes, 'that sex is just another form of talk, where you act the words instead of saying them. . . . Sex might be a sort of normal physical conversation between a man and a woman.'

Whatever irony Lawrence may have intended here (and some is certainly intended by that "just"), he has identified one of the essential functions of sexual intercourse in the novel. Most of the communication between Mellors and Connie is in fact physical, consisting of gestures and touches, a semaphore of small acts, as well as coitus. They speak the language of the body, which has for organs the eyes and skin rather than the ears and brain. It is as if Lawrence, while forced to communicate by words to *us*, struggled to free his lovers from the constraints of language in their dealings with each other. The point has a much more general bearing on his work, for many of his distinctive effects as a novelist involve this representation of "physical conversation between a man and a woman," often involving gestures, touch, or the lexicon of natural things. There are the flower rituals in *Sons and Lovers*; the sheaf-gathering and moonlit dancing scenes in *The Rainbow*; the catching of a rabbit and stoning of the moon in *Women in Love*; the pheasant-hatching and lovemaking scenes in *Lady Chatterley's Lover*. Returning to the point from which this section began, we can take as an example the scene in which Connie discovers the gamekeeper washing himself in the wood:

in some curious way it was a visionary experience: it had hit her in the middle of the body. She saw the clumsy breeches slipping down over the pure, delicate, white loins, the bones showing a little, and the sense of aloneness, of a creature purely alone, overwhelmed her.

No word is exchanged, but a physical communication has taken place. Connie is aroused from her spiritual stupor by the sight of a man's body, she is inwardly moved, *physically* affected, even though her mind scoffs, as Lydia Lensky was aroused from her emotional coma in *The Rainbow* by the insistent and speechless force of spring. At its most characteristic Lawrence's fiction creates the impression that dialogue between his characters, albeit often conducted in words, somehow transcends language, becoming really less a matter of communication—as previous novelists had normally rendered it—than of communion, a being together.

5 *Uses of Myth*

Lawrence was notoriously impatient of aesthetic form, but he was also impatient of language itself, and for the same reason: because it seemed an abstraction separating him from reality. Facing the same dilemma, hating words because they were "always coming between her and life," Connie fled to the ancient woods, where lived the dark prince with whom she could commune silently among the silent trees. Lawrence himself could only have escaped the Word by abandoning writing—from which he was restrained by habit, messianic impulse, and moderate financial need. Various features of his last novel seem to reflect a disillusionment with language, a loss of faith in the novel form itself. The didacticism, the endless conversations, the translation of silent Parkin into loquacious Mellors, register an uneasiness about his dramatic rendering of experience, an uncertainty about whether the message is really getting through. The insistent sexual realism, while narrowing Lawrence's earlier vision, displays a narrowed range of expression, neglecting many devices of metaphor, gesture and symbol with which he had previously depicted the varied interchange between man and woman. The programmatic use of taboo words reflects a similar uncertainty about his expressive resources; and his defense of their use turns upon a naïve view about the social function of such words. The stress upon coitus suggests that other modes of physical conversation, which he had explored with compelling immediacy in the earlier novels, have become suspect by the period of writing *Lady Chatterley's Lover*. And judging from the experience of Michaelis, Mellors and Connie herself, even this ultimate form of communion may distort one's meaning, or may communicate nothing at all.

By comparison with the earlier novels *Lady Chatterley* appears schematic. To use Lawrence's terms, it stands much nearer the pole of allegory than the pole of myth:

> Allegory is narrative description using, as a rule, images to express certain definite qualities. Each image means something, and is a term in the argument and nearly always for a moral or didactic purpose, for under the narrative of an allegory lies a

didactic argument, usually moral. Myth likewise is descriptive narrative using images. But myth is never an argument, it never has a didactic nor a moral purpose, you can draw no conclusion from it. Myth is an attempt to narrate a whole human experience, of which the purpose is too deep, going too deep in the blood and soul, for mental explanation or description.[17]

His last novel presents a moral argument by means of images—in this case characters—which have the clarity and stability of figures in a parlor game, and which act out their parts against a stark background of forest, cottage, collieries, and stately home. Gone are the disturbing but untranslatable horses of *The Rainbow*, the lambent moon of *Women in Love*, the awesome desert of *The Plumed Serpent*.

Yet there are unmistakable mythic echoes in *Lady Chatterley*, which account for much of the novel's power as a moral fable. There is, for example, the basic fertility myth which was delineated by Sir James Frazer in *The Golden Bough*: the crippled and sterile king (Clifford) rules a barren country (the mining district); his queen (Connie), who suffers from the barrenness of his realm, is restored to fertility by a potent prince (Mellors), who has survived various ordeals (the war, pneumonia, his first wife) to reach her. Only the final segment of the myth is lacking: the restoration of fertility to the land and its people. But the shock of the war seemed too great, the reserves of class hatred too deep, the disease of poverty and alienation too widespread to permit Lawrence hope of such recovery. While he continued to dream of this social rebirth in that late fable about the Midlands called "Autobiographical Fragment," and in the earlier drafts of *Lady Chatterley*, by the final draft he had all but abandoned hope that it would come to pass in his time, in his land. The condition of England was too grave. The cancer of money and class and machine had spread too far. Even Mellors—who breeds pheasants which are still the King's Beasts, who retreats in the end to till the earth which still provides feed for the pit ponies—cannot escape across the border from the barren land of industry and intellect.

The novel also suggests an inverted form of the Eden myth: Adam and Eve are cast back *into* the garden, where they redis-

[17] "Preface" to *The Dragon of the Apocalypse*, by Frederick Carter, PI 295–6.

cover innocence by destroying shame, which was only a product of the mind. In Sherwood Forest, last remnant of the virgin world, the lovers recover that state of primal oneness between man, woman and nature which had been dissolved by consciousness, and by mind's chilling instrument—language. "Adam and Eve fell," Lawrence maintained,

> not because they had sex, or even because they committed the sexual act, but because they became aware of their sex and of the possibility of the act. When sex became to them a mental object— that is, when they discovered that they could deliberately enter upon and enjoy and even provoke sexual activity in themselves, then were they cursed and cast out of Eden.[18]

> At a certain point in his evolution, man became cognitively conscious: he bit the apple: he began to know. Up till that time his consciousness flowed unaware, as in the animals. Suddenly his consciousness split.[19]

Lawrence could never quite accept the logical implication of this view: silence. Whether or not the fall can be reversed—and he seems to have been under no delusion that it can—the prelapsarian and preconscious state is *better*, and therefore any further effort of consciousness only compounds the evil. Yet Lawrence's whole adult life was taken up with what he called the "struggle for verbal consciousness."

We can observe this struggle in the evolution from *The First Lady Chatterley* to *Lady Chatterley's Lover*: the struggle to *know* sex, to make it available to the mind. Of this effort Lawrence himself was fully aware, as his remarks on the novel show:

> this is the real point of this book. I want men and women to be able to think sex, fully,· completely, honestly and cleanly. . . . Now our business is to realize sex. Today the full conscious realization of sex is even more important than the act itself.[20]

> I believe the consciousness of man has now to embrace the emotions and passions of sex, and the deep effects of human physical contact. This is the glimmering edge of our awareness and our field of understanding, in the endless business of knowing ourselves.[21]

[18] *Psychoanalysis and the Unconscious*, 202.
[19] Review of *The Social Basis of Consciousness*, by Trigant Burrow, PI 378.
[20] *À Propos*, PII 489–90.
[21] Letter to Morris L. Ernst, CL 1099. 10.xi.28.

I quote Lawrence against himself—man fell when he made sex conscious; we must make sex conscious—not to show that he was inconsistent, which is easy enough to prove against any ambitious and unsystematic thinker, but rather to indicate how sharply this particular novel focused his recurrent problem: given that we are outside of Eden, how can the tools of consciousness serve to restore the body's innocence and integrity? It will be recalled that in *The Rainbow* Ursula rejected the love of Anthony Schofield—and was approved for her action—because like Parkin the young man had *not* fallen into consciousness, while she had: "He did not see it. He was one with it. But she saw it, and was one with it. Her seeing separated them infinitely." Similarly in *Lady Chatterley's Lover* the return to Eden is impossible: Mellors has long ago rejected the sterile world represented by Wragby, which he sampled in the army, but he cannot return to the naïve state of Anthony Schofield or Parkin, for his experience cannot be unlearned. No more can Connie's. Their seeing separates them infinitely from Eden.

Other mythic parallels are scarcely less evident than that of Eden and the fertility cycle. Mellors, who nearly died of pneumonia, is a resurrected figure, like so many others in Lawrence's fiction: Paul Morel, Birkin, Dionys in *The Ladybird*, Aaron Sisson, Don Ramon, the gipsy in *The Virgin and the Gipsy*, Gethin Day in "The Flying Fish," and pre-eminently the Christ figure from *The Man Who Died*.[22] But none of them, not even Lawrence's sensual Christ, is fully reborn into the world; all remain outcasts, like Lawrence himself, nomads dwelling on the fringes of civilization. Within this typology, Clifford, who returned broken from the war, but never recovered his potency, may be seen as a victim of partial resurrection. Connie's rebirth is also incomplete. Her story evokes the *rite de passage*, which involves retreat from the world, contact with some fundamental source of power, and return to the world. But here again the last stage is omitted, as the restoration of

[22] Like mythical quest figures, Lawrence's resurrected men have survived an ordeal, through which they have gained a nearer vision of the truth. In *À Propos of "Lady Chatterley's Lover"* he implicitly related this experience of near-death and resurrection with the quest for truth: "The tragic consciousness has taught us . . . that one of the greater needs of man is a knowledge and experience of death; every man needs to know death in his own body" (PII 509).

fertility to the land and the recovery of the prelapsarian state had been omitted from the other myths.

Whichever form one traces—the myth of fertility, of Eden, of resurrection, or the *rite de passage*—it is obvious that Lawrence's despairing view of contemporary England interfered with his mythic intention. If, as Lévi-Strauss claims, the main function of myth is to resolve contradictions, then *Lady Chatterley's Lover* may be said to offer a partial mythic resolution, rather than a sociological solution. "I want, with Lady C.," Lawrence wrote in 1928, "to make an *adjustment in consciousness* to the basic physical realities."[23] By his creed, the social change, if it comes at all, will follow the change in consciousness. Myth deals with precisely such an adjustment, reconciling opposites, enabling men to dwell amidst contradictions. The basic opposition between mind and body—variously manifested in *Lady Chatterley's Lover* as talk vs. life, owners vs. workers, industry vs. forest, Wragby vs. cottage, language vs. silence—is partially overcome through the intercourse between Mellors and Connie. The lady is messenger from one sphere to the other. Their love solves nothing, only witnesses to a faith in the possibility of reconciliation.

Thus after two decades of writing, after travelling round the world, after ransacking history and mythology in search of a cure that would mend the breach between flesh and spirit, Lawrence returned to the point from which in *Sons and Lovers* he had begun. Once again in *Lady Chatterley's Lover* we see clearly that the division between body and mind reflects the social division between those who are required to labor without thinking and those who are privileged to think without laboring. It is the division between the mining village of Tevershall and the aristocratic retreat of Wragby. It is the split, which he struggled all his life to bridge, between his father's people and his mother's people. "Why is there so little contact between myself and the people whom I know?" Lawrence asked himself in a late, revealing "Autobiographical Sketch":

[23] Letter to Ottoline Morrell, CL 1111. 28.xii.28. The italics are Lawrence's own, and the italicized phrase was almost certainly borrowed from Trigant Burrow's *The Social Basis of Consciousness* (London, 1927), p. 226, which Lawrence was reading at the time.

The answer, as far as I can see, has something to do with class. Class makes a gulf, across which all the best human flow is lost. . . . As a man from the working class, I feel that the middle class cut off some of my vital vibration when I am with them. I admit them charming and educated and good people often enough. *But they stop some part of me from working.* Some part has to be left out.

Then why don't I live with my working people? Because their vibration is limited in another direction. They are narrow, but still fairly deep and passionate, whereas the middle class is broad and shallow and passionless. . . . But the working class is narrow in outlook, in prejudice, and narrow in intelligence. This again makes a prison. One can belong absolutely to no class.[24]

Like his creature Mellors, Lawrence hovered between classes, familiar with both spheres, at home in neither. "Class makes a gulf, across which all the best human flow is lost": a gulf within man and a gulf between men. Healing the split within the psyche waits upon healing the split within society.

In the process of revising *The First Lady Chatterley* into *John Thomas and Lady Jane,* and then again into *Lady Chatterley's Lover,* Lawrence gradually stripped away the social moral from his sexual myth. Beginning from the spectacle of suffering and class hatred in the industrial Midlands, he sought to apply his doctrine of sexual renewal to a concrete historical problem. But with each restatement of the erotic solution he abstracted further and further from the social problem, until by the last version Connie and Mellors have become, like Ursula and Birkin at the close of *Women in Love,* two isolated souls who have severed all ties with the degraded world and who seek their own private salvation through passion and flight. Personal regeneration is once again divorced from social regeneration. Communal ailments are deflected into the psyche, where they take on a life of their own, and where they admit of only private remedy. In this transition from first draft to third, *Lady Chatterley's Lover* reflects the general shape of Lawrence's career. Grieved by the division of men into classes, by the crippling effects of industrialization, by the growth of centralized authority and the abridgment of freedom, he strove to articulate a gospel which would speak to the needs of his time. But the

[24] Op. cit., PII 595–6.

maladjustment between pristine human nature and the contemporary social reality seemed to him so grave, the necessary revolution so radical and therefore so unlikely, that he was driven again and again to flee history into a mythical realm in which the passions of the body redeem the cruelties of the world.

6

Lawrence and the Novel

In his essay of 1914 on "The New Novel" Henry James complained that contemporary practitioners of the art of fiction—among them the Lawrence of *Sons and Lovers*—had become obsessed with the depiction of environment and the notation of consciousness, to the neglect of those virtues of selection, emphasis and design which characterized the works of Austen, Dickens, Trollope, Thackeray, and, implicitly, James himself.[1] These new novels by Wells, Bennett and Lawrence seemed to James fairly saturated with naturalistic details, without any discrimination, without any over-all imaginative control, as if they had been transcribed from experience rather than composed. Amidst such jumble, James further complained, the critic looks in vain for a centre of interest or a sense of the whole. However just or unjust such criticisms may have been for those older authors who dominated the world of English fiction at the time Lawrence began writing, they do point to an important difference between the novel form as handled by Austen, Eliot, Thackeray and James, and the novel form as developed by the author of *Sons and Lovers*.

In his rendering of the formation of Paul Morel within the concentric circles of family, colliery village and industrial Midlands, Lawrence followed the best nineteenth century realist tradition of representing the development of consciousness and affection

[1] The original version appeared in the *Times Literary Supplement*, No. 635 (19 March 1914), pp. 133–4 and No. 637 (2 April 1914), pp. 157–8; a revised and expanded version appeared in *Notes on Novelists* (London, 1914), and has been collected in *The Art of Fiction and Other Critical Essays*, ed. Morris Roberts (New York, 1948).

within a particular social context, at a particular time. Where he differs from his predecessors, however—even from Emily Brontë, Dickens and Hardy whom he most nearly resembles in this respect —is in the degree to which he treats that social context as alien, as something neither created nor sustained nor comprehended by those who are forced to live within it, something imposed from without upon the Bestwood community, upon the Morel family and upon young Paul. The world of *Sons and Lovers* seems *given*, to the novelist as to the protagonist.

As I argued in my analysis of the novel, the ties between environment and psyche are indeed closer than Lawrence was at that time prepared to acknowledge. The activities and pressures of Bestwood life are not some picturesque backdrop for the human drama, but rather form the substance of that drama itself, they mold personal relations and direct the growth of character. The shaping and connecting role of social forces is everywhere implicit in *Sons and Lovers*, demonstrating an historical awareness which rivals that of Dickens and George Eliot. Like those Victorian critics of society, Lawrence underwent a social dislocation which made him sensitive to the determining influences of education, wealth, class position and sexual roles. Yet because, to his mind, he had escaped the confines of Eastwood, he tended to overestimate the power of the individual to struggle free of community. In other words his awareness of the determining influence of social forces was accompanied by an exaggerated appraisal of individual freedom. Hence the contradiction one often encounters in Lawrence's fiction: a character who appears enmeshed in society on one level of the novel may appear on another as a free agent. Man is governed by culture: man is freed by nature.

Certainly the novel shows design and discrimination, but not such as to reduce all elements of the fictional world to some aesthetic, moral or thematic order. Of course Lawrence condemned the very desire for reducing unruly life to aesthetic rule, taking the works of Flaubert and Mann as samples of art's pernicious inclination to dominate life; hence the given-ness of the fictional world in *Sons and Lovers* may be accounted for in part as a sign of his temperamental anti-formalism. But this antiformalism, which has annoyed many critics besides James, was only one expression of Lawrence's general suspicion of reason.

As we have seen, this challenge to reason took two inter-related forms: a loss of faith in man's capacity to understand and control his history; and a loss of faith in the dominion of consciousness over the self. Such skepticism, directed simultaneously outward into the world and inward into the psyche, had important effects on Lawrence's depiction of character and community.

The earlier Victorian novelists presented both community and individual as knowable, either by the narrator, as in Scott, or by a central observer, as in Austen; and the same novelists treated the social order, however imperfect, as the product of human reason and desire.[2] The fictional world appears progressively less rational and intelligible after 1848, particularly in the later works of Dickens, Eliot and Hardy, and in Gissing and Conrad. Lawrence reproduces this century-long evolution within the space of his own career. He starts from the earlier position in *The White Peacock*, assuming intelligibility; but already in *Sons and Lovers* he is uncovering wild zones within the self and inhuman zones within society; and by the writing of *Women in Love* he is depicting contemporary society as so irrational and destructive, so utterly alien to all human reason or desire, that it must be escaped altogether if the individual—who is himself already unstable—is to survive. Just as *The Rainbow* continues and develops the work of George Eliot, so *Women in Love* extends the work of Hardy, taking up the moral issues where they were left tangled at the end of *Jude the Obscure*. Although in that novel Hardy several times blames the suffering of Jude Fawley and Sue Bridehead upon indifferent nature, the deeper implication of their story—as Lawrence pointed out in his analysis of the novel and as Hardy certainly intended— is that the social code itself is at fault: at fault for frustrating Jude's ambition to become scholar or priest; at fault for endorsing the barren marriage with Arabella while condemning the union with Sue; at fault for the suffering which follows on that union. What was implicit in *Jude the Obscure* becomes explicit in

[2] My reading of the evolution of the Victorian novel, and my placement of Lawrence in that development, has been influenced by John Holloway's *The Victorian Sage* (London, 1953; Hamden, Conn., 1962), J. Hillis Miller's *The Form of Victorian Fiction* (Notre Dame, 1968) and especially Raymond Williams' *The English Novel from Dickens to Lawrence* (London and New York, 1970).

Women in Love. Birkin and Ursula pursue their passion in soli-
tude; sex becomes a region which they inhabit instead of society.
Their fulfillment is to be sought no longer through activity in the
world, but through more and more private, intense physical experience. Hence Birkin's assumption that the first step towards "completeness of being" was to drop all social responsibilities and quit
his school inspector's job. There is nothing whatsoever triumphant
about this alienation in Lawrence's work, nothing of the defiant
exile we have come to expect as a stock feature of twentieth century literature; rather there is a deep sense of loss, not simply
of the knowable community, but of the inhabitable community.

Adrift, the isolate self, like Ursula alone in the horse pasture at
the close of *The Rainbow*, is subject to incomprehensible influences
from within and from without. So far as Lawrence can see, there
is no longer any "cultivated field" of human activity which will
guarantee an authentic existence, no longer any settled community in which the self can discover its identity, no longer any agreed
code by which the self can gauge its conduct. Thus he cannot provide
that sense of the whole which James desired, that impression
of a range of life wholly encompassed within the artist's organizing
vision, for Lawrence's subject stretches obstinately beyond his ken;
outward, into the destructive realm of social forces, and beyond
that to the enveloping process of nature; inward, into the irrational
recesses of the self, where the divine life impulse stirs with unpredictable motions. There is no still centre from which this can
all be measured, no circumference within which it can all be con-
tained.

The indeterminacy of character and of community are clearly
inter-related: if the individual is subject to irrational influences,
then society, multiplying this effect a thousandfold, may act irra-
tionally on a vast scale, as in the First World War; on the other
hand, if community disintegrates, as it does in the transition from
Marsh Farm to industrial Wiggiston in *The Rainbow*, then character must also fragment. This is the meaning of Lawrence's celebrated warning, with reference to early drafts of *The Rainbow*, that
"You mustn't look in my novel for the old stable *ego*—of the
character." The stable ego is product of a coherent society, and
the unstable ego of an incoherent society. Beginning with the wartime novels, Lawrence no longer presents character as a develop-

ing psychic continuity, but rather as a variable, discontinuous, un-predictable manifestation, almost a form of energy. The demands such a reconception of character made upon language were ex-treme, particularly noticeable in *Women in Love*.

In conscious opposition to his nineteenth-century predecessors, Lawrence was unwilling or unable "to conceive a character in a certain moral scheme and make him consistent." The impression of self-sufficiency and solidity created by *Emma, David Copperfield, Middlemarch* or *The Portrait of a Lady* depends in large part upon the assumption of a shared moral scheme linking narrator and audience, and upon the further assumption that the fictional world is essentially knowable. Lawrence could no longer make those assumptions, for the inherited moral schemes seemed to him bankrupt, while life itself seemed too vast and mysterious for reason to comprehend. Victorian novels could generally get by with-out God, without seriously invoking any superhuman order, be-cause the social code itself seemed adequate for defining personal relationships and for assessing individual lives. Specific faults with-in society were of course denounced, notably by Dickens; but they were denounced through appeal to a set of assumptions, a scale of values, which the writer held in common with his audience. Whereas the Victorian novelist typically spoke with the moral force of the first person plural, Lawrence speaks in the first person singular. As J. Hillis Miller has argued in *The Form of Victorian Fiction*, the narrator of Dickens, Eliot, Thackeray or Hardy plays the role of a generalized social consciousness, speaking for the whole community. Lawrence more nearly appears to speak *against* the community, from the solitary prominence of his own con-science.

His abandonment of the stable, coherent, knowable character of Victorian fiction coincided with economic and social develop-ments which during his lifetime were undermining that corner-stone of bourgeois ideology—the autonomous individual, who was theoretically free to pursue his own ends and who therefore bore the responsibility for his own destiny. Throughout the nineteenth century, as commodity relations—the buying and selling of pro-ducts on the market—displaced other forms of human inter-course, as the power of financiers, governors, industrialists and bureaucrats grew, society increasingly thwarted the free develop-

ment of the individual. The atomic self had been a myth from the beginning, but one easier to maintain in the age of Adam Smith than in the age of Marx. The rapid growth of sociology and depth psychology during the latter decades of the nineteenth century and the early decades of the twentieth, were an ideological expres- *
sion of the changed circumstances of the individual. The sociologists attacked his autonomy from the outside, revealing his subjection to economic and political forces; while the psychoanalysts attacked him from the inside, revealing his subjection to unconscious psychic forces. Lawrence's unstable, frustrated characters, prey to irrational impulses and thwarted by society, clearly reflect these vast, gradual changes in the real world. Like every great inventive artist, he developed new literary forms to express a changed historical content.[3]

Obviously I am not suggesting that the nature of community and character suddenly became problematic in Lawrence's mature fiction; or that his great predecessors never questioned the moral schemes on which their fictions were built. The pressure of these concerns was increasing throughout the latter half of the century, conspicuously in the work of Hardy and Conrad. But for Lawrence the pressure became so intense, the problems of character and community so acute, that he had to devise what was practically a new language in order to express his altered conception of man, '
and he had to radically modify the novel form in order to express his altered perception of society. *Sons and Lovers* still follows the pattern of much nineteenth century fiction: a child grows to young manhood within the context of family life, in organic relation to a richly evoked community; his personal relationships and his psychological development are inextricably woven out of that common life, even when he is in conscious opposition to his surroundings.

[3] I wish to acknowledge here a general debt to Lucien Goldmann's studies of the novel form, particularly *Pour une sociologie du roman* (Paris, 1964) and his "Introduction aux premiers écrits de Georges Lukács," in Lukács, *La Théorie du roman* (Paris, 1963); to the work of Georg Lukács: in addition to *The Theory of the Novel* (English translation by Anna Bostock, London and Cambridge, Mass., 1971; originally Berlin, 1920), his study of *The Historical Novel* (English translation by Hannah and Stanley Mitchell, London, 1962; New York, 1965; originally Berlin, 1955); and to Frederick Jameson for his *Marxism and Form* (Princeton, 1971).

The Rainbow begins on very much the same pattern, but over the course of three generations personal relations are progressively isolated from community. This development is then carried to its extreme in *Women in Love*, where four individuals appear as atomic units, fully developed at the opening of action, independent of family, cut off from all social involvement (with the partial exception of Gerald, whose involvement is wholly predatory). Problems of meaning, value and relationship have been *abstracted* from the social context, and the offered solutions, such as they are, appear in almost algebraic form. Birkin's ultra-individualistic love-ethic seems to be a last desperate attempt to salvage the self in face of a uniformly destructive society, and to defend the self against all claims, either personal or communal.

In the early novel, identity was still to be found in community; in the later it was to be found, if at all, in isolation. This change of perspective is graphically displayed in *The Lost Girl*. The first half of that novel, written before the War, represents the petit-bourgeois upbringing of Alvina Houghton within a shopkeeper's home in a Midlands mining town, all of it rendered with Dickensian gusto and concreteness; the second half of the novel, written after the War, dispenses with family and community, and drives the heroine (in dubious partnership with a vaudeville performer) to the desolate, remote and defiantly inhuman wastes of a mountain settlement in southern Italy; at the end Alvina is cut off even from her improbable husband, who is called away to battle. The difference between the first and second halves of *The Lost Girl*, like the difference between the first and third versions of *Lady Chatterley's Lover*, like the difference between *Sons and Lovers* and *Women in Love*, is a measure of Lawrence's disillusionment with the available forms of community.

His works record a constant attempt to articulate a new moral scheme, which would serve as the framework for a new community. Like Hawthorne and Melville, whom he admired, and like James, whom he did not, Lawrence inherited the powerful ethical sensibility characteristic of the greatest Christian writers, yet without accepting their theology. He was preoccupied with religious questions, which he posed with religious intensity, but for which he could no longer offer an orthodox religious solution. This dilemma, the dilemma of secular man consumed by religious concerns, lies at the heart of his work. Like Gerald Crich in *Women in Love*,

> He did not inherit an established order and a living idea. The whole unifying idea of mankind seemed to be dying . . . , the centralizing force that had held the whole together seemed to collapse . . . , the parts were ready to go asunder in terrible disintegration.

In his mature works we witness this disintegration of the community and the self, a process resisted with all the powers of genius, but finally, for a man of Lawrence's honesty and experience, irresistible.

Since community was dissolving, since the social personality was disintegrating, Lawrence suggested that nature might replace culture as the matrix within which man discovers his identity. Throughout his works, above all in *The Rainbow*, he intimates the form that such a natural identity might take, employing in the process language which relates him directly to Wordsworth, Coleridge and Shelley. But he was inclined to oppose nature to culture with a rigor unrivalled even by his Romantic forebears. He tended increasingly, from *Sons and Lovers* through *The Plumed Serpent*, to equate a particular repressive social order with social order as such; and in proportion as he completed that equation, he made of nature an alternative to culture, rather than a measure of contemporary society. This as I say was only a tendency, an inclination which he recognized and never fully indulged; but insofar as he divorced man's nature from his social existence, as if the two were distinct and opposed terms, he was reacting defensively rather than critically to his age. The logical consequence of such a divorce is dramatized in "The Man Who Loved Islands", where the affluent hermit, voluntarily cut off from all society of man or beast, dissolves back into the material elements of which he has been composed. This corresponds exactly to the reduction of personality to material terms in *Women in Love*; and it has a disturbing resemblance to the effects of an exploitive industrial system upon its workers, as presented in *Sons and Lovers*.

Although he began from the biographical, individualistic focus of the bourgeois novel, Lawrence ended by radically challenging the liberal conception of the self. The Victorian novelists approached society through biography, since the individual was held to be the locus of value and meaning. "Human beings in society," wrote John Stuart Mill, "have no properties but those which are derived from and may be resolved into the laws of the nature of individual man."[4] Lawrence worked from the same explicit assumption, echoing Mill's words some eighty years later in *Kangaroo*: "the only way to make any study of collective psychology is to study the isolated individual. Upon your conception of the single individual, all your descriptions will be based, all your science established." But like Freud who also commenced with the isolated individual, Lawrence burrowed through the walls of the psyche to explore those physical strata of instinct and desire which unite rather than separate men. Under the magnification of his regard the autonomous self dissolved into a chaos of psychic forces. The characters of Joyce, Proust, Mann or Virginia Woolf are by comparison insulated and secure within the shell of cultivated consciousness. In the brotherhood of the flesh and in men's shared relation with nature, Lawrence offered a basis for a community that was ultimately subversive of bourgeois ideology.

Stronger than his inclination to reject society as irredeemably corrupt and corrupting, was his belief in man's capacity to conceive and create a more humane social order. His fictions and essays continually pose the question, "What is the underlying impulse in us that will provide the motive power for a new state of things. . . ?"

In agreement with Blake, indeed with all revolutionary thinkers, Lawrence maintained that the impulse is *there*, inherent in man. Like Blake in particular he identified that impulse with Eros, the creative force which prevailing social forms had perverted to acquisitive or destructive ends. Individually, this meant the repression of spontaneous desire. Socially, it meant the repression of particular classes, and the squandering of human energies on a vast scale, through war or frenzied material accumulation. Just as Blake gives a sexual as well as a political meaning to the enslavement and revolt of Orc in *America*, so Lawrence insists upon the connection between repression on the personal and on the social level. He was convinced by direct experience that an

⁴ *System of Logic*, Book VI, Chapter vii (1843).

entire class had been repressed, a class represented by the industrial communities of Bestwood in *Sons and Lovers*, Wiggiston in *The Rainbow*, Beldover in *Women in Love*, and Tevershall in *Lady Chatterley's Lover*. He showed that the power to shape these communities had passed from the people themselves, and had been alienated to landowners, industrial magnates, planners, engineers and politicians. This identification between the cause of the id and the cause of the working people gave to Lawrence's protests a force and significance that has not been surpassed in the work of any other modern writer. By comparison the social views of Proust, Joyce, Eliot, Mann and even Gide seem the expression of a narrower class interest, a more private frustration. Although Lawrence offered no program for the recovery of that alienated power which had been lost from the enslaved body and from the laboring community, he continually witnessed, both in the activity of his own mind and in the vitality of his characters, to the creative energy potential in all men.

Almost everything Lawrence wrote manifests that quality which Coleridge took to be the true sign of genius: an intense activity of mind, which demands a correspondingly active response from the reader. If one had to choose which of DeQuincey's two categories best fitted Lawrence's work—the literature of knowledge or the literature of power—surely the choice must fall to the latter. For through the novels and essays he is constantly acting on the reader's understanding and perception, disintegrating old forms of consciousness and shaping new ones. On a large scale, one recognizes the imaginative effort required to transmute the nineteenth century novel form used in *The White Peacock* into the very different (in some ways more comprehensive, in other ways more restricted) form of *Women in Love*, and then to continue evolving the fabulous and mythic shapes of his later works. On a smaller scale one recognizes, in the details of metaphor and syntax, the continual pressure to extend the expressive resources of language. We can with justice apply to all of Lawrence's work the words that he offered in defense of *Women in Love*:

> Man struggles with his unborn needs and fulfilment. New unfoldings struggle up in torment in him, as buds struggle forth

215

from the midst of a plant. Any man of real individuality tries to know and to understand what is happening, even in himself, as he goes along. This struggle for verbal consciousness should not be left out in art. It is a very great part of life. It is not superimposition of a theory. It is the passionate struggle into conscious being.

Everywhere in his work one recognizes this unremitting "struggle for verbal consciousness", and it is precisely this constant pushing at the limits of expression which makes study of his novels so rewarding. It was Lawrence's achievement to bring to verbal consciousness certain of the more important social pressures, some of them active, some of them still latent, in contemporary England; to register the effects of profound social changes upon community, personal relations and individual consciousness; and to offer a high estimate of human potential in a repressive and destructive age.

Bibliographical Note

Unless otherwise specified, all quotations from Lawrence are taken from the Heinemann Phoenix Edition, London. This is in most cases identical with the Viking Compass Edition, New York. The standard bibliography remains that by Warren Roberts, *A Bibliography of Lawrence* (London, 1963). More recent criticism of Lawrence has been catalogued by Richard D. Beards and G. B. Crump, "D. H. Lawrence: Ten Years of Criticism, 1959–1968: A Checklist," *The D. H. Lawrence Review*, I, No. 3 (Fall 1968), 245–85. Since 1968 the *DHLR* has published an annual checklist of criticism.

The standard biography remains that by H. T. Moore, *The Intelligent Heart* (New York, 1954; London, 1955). A better study of Lawrence's development as a writer, from childhood through the completion of *Women in Love*, has now been provided by Emile Delavenay, in his fine *D. H. Lawrence: the Man and His Work: the Formative Years, 1885–1919* (London and New York, 1971; originally Paris, 1970). Lawrence's own letters, poems and essays offer a penetrating commentary on his fictions.

A brief list of essential Lawrence criticism should also include the following:

Draper, R. P. (ed.). *D. H. Lawrence: The Critical Heritage* (London and New York, 1970).

Freeman, Mary. *D. H. Lawrence: A Basic Study of His Ideas* (New York, 1955).

Goodheart, Eugene. *The Utopian Vision of D. H. Lawrence* (Chicago, 1963).

Hochman, Baruch. *Another Ego: The Changing View of Self and Society in the Work of D. H. Lawrence* (Columbia, S.C., 1970).

Hough, Graham. *The Dark Sun: A Study of D. H. Lawrence* (London, 1956; New York, 1957).

Leavis, F. R. *D. H. Lawrence: Novelist* (London, 1955; New York, 1956).

Moore, H. T. (ed.). *A D. H. Lawrence Miscellany* (Carbondale, Ill., 1959; London, 1961).

—— and F. J. Hoffman (eds.). *The Achievement of D. H. Lawrence* (Norman, Oklahoma, 1953).

Moynahan, Julian. *The Deed of Life: The Novels and Tales of D. H. Lawrence* (Princeton, 1963).

Schorer, Mark. *The World We Imagine* (New York, 1968; London, 1969).

Spilka, Mark. *The Love Ethic of D. H. Lawrence* (Bloomington, Ind. and London, 1955).

—— (ed.). *D. H. Lawrence: A Collection of Critical Essays* (Englewood-Cliffs, N.J., 1963).

Index

219